MEDIEVAL JEWRY IN NORTHERN FRANCE

THE JOHNS HOPKINS UNIVERSITY STUDIES IN
HISTORICAL AND POLITICAL SCIENCE

NINETY-FIRST SERIES (1973)

1. Daniel Webster and Jacksonian Democracy *(not included in this volume)*
   BY SIDNEY NATHANS

2. Medieval Jewry in Northern France:
   A Political and Social History
   BY ROBERT CHAZAN

MEDIEVAL JEWRY IN NORTHERN FRANCE

A Political and Social History

by Robert Chazan

THE JOHNS HOPKINS UNIVERSITY PRESS
BALTIMORE AND LONDON

The Johns Hopkins University Press, Baltimore, Maryland 21218
The Johns Hopkins University Press Ltd., London

Library of Congress Catalog Card Number 73-8129
ISBN 0-8018-1503-7

Library of Congress Cataloging in Publication data
will be found on the last printed page of this book.

To Saralea

ACKNOWLEDGMENTS

I T IS MY PLEASANT obligation to acknowledge the influence and aid of a series of teachers and friends. Much of my graduate study at the Jewish Theological Seminary of America was devoted to Talmudic texts. It was my privilege to enjoy the instruction of Professors Saul Lieberman, Moses Zucker, and H. Z. Dimitrovsky. These distinguished scholars taught me more than Talmud; they imparted a strong sense of the methods of intensive textual analysis, which I have attempted to use on other materials as well. In my historical studies at Columbia University I was guided by Professors Salo Baron, John Mundy, Zvi Ankori, and Gerson Cohen. Professor Ankori supervised my masters essay, and Professor Cohen was the principal reader of my doctoral dissertation. I am deeply indebted to these gifted and concerned teachers, who gave so unstintingly of their time, energy, and funds of knowledge. During a year of research in France, I benefited greatly from extended conversations with two major students of medieval French Jewry, Bernhard Blumenkranz and Gérard Nahon. Over the years, a host of colleagues and students at The Jewish Theological Seminary of America, at The Ohio State University, and elsewhere have enriched my understanding of medieval French Jewry. To all I owe deepest thanks.

ACKNOWLEDGMENTS

The research for this project was sponsored by a variety of grants, including a Columbia University Travel Fellowship, a travel grant from The Jewish Theological Seminary of America, grants-in-aid from The American Council of Learned Societies and The National Foundation for Jewish Culture, a summer study grant from The Ohio State University Development Fund, and continuing support from funds established as part of The Samuel and Esther Melton Chair of Jewish History and Studies at The Ohio State University. To all these institutions I extend my appreciation.

The staff at The Johns Hopkins University Press have been extremely cooperative. From our first contacts they have been uniformly interested, cordial, and efficient. I am particularly obliged to Kenneth Arnold and Joanne Allen for their deep concern for this book and their extensive efforts to produce it as quickly, accurately, and handsomely as possible. Special thanks also go to Mr. Terry Campbell of the Graphics Services Department of The Ohio State University for his careful preparation of the two maps and to Rabbi and Mrs. David Zisenwine for their painstaking and good-natured assistance in reading proofs.

Finally, dedication of the book to my wife indicates that my debt to her exceeds all others. She contributed to completion of the manuscript in innumerable ways—by aiding in preparation of the maps, compiling the bibliography, composing the index, and through scores of insightful suggestions. More important, she provided the rich and happy setting which made the entire enterprise meaningful.

CONTENTS

MEDIEVAL JEWRY IN NORTHERN FRANCE

Abbreviations

BEC	*Bibliothèque de l'École des Chartes*
Comptes du Trésor	Robert Fawtier, ed., *Comptes du Trésor*
Comptes royaux	Robert Fawtier, ed., *Comptes royaux (1285-1314)*
Journaux	Jules Viard, ed., *Les Journaux du Trésor de Philippe IV le Bel*
JQR	*Jewish Quarterly Review*
Layettes	Alexandre Teulet et al., eds., *Layettes du Trésor des Chartes*
Mignon	Charles-Victor Langlois, ed., *Inventaire d'anciens comptes royaux dressé par Robert Mignon*
Olim	Arthur Beugnot, ed., *Les Olim ou registres des arrêts*
Ordonnances	Eusèbe de Laurière et al., eds., *Ordonnances des roys de la troisième race*
PAAJR	*Proceedings of the American Academy for Jewish Research*
PL	J. P. Migne, ed., *Patrologiae cursus completus, series Latina*
Registres	Robert Fawtier et al., eds., *Registres du Trésor des Chartes*
REJ	*Revue des études juives*
RHF	Martin Bouquet et al., eds., *Recueil des historiens des Gaules et de la France*

INTRODUCTION

THE JEWS OF medieval northern France occupy a distinguished niche in the long and rich history of their people. They constituted an important element in early Ashkenazic Jewry, the biological source of the major portion of modern Jewish population. They were highly innovative in fashioning for themselves useful—although not always popular—economic roles in a hostile environment and in elaborating effective techniques for ordering their internal affairs, legacies which they passed on to their descendants. Perhaps their greatest renown lies in the intellectual sphere. A number of the most significant scholarly creations of medieval northern French Jewry are to this day vibrant staples of traditional Jewish curricula.

All this was effected under most difficult circumstances. Medieval French society was in a state of unremitting struggle, slowly lifting itself out of chaos and striving towards greater power and more civilized living. While the Jews were accepted for the contribution they might make towards this struggle, they were almost always viewed with suspicion or with outright animosity. All aspects of Jewish life were hedged about with serious constraints, some unarticulated and some carefully formalized. Against this background of antipathy and limitation, the achievements of these Jews loom all the more impressive.

1

While much of the excitement generated by the study of medieval northern French Jewry flows from this sense of creative adaptation to trying conditions, there is also a sobering side to this history. For ultimately all efforts, both Jewish and non-Jewish, proved unavailing. The attempt to mold viable options for Jewish existence in northern France failed. By the thirteenth century ominous signs were in evidence; all major facets of Jewish life were being increasingly constricted by pressures from a number of directions. In 1306, with terrifying suddenness, the curtain dropped.

An account of medieval northern French Jewry must thus include both the successes and failures of the French and the Jews in fostering Jewish presence, the conditions under which the Jews lived, and Jewish achievement within the limits set forth. Such a depiction is of interest first and foremost to the student of Jewish history. It has meaning, however, for the historian of medieval France as well, since it highlights aspects of French life from an unusual perspective. Features of medieval French society reflected in majority sources take on new qualities when seen from the minority point of view. Finally, this story is of significance to all who share a concern for investigating the capacity of human groups to respond creatively to the limitations imposed on them by the circumstances of their existence.

Despite the undisputed importance of this community and the availability of a wide range of source materials, there has been no concerted effort to reconstruct its history. The development of northern French Jewry during the Middle Ages has been discussed in general Jewish histories,[1] in broad surveys of French Jewish life throughout the ages,[2] and in studies of medieval France;[3] it has also been mentioned in biographical and literary accounts of key intellectual figures.[4] This sig-

---

[1]The two most significant treatments of medieval French Jewry in general Jewish histories are Georg Caro, *Sozial- und Wirtschaftsgeschichte der Juden im Mittelalter und der Neuzeit*, 2 vols. (Frankfort, 1908-20), and Salo Baron, *A Social and Religious History of the Jews*, 2nd ed., 14 vols. (New York, 1952-69), vols. 4 and 10.

[2]The standard surveys of French Jewish history are Léon Berman, *Histoire des Juifs de France des origines à nos jours* (Paris, 1937); Mosche Catane, *Des Croisades à nos jours* (Paris, 1956); Simon Schwarzfuchs, *Brève histoire des Juifs de France* (Paris, 1956); and Bernhard Blumenkranz, ed., *Histoire des Juifs en France* (Toulous, 1972). None of these treats medieval northern French Jewry in great depth.

[3]Among the fullest treatments in general histories of medieval France are Nicolas Brussel, *Nouvel examen de l'usage des fiefs en France*, 2 vols. (Paris, 1750), vol. 1, pp. 569-628; Adolphe Vuitry, *Études sur le régime financier de la France* (Paris, 1878), pp. 315-31; and idem, *Études sur le régime financier de la France. Nouvelle série*, 2 vols. (Paris, 1883), vol. 1, pp. 91-102.

[4]See, for example, Henri Gross, *Gallia Judaica* (Paris, 1897); Ernest Renan, *Les rabbins français du commencement du quatorzième siècle* (Paris, 1877); idem, *Les écrivains juifs*

2

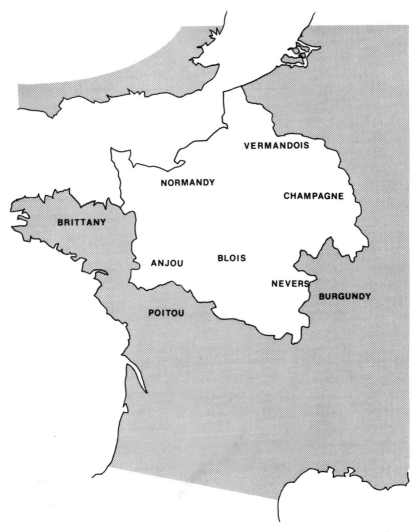

Areas of Northern France Included in this Study

nificant Jewry has not, however, been accorded the separate mono-graphic treatment which it so obviously merits.

The sources for such a study vary widely. For the early period, there is very little documentary evidence. There are occasional references to Jews in Christian histories or polemics. Jewish sources, while not copi-ous, are useful; particularly noteworthy are the random chronicles and the rabbinic responsa.

In general, as we proceed into the thirteenth century the volume of evidence mounts. Documentary materials in particular increase substan-tially. Beginning with the reign of Philip Augustus, royal records were kept with stricter care. By the time of Philip the Fair, there is documen-tation that far exceeds that of any of his predecessors.[5] The records left by lesser rulers and by private institutions show similar expansion dur-ing the course of the twelfth and thirteenth centuries. Much of this material has now been carefully edited and published. Although this evidence still leaves gaps in our knowledge, its utilization can enhance enormously our understanding of many aspects of Jewish life.

Curiously, at the point when non-Jewish documentary records begin to proliferate, Jewish sources diminish. Much of the decline can be directly attributed to the ecclesiastical-royal assault on the Talmud and related literature, which resulted immediately in the destruction of much important material and ultimately in the long-range attrition of Jewish academic life in northern France.[6] When the further upheavals occasioned by the expulsion of 1306 are considered, the lack of later Jewish sources becomes even more understandable. The result of this dearth of Jewish materials is a marked decrease in our information on the internal workings of Jewish community life during the latter part of the period under investigation. Clearly the Jewish community did not cease functioning; however, our ability to trace its operations has suf-fered.

There are thus many different kinds of sources available for this study. Each genre presents insight into only certain facets of Jewish

---

français du XIVe siècle (Paris, 1893); Samuel Poznanski's essay on French Biblical exegesis in his edition of the commentary of R. Eliezer of Beaugency to Ezekiel and the Minor Prophets; and Ephraim Urbach, Ba'aley ha-Tosafot (Jerusalem, 1955). An attempt to utilize the literary materials for their historical implications has been made by Louis Rabinowitz, The Social Life of the Jews of Northern France in the XII–XIV Centuries (London, 1938). Unfortunately the value of this work is mitigated by certain methodological weaknesses, such as indiscriminate use of data from France, Germany, and England and a failure to distinguish between sheer literary discussion and direct concern with contemporary reality.

[5] On the development of royal records, see the broad sketch by Robert Fawtier, The Cape-tian Kings of France, trans. Lionel Butler and R. J. Adams (London, 1960), pp. 6–11.

[6] See below, chapter 4.

life. A number of these types of evidence must be used with extreme caution, making allowance for potential distortions in their depictions of the Jews. Intensive utilization of limited data is indispensable; there is nothing like the *embarras de richesses* that sometimes confronts the student of modern history. Yet, in the final analysis, there is sufficient material and a wide enough variety of perspectives to allow a plausible reconstruction of major aspects of Jewish life in medieval northern France. While there will be occasional frustration for lack of additional evidence and insight, the portrait that emerges is relatively full.

The limits of this study are important to specify. As indicated in its title, this study is concerned primarily with political and social history. This includes consideration of Jewish political status, the Jews' relations with key elements in Christian society, Jewish demographic development, Jewish economic outlets, internal communal organization, and Jewish attitudes towards the Christian environment. An obvious omission is extensive treatment of Jewish intellectual life. This area has been neglected partially because it is the one aspect of this community's history that has been treated in depth. More important, the intellectual creations which later Ashkenazic Jewry saw fit to preserve were precisely those works which were "timeless," that is, only minimally related to the actual circumstances of twelfth- and thirteenth-century France. Where Jewish intellectual expressions reveal responses to contemporary reality they will be considered. Such instances, however, are lamentably few.

A chronological *terminus a quo* presents some problems. Jews had been settled in northern France in Merovingian times and even earlier.[7] The Carolingian emperors had had substantial contact with Jews.[8] Yet, for the purpose of this inquiry, attention will be focused on post-Carolingian France, on the new civilization that began to emerge in the tenth century and to blossom in the eleventh.[9] The Jewish life which we are setting out to investigate is very much a product of this new European society, in its economic structure, in its political status, and in the forms of its intellectual creativity.

[7] See, for example, Solomon Katz, *The Jews in the Visigothic and Frankish Kingdoms of Spain and Gaul* (Cambridge, Mass., 1937).

[8] See, for example, Simon Schwarzfuchs, "France and Germany under the Carolingians," in *The Dark Ages: Jews in Christian Europe 711–1096*, ed. Cecil Roth (Tel Aviv, 1966), pp. 122–42.

[9] On these developments, see *inter alia* Marc Bloch, *Feudal Society*, trans. L. A. Manyon (Chicago, 1961), pp. 3–71, and R. W. Southern, *The Making of the Middle Ages* (London, 1953), pp. 11–14.

A *terminus ad quem* is easier to establish and far more clear-cut. In 1306, Philip IV expelled the Jews from royal France.[10] While Jews were readmitted in 1315, the terms of settlement reveal a new status imposed on those Jews interested in returning.[11] Although the Jews were recalled sporadically during the fourteenth century, at no point did they succeed in reestablishing the foundations of flourishing community existence.[12] The summer of 1306 affords then a sensible and sharp termination to the study.

Geographic limits are more difficult to define. The focus of this study, it must be emphasized, is a set of similar Jewish communities. Unfortunately no simple political boundaries encompass this group of settlements. While most of northern French Jewry had, by 1306, come under the direct authority of the French monarchy, this process of political consolidation was a slow one.[13] Moreover, by 1306 other French Jewries had also been absorbed into royal France. These southern Jewries differed from their northern confreres in political status, in demographic and economic patterns, and in cultural and religious heritage.[14]

Since no simple political borders correspond to the recognizable unit of Jewish communities under consideration, the geographic boundaries will be somewhat loose. The area covered will range from Flanders in the north to a line slightly south of the Loire valley in the south and from Normandy and Anjou in the west through Champagne in the east.[15] These territories showed remarkable unity of political, economic, and intellectual life even before they were formally united under royal rule. Jewish life in this area also reveals common traits.

---

[10] See below, chapter 6.

[11] Ibid.

[12] Isidore Loeb, "Les expulsions des Juifs de France au XIVe siècle," *Jubelschrift zum siebzigsten Geburtstage des Prof. Dr. H. Graetz* (Breslau, 1887), pp. 39–56. There is much documentary evidence available for Jewish life in northern France between 1315 and 1394. It is a period that merits further study.

[13] See Auguste Longnon, *Atlas historique de la France* (Paris, 1888), maps 12, 13, and 14, and Auguste Longnon and H.-François Delaborde, *La formation de l'unité française* (Paris, 1922).

[14] The classic work on southern French Jewry is Gustave Saige, *Les Juifs du Languedoc antérieurement au XIVe siècle* (Paris, 1881). Much useful monographic study has since been done. For a recent overview, see Isidore Twersky, "Aspects of the Social and Cultural History of Provençal Jewry," *Cahiers d'histoire mondiale* 11 (1968): 185–207.

[15] By the latter decades of the thirteenth century, this had all become royal territory. Brittany in the west and Burgundy in the east, both of which remained outside royal control, have not been included in this study.

6

These Jews spoke the same vernacular, plied the same trades, enjoyed similar political privileges, suffered similar liabilities, and shared comparable cultural horizons.

It is to the history of this Jewry that we now proceed.[16]

---

[16] A word as to the system of noting sources is in order. Wherever an English translation is available, it will be cited; it is assumed that the original can be readily traced. Where there is no English translation, the best edition of the text will be cited. Occasionally a second and more accessible version will be added.

I

TENTH- AND ELEVENTH-CENTURY

BACKGROUND

DURING THE TENTH and eleventh centuries northern France slowly rose from its torpor. Population increased, the economy developed, and cities grew. This progress contributed to—and benefited from—the establishment of more effective political units. The dukes and counts of northern France carved out for themselves ever larger territories and began to control their domains with increasing authority. The most powerful of these magnates, William of Normandy, was able, during the 1060's, to muster sufficient force to conquer for himself a kingdom across the English Channel. Unobtrusively the king of France, overshadowed often by his mighty vassals, was subduing the Île-de-France and bending it to his will, slowly laying the groundwork for the sudden expansion of royal power that materialized at the end of the twelfth century.[1]

---

[1] An important overview of this period is provided in the volume by Auguste Longnon on "Les Premiers Capétiens (987-1137)," in Ernest Lavisse, *Histoire de France*, 9 vols. in 18 (Paris, 1900-1911), vol. 2, pt. 2. More detailed information on the specific tenth- and eleventh-century reigns can be found in Ferdinand Lot, *Études sur le règne de Hugues Capet et la fin du Xe siècle* (Paris, 1903); Charles Pfister, *Études sur le règne de Robert le Pieux* (Paris, 1885); and Augustin Fliche, *Le règne de Philippe Ier, roi de France (1060-1108)* (Paris, 1912). Significant studies of major northern French baronies in this early period include Henri d'Arbois de Jubainville, *Histoire des ducs et des comtes de Champagne*, 7 vols. in 8 (Paris, 1859-69); Louis Halphen, *Le comté d'Anjou au XIe siècle* (Paris, 1906); Robert Latouche, *Histoire du comté du*

The revival of trade and of urban centers must have vitally affected the Jews of northern France; however, evidence from this period is sparse. Documentary records, generally meager for this early age, shed no light whatsoever on the role and position of the Jews. The only non-Jewish materials available are the random observations of church-men, in some instances enlightening, in others misleading. Jewish sources likewise are slim, consisting of a few brief chronicles, a substantial number of rabbinic responsa, and commentaries on the classics of Biblical and Talmudic literature.[2] While the paucity of evidence precludes a detailed reconstruction of Jewish history during this period, enough remains to sketch in outline the condition of northern French Jewry prior to the First Crusade.[3]

A precise geography of pre-Crusade northern French Jewry is impossible.[4] There are, however, a number of locales for which Jewish settlement is attested: Auxerre, Blois, Châlons-sur-Marne, Le Mans, Orléans, Paris, Reims, Rouen, Sens, Troyes.[5] These are major urban centers, all

---

Maine pendant le Xe et le XIe siècle (Paris, 1910); David Douglas, "The Rise of Normandy," in *Proceedings of the British Academy* 33 (1947): 101–30; and idem, *The Norman Achievement: 1050–1100* (Berkeley, 1969).

[2] The two chronicles, both highly useful, were originally published by Abraham Berliner in *Oẓar Tov* (1878), pp. 46–52, and were republished by Abraham Habermann in *Sefer Gezerot Ashkenaz ve-Ẓarfat* (Jerusalem, 1945), pp. 11–15, 19–21. On these narratives, see Robert Chazan, "The Persecution of 992," *REJ* 129 (1970): 217–21, and idem, "1007–1012: Initial Crisis for Northern-European Jewry," *PAAJR* 38–39 (1970–71): 101–18. A substantial number of rabbinic responsa have been collected and translated by Irving Agus in *Urban Civilization in Pre-Crusade Europe*, 2 vols. (New York, 1965). The most important of the commentaries are those of R. Solomon b. Isaac of Troyes, readily available in standard editions of the Bible and the Talmud. His commentary on the Pentateuch has been translated by Morris Rosenbaum and Abraham Silbermann.

[3] General treatments of tenth- and eleventh-century European Jewry include Salo Baron, *A Social and Religious History of the Jews*, 2nd ed., 14 vols. (New York, 1952–69), vol. 4; Bernhard Blumenkranz, *Juifs et chrétiens dans le monde occidental, 430–1096* (Paris, 1960); Cecil Roth, ed., *The Dark Ages: Jews in Christian Europe 711–1096* (Tel Aviv, 1966); and Irving Agus, *The Heroic Age of Franco-German Jewry* (New York, 1969). For specific studies of northern French Jewry, see Robert Anchel, "Les Juifs des origines aux Croisades," in his *Les Juifs de France* (Paris, 1946), pp. 19–40, and Solomon Schwarzfuchs, "France under the Early Capets," in Roth, *The Dark Ages*, pp. 143–61.

[4] The standard geographic study of medieval French Jewry is Henri Gross, *Gallia Judaica* (Paris, 1897). The value of Gross's work is limited by its excessive reliance on rabbinic sources. Plans for an expansion of Gross's efforts have been announced by Bernhard Blumenkranz, "Pour une nouvelle *Gallia Judaica*," *L'Arche* 106 (December 1965): 42–47, with exploratory findings in his "Contributions à la nouvelle *Gallia Judaica*," *Archives juives* 4 (1967–68): 27–29, 35–37.

[5] Evidence for these Jewish settlements can be found *inter alia* in the following: for Auxerre, see Agus, *Urban Civilization*, vol. 1, p. 174; for Blois, Berliner, *Oẓar Tov*, p. 49, and Habermann, *Sefer Gezerot*, p. 11; for Châlons-sur-Marne, Agus, *Urban Civilization*, vol. 1, p. 174 (Châlons-sur-Marne seems more plausible than Chalon-sur-Saône); for Le Mans, Berliner, *Oẓar Tov*, p. 49, and Habermann, *Sefer Gezerot*, p. 11 (for the identification with Le Mans, see Chazan, "The Persecution of 992"); for Orléans, Raoul Glaber, *Les cinq livres de ses histoires*

the seats of dioceses. Random evidence indicates Jewish presence in smaller towns as well. Thus, in the incident of 992, the villain, a convert from Judaism to Christianity, moved from Blois to Le Mans, visiting (and duping) a number of Jewish communities in western France along the way.[6] Likewise the so-called Rashi ordinance, which dealt with taxation procedures in the Jewry of Troyes, reflects Jewish settlement in smaller towns. The ordinance was enacted by a major Jewish community surrounded by smaller satellites: "We the inhabitants of Troyes, along with the communities in its environs. . . . "[7] By 1096 the Jews had begun to spread beyond the confines of the major cities of northern France.

Widespread insecurity had destroyed the centralized authority of the Carolingians and had brought to power the feudal barony of northern France. Endangered French society had reconstructed itself through a network of immediate personal ties; the unity embodied in Carolingian rule gave way to a host of localized principalities. The Jews, as perhaps the most exposed element in this society, had the deepest need for the protection that only these magnates could offer. They were thus cast into permanent dependence upon a plethora of seigneurs, ranging from king to petty noble.[8]

It is difficult to trace the implications of this dependence in the pre-Crusade period. The political status of northern French Jewry was never specified in comprehensive charters, as was the case in Germany. It is only with the passage of time and the proliferation of records that a detailed picture of Jewish political circumstances emerges. In general it is obvious that even in this early period the political authorities were responsible for basic Jewish security. This included both protection of Jewish life and property and judicial jurisdiction over the Jews. In 992, when a serious charge was leveled at the Jews of Le Mans, the count not only constituted the court before which the Jews were to be tried; he in fact stipulated the procedure to be utilized.[9] It is also possible that even at this early stage governmental support for the Jews included aid in Jewish business affairs. Detailed information on this comes only in the twelfth century, however.

(900–1044), ed. Maurice Prou (Paris, 1886), p. 72; for Reims, Agus, Urban Civilization, vol. 1, p. 174; for Rouen, Berliner, Ozar Tov, p. 47, and Habermann, Sefer Gezerot, p. 20; for Sens, Agus, Urban Civilization, vol. 1, p. 174; for Troyes, ibid.

[6] Berliner, Ozar Tov, p. 49; Habermann, Sefer Gezerot, p. 11.

[7] Louis Finkelstein, Jewish Self-Government in the Middle Ages (New York, 1924), p. 149.

[8] A great deal has been written concerning the breakdown of Carolingian government and the development of new societal bonds. Perhaps the most useful treatment for our purposes is Marc Bloch, Feudal Society, trans. L. A. Manyon (Chicago, 1961).

[9] Berliner, Ozar Tov, p. 51; Habermann, Sefer Gezerot, p. 14.

Willingness to extend to the Jews protection and aid was contingent, of course, on significant advantage to be derived from these Jews. Governmental authorities anticipated two major benefits from Jewish presence: general stimulation of trade and and urban life and, more tangible, the immediate profit to be realized from taxation. Tax records from the early period no longer exist, and information in the Jewish sources is fragmentary. There can be little doubt, however, that the flow of income from this taxation was the major factor in the protective stance taken by the barony of northern France.[10]

The dangers inherent in this alliance with the ruling class were manifested early. While the authorities were relatively successful in protecting the Jews from others, there was no power that could effectively interpose itself between the Jews and their protectors. Only two incidents of any proportion mar the calm of Jewish life in northern France prior to 1096; in both cases it was rulers with unrestricted power over the Jews who were responsible for the persecutions.

The first crisis took place in 992 in the city of Le Mans. A convert from Judaism, one Seḥok b. Esther, after earlier clashes with the Jews of Le Mans, deposited a waxen image in the synagogue ark and then unearthed it in the presence of the count of Maine, Hugh III, claiming that the Jews pierced the image regularly in hopes of destroying the count. In the face of adamant Jewish denials, Hugh of Maine ordered the Jews to be tried by combat with their accuser. The chronicle breaks off at this point, with the Jewish community seemingly on the brink of catastrophe. From the opening remarks of the communal letter which describes the incident, it is obvious that the community emerged unscathed. How this came about is unknown. Perfectly clear, however, is the danger stemming from the Jewish community's total reliance on the will of the governing authorities.[11]

The second major incident was far more serious, both in scope and in consequences. According to a variety of extant sources, the years between 1007 and 1012 saw a series of edicts across northern Europe, posing to the Jews the alternatives of conversion to Christianity and expulsion or, on occasion, death. Most of the Jews seem to have chosen expulsion. In some cases, however, there was loss of life, the first instances of that readiness for martyrdom which became a significant characteristic of Ashkenazic Jewry. Although the factors in this perse-

---

[10]The Jewish sources were concerned primarily with the internal issues of Jewish community affairs, particularly the apportionment and collection of taxation. For later information on taxation of the Jews, see below.

[11]Berliner, *Oẓar Tov*, pp. 49–52; Habermann, *Sefer Gezerot*, pp. 11–15; Chazan, "The Persecution of 992."

cution were of a religious nature, primarily a concern with the spread of heresy in northern Europe, the decision to convert or expel the Jews could only be made by those feudal lords who controlled Jewish fate—once more an important index of the potential dangers inhering in Jewish political status.[12]

While the local lord exercised effective power over the Jews of his domain, there were other forces striving to make their influence felt. Chief among these was the Church. In some cases, churchmen were themselves feudal lords holding direct rights over Jews. Such overt control, however, was not so prominent in northern France as it was elsewhere.[13] The normal channels of Church influence were twofold. The first was the Church's strong moral pressure on the barony. Clerics close to the feudal dignitaries would utilize this intimacy to further their views on the Jews. Thus, for example, in the 992 incident an anonymous churchman strongly bolstered the anti-Jewish animus by his inflammatory speech to the count of Maine.[14] A more circuitous and less effective mode of influence was through the masses. This involved specifying the Jewish behavior which was unacceptable to the Church and threatening excommunication of those Christians having contact with recalcitrant Jews. According to Raoul Glaber, part of the early-eleventh-century program to eliminate Judaism entirely from sections of northern France was abetted by an episcopal decree outlawing all contact with Jews.[15] The major problem with such boycotts was the difficulty of enforcement.

From the point of view of the Jews, ecclesiastical influence could be either beneficial or baneful. In the instance cited, the cleric of Le Mans much inflamed anti-Jewish passions. On the other hand, it was the awareness of potential Church protection that led a Jew of Rouen, Jacob b. Yekutiel, to deny the right of Richard II of Normandy forcibly to convert the Jews: "You lack the necessary jurisdiction over the Jews to force them from their faith or to harm them. This can only be done by the pope at Rome."[16] The claim of Jacob was not a negation of the feudal rights of Richard over the Jews of Normandy; it was an assertion that the program undertaken ostensibly in the name of the Christian faith was in fact a perversion of Christian principles and had

[12] Chazan, "1007–1012: Initial Crisis."

[13] Note, for example, the extensive political power exercised by the bishops of Germany over the Jewish communities of that area.

[14] Berliner, *Ozar Tov*, p. 52; Habermann, *Sefer Gezerot*, p. 15.

[15] Glaber, *Les cinq livres de ses histoires*, p. 72.

[16] Berliner, *Ozar Tov*, p. 47; Habermann, *Sefer Gezerot*, p. 20.

to be brought before the highest ecclesiastical officials for sanction or annulment. According to the Hebrew account, Jacob proceeded to Rome, pleaded his case, and secured a papal decree halting the program of forced conversion.[17]

At this juncture the king exercised no special regalian rights over the Jews. He did, of course, possess normal baronial jurisdiction over the Jews of his own domain. Beyond this, he could on occasion exercise his prerogative as suzerain. It was on this basis that Robert the Pious intervened in the affairs of the county of Sens, deposing Count Raynaud on charges of Judaizing.[18] In the incident of 1007–1012, the king exhibited strong moral leadership in the campaign of forced conversion. While the Hebrew chronicle emphasizes the king's central role in the affair, it also underscores the necessity of agreement by his vassals.

> Then the king and queen took counsel with his officers and his vassals throughout the limits of his kingdom. They charged: "There is one people dispersed throughout the various principalities which does not obey us. . . ." Then there was perfect agreement between the king and his officers, and they concurred on this plan.[19]

Thus the king could suggest action; its execution, however, depended on the consent and the support of the local authorities.

Yet another potential influence on the destiny of the Jews was the municipality and its burghers. In an early stage of development at this point, its lack of authority over the Jews was already manifest. For the Jews, this powerlessness was a boon. If to the princes the Jews promised economic advantage, to the burghers they offered primarily competition. It was all to the Jews' advantage to be removed from the jurisdiction of the growing communes. Yet this removal added political animosity to the religious and economic antipathies already harbored by the townsmen towards the Jews.

During this early period, the populace at large does not appear as a major instigating force in anti-Jewish activity. This was, to be sure, an epoch of substantial violence, and the Jews felt this lawlessness on occasion. The chronicle of 992 mentions in passing economic competition between the renegade Sehok and a member of the Jewish community. This rivalry led eventually to assassination of the Jew by hired

---

[17] Berliner, *Ozar Tov*, pp. 47–48; Habermann, *Sefer Gezerot*, pp. 20–21.

[18] Glaber, *Les cinq livres de ses histoires*, pp. 69–71; Bernhard Blumenkranz has raised doubts about the dating and the authenticity of this incident in *Les auteurs chrétiens latins du moyen age sur les juifs et le judaisme* (Paris, 1963), p. 258, n. 7.

[19] Berliner, *Ozar Tov*, p. 46; Habermann, *Sefer Gezerot*, p. 19.

killers from Blois.[20] The responsa literature reflects the same instability. There is, for example, an interesting responsum dealing with Jewish merchants captured and held for ransom.[21] More striking, however, is the frequency with which governmental oppressions such as those of 992 and 1007–1012 were accompanied by outbursts of popular antipathy. This is attested by the Hebrew chronicle for 992 and by a number of the sources for 1007–1012.[22] The breakdown of official protection allowed the overt expression of that popular hatred normally suppressed by the authorities.

The Jews of northern France were by the eleventh century already supporting themselves primarily by commerce, and, as the century progressed, this led them increasingly into moneylending. The reliance on commerce and usury is reflected in a most interesting responsum from the early eleventh century. The community had "levied on every man and woman, while under the ban, a fixed amount per pound of value of his or her *money, merchandise,* and *other saleable possessions*"; trade and banking were obviously primary.[23] Despite the ordinance's orientation towards taxation of merchandise and money, the community attempted to levy taxes on a local Jewess's vineyard, demanding a portion of the value of both the land and its produce. The terms in which the issue was debated are revealing:

They [the community] claimed that vineyards were in the same category as the capital of a loan, while the harvested crop was equivalent to the interest. One derived no benefit from the vineyard itself, nor from the capital of the loan, during the first half year or year of its investment. Since they paid taxes from both the capital and the interest of their money investments, from their merchandise as well as from its profit, they held that L should do likewise. L, on her part, pointed out that a vineyard could not be compared to the capital of a loan, nor even to merchandise. . . . Thus they argued back and forth.[24]

---

[20] Berliner, *Ozar Tov*, p. 50; Habermann, *Sefer Gezerot*, p. 12.

[21] Agus, *Urban Civilization*, vol. 1, p. 174.

[22] For 992, see Berliner, *Ozar Tov*, p. 52; Habermann, *Sefer Gezerot*, p. 15. For 1007–1012, see especially Berliner, *Ozar Tov*, p. 47; Habermann, *Sefer Gezerot*, pp. 19–20; and Raoul Glaber, *Les cinq livres de ses histoires*, p. 72.

[23] Agus, *Urban Civilization*, vol. 2, pp. 438–39 (italics mine).

[24] Ibid., p. 439. The translation is somewhat free. Agus notes the primacy of commerce in his comments on this responsum; compare his *The Heroic Age of Franco-German Jewry*, pp. 101–2.

What is plainly assumed by both sides in the dispute is the centrality of wares and capital in communal taxation. The reply of R. Joseph Bon Fils agreed with the position that *only* merchandise, money, and the profits from both are taxable.

The economic reliance on commerce and moneylending emerges also from the famous ordinance of Rashi, dating from the end of the eleventh century.

> We, the inhabitants of Troyes, along with the communities in its environs, have ordained—under threat of excommunication—upon every man and woman living here that they be forbidden to remove themselves from the yoke of communal responsibility. . . . Each one shall give per pound that which is enjoined by the members of the community, as has been practiced since the very day of its founding. We have likewise received from our predecessors the practice of paying on all possessions, except household items, houses, vineyards, and fields.[25]

A community which exempts "household items, houses, vineyards, and fields" from taxation is obviously heavily involved in mercantile pursuits.

Jewish commerce was probably largely local. As noted, evidence for settlement shows the Jews primarily in major urban centers. A number of responsa, however, indicate Jews traveling through northern France, trading at the fairs of this period. Insecurity made such travel hazardous on occasion; Jewish traders were seized and their goods confiscated.[26] Sometimes the inherent dangers of commerce were magnified by involvement in shady dealings. An early–eleventh-century responsum deals with the legal complications arising from the disappearance and presumed death of an unscrupulous Jewish merchant. The questionable practices, which probably led to his violent demise, are described as follows:

> A was accustomed to travel to many places and to many towns situated within a day or two of his residence. He would sell to and buy from the overlords of these towns, his regular clientele. Whenever they were short of cash, he would sell to them on credit, against pledges of gold or silver, or exchange his merchandise for cattle (or horses) which they had robbed from their enemies. These cattle he would accept at a low price, bring them home and sell them for a much higher price. His activities aroused the anger and hatred of the

---

[25] Finkelstein, *Jewish Self-Government*, p. 149.

[26] Agus, *Urban Civilization*, vol. 1, p. 174.

plundered villagers, and of their feudal lords, who would say: "This Jew, by the very fact that he is always ready to buy looted goods, entices our enemies to attack and plunder us. . . ." Moreover, occasionally the overlords quarrelled with him on account of the pledges which A would eventually sell and because of the high interest he charged.[27]

The normal hazards of eleventh-century trade were here much enhanced.

The same responsum reveals the very fluid transition which many Jews made from commerce to lending. When his customers lacked the necessary cash at hand to make their purchases, the Jewish merchant would extend credit. In fact, there is an indication of the mechanism utilized for safeguarding this investment. The debtors gained the necessary credit by depositing pledges, which were held as security for repayment of the obligation. In case of eventual nonpayment, these pledged objects could be sold. No litigation or third party was needed, and the creditor was amply protected from the moment that the loan was extended. Safeguarding loans through retention of a pledge is, of course, the simplest expedient available, and it was probably the most common method used during this period.[28]

There are, nonetheless, fragmentary signs of more sophisticated arrangements. A responsum of Rashi deals with a dispute between a widow and her brother-in-law concerning gifts allegedly given to the widow and her deceased husband by his parents. Chief among these gifts was "the tithe collectible from a certain village, which tithe had been pledged with L and J [the parents] for a loan of seven rotl. L and J thus empowered R and A to collect the produce of that tithe and the principal of the loan in the event the original owner of the tithe should come to repay the loan and redeem his pledge."[29] While this arrangement is also designated a pledge (mashkon), it is quite different from the pledges indicated earlier. The former were physical objects which were deposited at the time of the loan. When the debt was repaid, the pawn was returned; if the borrower defaulted, it would be kept or sold. In the case of the tithe, however, it was not a physical object that changed hands; it was a right. The difference in practical terms was twofold. First, there was constant revenue; the lender collected regular

[27] Ibid., p. 99.

[28] For a comprehensive study of Jewish pawnbroking during this period, see Haym Soloveitchik, "Pawnbroking: A Study in *Ribbit* and of the Halakah in Exile," *PAAJR* 38–39 (1970–71): 203–68.

[29] Agus, *Urban Civilization*, vol. 1, p. 407.

income, which was probably seen as the interest on the loan. More important, this was an arrangement that involved more than simply a creditor and a debtor; the implicit aid of a governmental agency was necessary. The creditor did not physically control the pledge; hence, should contention arise, he had to have the certainty of powerful support. Lending of the kind revealed in the responsum of Rashi is far more complex and generally more lucrative; it had as its result the further tightening of the crucial bond between Jew and baron. As Jews turned increasingly towards this kind of business operation, they began to depend on their overlords not only for physical protection but for buttressing their financial investments as well. Prior to the First Crusade this more complex method of lending may have remained rather uncommon. It was, however, destined to play an increasingly important role in Jewish economic life.

The aspect of pre-Crusade Jewish life that has attracted the most scholarly attention has been its communal organization.[30] The Jewish communities of northern France were small, with a high level of internal cohesion and a broad range of activities. Yitzhak Baer has delineated three major functions in this community: the preservation of satisfactory relations with the ruling powers, the securing of internal discipline and order, and the establishment of necessary internal economic limitations and controls.[31]

The alliance fashioned between the Jews and the barony was fueled by the tangible advantages realized by the feudal magnates. The most immediate expression of this was taxation. Collection of taxes was certainly one of the major functions assumed by the communal agencies. The responsum specifying those holdings open to taxation indicates that the purpose of the levy was "to collect the king's tax."[32]

The methods for apportioning taxation were well-established and reflect the cohesiveness of the community. One method was that indicated in the above-noted responsum. This involved levying "on every man and woman, while under the ban, a fixed amount per pound of value of his or her money, merchandise, and other saleable possessions."[33] This system depended for its effectiveness upon honest evalu-

---

[30] Yitzhak Baer, "The Origins of the Organisation of the Jewish Community of the Middle Ages" (Hebrew), *Zion* 15 (1950):1–41; Irving Agus, "Democracy in the Communities of the Early Middle Ages," *JQR* 43 (1952–53): 153–76; Shlomo Eidelberg, "The Community of Troyes before the Time of Rashi" (Hebrew), *Sura* 1 (1953–54): 48–57; Agus, *The Heroic Age of Franco-German Jewry*, pp. 185–276.

[31] Baer, "The Origins of the Organisation," pp. 32–36.

[32] Agus, *Urban Civilization*, vol. 2, p. 438.

[33] Ibid., pp. 438–39.

ation, by each member of the community, of his possessions. The likelihood of such honesty was enhanced by the religious sanctions mentioned and by the closeness of a small community, where the temptation to underevaluate would be tempered by the difficulty of concealing the truth. Occasionally, however, this arrangement broke down. R. Joseph Bon Fils was asked to resolve a complicated issue that began with the following circumstance:

> The people of T came to pay the king's tax. They complained against one another, saying: "You lightened your own burden and made mine heavier." Whereupon they selected trustees, the noble and great of the town, the experts of the land, from the community, and (agreed) to abide by their decision, for they dealt faithfully.[34]

The role of the Jewish community organization as a liaison between the Jews and the ruling authorities was not exhausted by the collection of taxes. On occasion the organized community had to make representation before the authorities on matters affecting the security of the Jews. Thus, in 992, when faced with the danger of trial by combat, the Jewish community made vehement protestations before the count of Maine. They appealed to precedent, on the one hand, and offered substantial material inducements, on the other.[35] While in this instance there was large-scale community response, in periods of crisis a prominent individual could take the initiative, thrusting himself to the fore as the community's spokesman. It was in this manner that Jacob b. Yekutiel ventured to step forth before the duke of Normandy and ultimately before the pope himself.[36]

In a community desperately anxious to preserve its insulation from the local municipality within whose boundaries it lived and to achieve a measure of distance from even the more favorably-disposed feudal authorities, there was an absolute necessity for maintaining inner discipline. While the small size of the Jewish community contributed to cohesiveness, close living could on occasion produce sharp conflicts between members of the community. In the face of such conflict, the community marshaled its forces and ordained limitations on intracommunal strife. The community's goal in such cases was the preservation of peace within the community, without the intervention of outside powers.

---

[34] Ibid., p. 466.

[35] Berliner, *Ozar Tov*, p. 51; Habermann, *Sefer Gezerot*, p. 14.

[36] Berliner, *Ozar Tov*, pp. 47–48; Habermann, *Sefer Gezerot*, pp. 20–21.

The economic outlets available to the Jews were not extensive. For this reason the community had to exercise significant control in the area of economics also. The two major thrusts of communal limitation were the granting of exclusive commercial privileges and the restriction of the right to settle. The former usually involved business dealings with important secular lords or ecclesiastical institutions. From the slim evidence available, it seems that the arrangement was not everywhere operative and that, even where the prerogative of the community to give such privileges was recognized, the rights of exclusive trade were not widely granted.[37] Restriction of settlement was directly related to the economic situation of the Jews. The small towns of northern France could absorb only so many Jewish traders and moneylenders. Over-population would simply force the available income of the community below the subsistence level. Again it must be noted, however, that the right of the community to declare a total or even a partial ban on new settlement was far from universally recognized.[38]

To the three major functions of the Jewish community delineated by Baer at least a fourth must be added. The Jewish community of necessity had to supply certain essential religious and social services to its membership. The centrality of the synagogue in the Jewish community of this period is undisputed. It was far more than a center of worship, serving as an educational and general communal center as well. Details of Jewish schooling at the time are almost nonexistent. The literacy demanded by the business pursuits of the Jews and the already high level of cultural achievement indicate a successful educational system. Within the medieval municipality there were of course no "neutral" social welfare agencies; such facilities as did exist were Church institutions and, as such, closed to the Jews; thus the Jews had to provide for their own indigent, ill, and unfortunate. The needs of the local community were often augmented by the requirements of Jews whose business took them from town to town. In the case of the central figure in the Le Mans letter, as he proceeded through the Jewish communities of northwestern France, the Jews "supported him, as is their custom, in every town to which he came."[39] Perhaps the most striking evidence of such concern is revealed in the following responsum:

Jews of Rheims, while on their way to the fair of Troyes, were attacked, plundered, and taken captive by "an adversary and an

[37] See Agus, *The Heroic Age of Franco-German Jewry*, pp. 79–86.

[38] See Finkelstein, *Jewish Self-Government*, pp. 10–15; Louis Rabinowitz, *The Herem Hayyishub* (London, 1945); and Agus, *The Heroic Age of Franco-German Jewry*, pp. 90–94.

[39] Berliner, *Ozar Tov*, p. 49; Habermann, *Sefer Gezerot*, p. 11.

enemy." The charitable Jews of Troyes risked their own lives, (negotiated with the enemy,) and agreed to a redemption price of thirty pounds. The greater part of the ransom money was paid by the captives themselves; while in order to raise the remainder, the community of Troyes levied a tax of one *solidus* per pound on themselves, as well as on the neighboring communities of Sens and Auxerre, and on the Jews of Chalon-sur-Saone.[40]

The locus of power in the Jewish community was the community membership itself. While the governing authorities benefited from the ability of the community to control its own affairs, particularly in the area of taxation, there was as yet no strong drive for more direct involvement in Jewish communal affairs or for more extensive exploitation of this useful and cohesive group. As noted, the community, for its part, was anxious to minimize outside interference.

The rhetoric of community enactments generally emphasized unanimous decisionmaking by the entire local Jewry: "The community of Troyes levied a tax. . ."; "the townspeople levied on every man and woman. . ."; "the community . . . heard about it and solemnly pronounced the ban. . . ."[41] There was, in fact, even question as to the right of the majority to exercise its will over the minority.[42]

At the same time, however, certain elements in the community did command special authority. Leadership was exercised by significant scholarly figures, such as Rashi, or by men of wealth and standing, such as Jacob b. Yekutiel. An interesting responsum indicates a more general tendency towards control by a segment of the community. In a conflict concerning the responsibility of individuals to accept the decisions of the majority, the following question was asked:

We are a small community. The humble members among us have always abided by the leadership of our eminent members, dutifully obeyed their decrees, and never protested against their ordinances. Now, when we are about to enact a decree, must we ask each individual member whether or not he is in agreement with it?[43]

Even at this early point a leadership class does seem to have emerged, although it certainly lacked the direct governmental support and the recognized religious authority that would later develop.

---

[40] Agus, *Urban Civilization*, vol. 1, p. 174. We have suggested earlier that Châlons-sur-Marne is more likely.

[41] Ibid., vol. 1, p. 174, and vol. 2, pp. 438, 499.

[42] Agus, "Democracy in the Communities of the Early Middle Ages."

[43] Idem, *Urban Civilization*, vol. 2, p. 448.

With the community itself as the fundamental authority, it is in no way surprising to find power highly localized. The question of the right of one Jewish settlement to legislate for others was raised a number of times. In general a distinction was drawn between daily administrative affairs—where each community was autonomous—and principles of Jewish religious behavior—where coercion could be exerted. One of a number of expressions of this distinction is phrased in the following way:

> As to your question whether the inhabitants of one town are competent to enact decrees binding on the inhabitants of another town, and to coerce the latter inhabitants while they are in their own town, the following ruling seems proper to us: If the decree that they are enacting deals with the needs of their place, such as taxation, weights, measures, and wages—in all such matters the inhabitants of one town are not competent to legislate for the inhabitants of another town. Thus we quoted above the Talmudic ruling: "The townspeople are permitted," which means that only the people of the town are competent to legislate in such matters but not outsiders. If, however, the inhabitants of a town transgressed a law of the Torah, committed a wrong, or decided a point of law or of ritual, not in accordance with the accepted usage—the inhabitants of another town might coerce them, and even pronounce the *ḥerem* against them, in order to force them to mend their ways. In that case, the inhabitants of the former town may not say to the latter: "we are independent of you, we exercise authority among ourselves, as you do among yourselves." For all Israel is then enjoined to force them (to mend their ways); as we find in the case of the "rebellious sage," or "the condemned city," that the Sanhedrin coerces them and judges them.[44]

Extensive authority was exercised by outstanding scholarly figures, whose enactments were generally considered binding over a wide number of settlements. Thus, Rashi affirms that the important edict of R. Gershom of Mayence would certainly be applicable in all Jewish communities.

> Should it become established through the testimony of reliable witnesses who are recognized authorities on this restrictive ordinance of the great teacher (R. Gershom), that he enacted this ordinance with greater rigor and strictness than all other anathemas and restrictive measures customarily enacted in the last generations; that in this enactment he used the awesome term *shamta*; and that he solemnly

---

[44]Ibid., vol. 2, p. 452.

prohibited to mention the disgrace (of temporary apostasy) not only to the culprits themselves who eventually returned to Judaism, but even to their descendants; and should it further become established that when A and his family were forewarned, the name of the great teacher (as author of the awesome ban) was mentioned to them—we cannot deal lightly with a ban of Rabbenu Gershom, since in our generation there is no scholar of his great eminence, capable to release a person from such a ban.[45]

The sanctions at the disposal of the community were of course conditioned by the bases of its power. One possibility lay in the direction of the secular authority, but it was an avenue only sparingly utilized because of the danger inhering in such an approach. Thus, an early-eleventh-century Jewish community faced with the overt recalcitrance of two of its members and the support of a neighboring community for the rebels was "about to ask the king to order his constables to collect his tax directly from A and B. Upon further deliberation, however, they changed their minds and decided first to inquire whether their solemn decree was still valid, i.e., whether the cancellation thereof by the community of S was of any consequence."[46] A turn to secular authorities was a step which most Jewish communities were reluctant to take.

Since the most tangible locus of power was the cohesive community itself, the ultimate weapon at the disposal of the Jews was the ban of excommunication. Given the importance of the Jewish community and its facilities to the individual Jew, the power of exclusion was a formidable one. The ostracized Jew was in a hazardous position politically, economically, socially, and religiously. At the same time, excommunication was not an infallible tool in the hands of the Jewish community. The realities of power within the community often limited the effectiveness of the ban. In one case, for example, "since the members of the community feared that B and his friends, living so near the synagogue, would remove the scrolls of the Law and other community articles, and that no one would be able to stop them from taking these articles, they transgressed the law on several occasions—all on B's instructions."[47] Another limitation on the effectiveness of excommunication was the localization of Jewish authority already noted. Thus two Jews excommunicated in community T "went to S and related there the whole incident. The people of S took A and B into their homes, wined and dined them, transacted business with them, lifted from them the ban of

[45] Ibid., p. 501.
[46] Ibid., p. 467.
[47] Ibid., p. 447.

community T, and gave them a written release of such ban."[48] While the action of community S was judged illegal, in fact the localization of power did weaken the impact of any such ban.

The Jewish community of northern France thus emerges, from earliest times, as a remarkably cohesive and comprehensive organization. The isolation of the Jews forced them to create for themselves all sorts of agencies—political, economic, social, educational, and religious. The small size of the individual Jewish settlements precluded the independence of each of these agencies. What emerged then was a total Jewish community responsible for filling every one of the vital needs of its constituents. Therein lies the secret of the wide range of powers and the effectiveness of the Jewish community organization even at its early stage of development.

Perhaps the most persuasive index of the level of maturity reached by northern French Jewry prior to the First Crusade is its intellectual creativity. It seems reasonable to conclude that a community capable of producing extensive scholarly achievement like that of R. Solomon b. Isaac of Troyes (Rashi) must have been well-established and effectively organized. Rashi, already noted as an outstanding communal authority—one of the few whose eminence was broadly recognized—wrote copiously. His works, which quickly became classics in Ashkenazic circles, included primarily extensive commentaries on the Bible and the Talmud.[49] While he was always revered as the beginning—and not the culmination—of a brilliant series of northern French scholars, his creations indicate that, by the last years of the eleventh century, northern French Jewry had come of age.

At the end of the eleventh century many of the creative forces that had been germinating steadily throughout western Europe burst forth into the passion, vision, and violence of the First Crusade. The Crusade was an expression of the new militance of Christendom against its external foes; it revealed also new potential for internal upheaval and disruption. While the goal of the pope and of the great barons was a military expedition against Islam, the feelings unleashed by the call to the Crusade could hardly be contained within the particular channels

<hr />

[48] Ibid., p. 466.

[49] On Rashi, see Maurice Liber, *Rashi*, trans. A. Szold (Philadelphia, 1906); *Rashi Anniversary Volume*, published by the American Academy for Jewish Research (New York, 1941); Judah Fishman, ed., *Sefer Rashi* (Jerusalem, 1956); Irving Agus, "Rashi and His School," in Roth, *The Dark Ages*.

delineated by its instigators. Thus the First Crusade brought more than the conquest of Jerusalem; it left a path of death and destruction within Christendom itself.[50]

The dispossessed who took up the chant "Deus lo volt" savagely vented pent-up furies upon many of their long-despised neighbors. Given the pervasive religiosity of medieval civilization and the distinctly religious hatreds that animated the Crusaders, it comes as no surprise that the prime object of the internal violence associated with the First Crusade was European Jewry.

France, particularly northern France, played a major role in the great drama of 1095–1099. It was in the French city of Clermont that Urban II issued his appeal; French barons were conspicuous in their leadership of the crusading forces; it was in the French countryside that Peter the Hermit began his preaching for a humble army of the pious to free the holy places from Moslem hands. Yet France, despite its prominence, was spared the upheavals that followed in the wake of Crusade preaching.[51] France's eastern neighbors bore the brunt of the devastation that crusading fervor unleashed.

The relative calm with which France weathered the Crusade is reflected in the fate of her Jews. The same Jewish and Christian sources that are so copious in their description of Jewish sufferings in the Rhineland area say almost nothing of Jewish fate in France. Although arguments from silence are always suspect, it is difficult to believe that this set of Jewish and Christian chroniclers and editors would have been unaware of, or uninterested in recounting, extensive Jewish tragedy in nearby France. The Rhineland Jews who compiled the Hebrew chronicles knew the reactions of the French Jews to the organization of the Crusade, and they detailed Jewish persecution over a broad area. It is inconceivable that large-scale catastrophe in France could have gone unknown or unreported.[52] Moreover, the longest of the Hebrew Crusade chronicles is embedded in a late–twelfth-century communal his-

---

[50] For a general description of the First Crusade, see Steven Runciman, *A History of the Crusades*, 3 vols. (Cambridge, 1951–54), vol. 1; Kenneth Setton, ed., *A History of the Crusades*, 2 vols. (Philadelphia, 1955–62), vol. 1, pp. 3–367; and Joshua Prawer, *Toldot Mamlekhet ha-Ẓalbanim be-Ereẓ Yisrael*, rev. ed., 2 vols. (Jerusalem, 1971), vol. 1, pp. 3–148.

[51] On the movement of the Crusaders through western Europe and the outbreak of violence, see Runciman, *A History of the Crusades*, vol. 1, pp. 119–71; Setton, *A History of the Crusades*, vol. 1, pp. 253–79; and Prawer, *Toldot Mamlekhet ha-Ẓalbanim*, vol. 1, pp. 92–103.

[52] The Hebrew First-Crusade chronicles were published by Adolf Neubauer and Moritz Stern, *Hebräische Berichte über die Judenverfolgungen während der Kreuzzüge* (Berlin, 1892), pp. 1–30, 36–46, 47–57, and were republished in Habermann, *Sefer Gezerot*, pp. 24–59, 72–82, 93–104; note my study of these chronicles to appear shortly in the *REJ*.

tory of Spires Jewry, which includes a series of letters detailing the Blois catastrophe of 1171 and its aftermath. The Spires editor would not have omitted information on Crusade tragedy in France had it been available.[53]

There is satisfactory evidence for but one specific persecution of Jews within the area of northern France, an attack which took place in the Norman city of Rouen. The fullest description of this assault is given by Guibert of Nogent as a backdrop to his account of a monk of the monastery of Fly.

> At Rouen on a certain day, the people who had undertaken to go on that expedition [that is, the Crusade] under the badge of the Cross began to complain to one another, "After traversing great distances, we desire to attack the enemies of God in the East, although the Jews, of all races the worst foe of God, are before our eyes. That's doing our work backward." Saying this and seizing their weapons, they herded the Jews into a certain place of worship, rounding them up by either force or guile, and without distinction of sex or age put them to the sword. Those who accepted Christianity, however, escaped the impending slaughter.[54]

The striking difference between the relative peace enjoyed by northern France and its Jews and the wholesale destruction, especially of Jewish life and property, further east can be accounted for in a number of ways. This difference is surely *not* a reflection of more benign French attitudes; as Norman Golb has argued, French Crusaders were deeply implicated in the wave of German atrocities associated with the First Crusade.[55] In France, however, their antipathy was not translated into deed, partially because France was the very first area of organization. The problems of the undisciplined Crusader bands tended to multiply the further eastward they moved, the larger their numbers, and

---

[53]On the composite Spires chronicle, see Robert Chazan, "A Twelfth-Century Communal History of Spires Jewry," *REJ* 128 (1969): 253–57. The position taken here diverges widely from that presented by Norman Golb in his "New Light on the Persecution of French Jews at the Time of the First Crusade," *PAAJR* 34 (1966): 1–64. While agreeing that Frenchmen were implicated in the attacks on German Jews, we find only the incident in Rouen attested for our area of northern France. Even with Golb's reconstruction of the persecution at Monieux (out of our domain), the evidence for Jewish suffering in France is extremely sparse. It seems to us that Golb has made far too much of Monieux and of the participation of Frenchmen in massacres elsewhere.

[54]John Benton, ed., *Self and Society in Medieval France* (New York, 1970), pp. 134–35. Guibert's rendition of the rationalization for attacks on the Jews corresponds perfectly to the reports of the Jewish chroniclers. See Neubauer and Stern, *Hebräische Berichte*, pp. 1, 4, 36–37, 47, and Habermann, *Sefer Gezerot*, pp. 24, 27, 72, 93.

[55]Golb, "New Light on the Persecution of French Jews," pp. 31–35.

the slimmer their provisions. The initial rallying of these crusading groups in France and their speedy movement towards the East played a major role in the safety of French Jewry. A second factor was the protection afforded by the less pretentious, but more effective, French political authorities. While the emperor was the most exalted political dignitary of Europe, the base upon which his power rested was a shaky one.[56] Thus, in town after town, the Jews found themselves separated from large and bloodthirsty mobs by the flimsy military and political power of the local bishop. Even the Hebrew chroniclers recognize that many of these bishops were sincere in their desire to protect their Jews; their failure resulted from a lack of the required force.[57] In France, on the other hand, where the Capetian monarchy advanced none of the grandiose claims of the German empire, firm political power had been slowly crystallizing in a series of well-organized principalities. Within these principalities the count and his growing retinue of administrative officials exercised effective authority. It was this political stability also that aided in harnessing the violence of the Crusaders and in sparing the Jews.

Although the Jews of northern France suffered little during the tumultuous first months of the Crusade, they were hardly oblivious to the dangers. In fact they were far more aware of the impending threat than any of their fellow Jews, for it was in their land that the Crusade was called, that the first active preaching took place, and that the first crusading groups began to form. The same Hebrew chronicle that said nothing of overt persecution in France recorded faithfully the fears of the French Jews.

At the time when the Jewish communities in France heard [of the beginning of the Crusade] they were seized with fear and trembling. They then resorted to the devices of their predecessors. They wrote letters and sent messengers to the Rhineland communities, that these communities fast and seek mercy on their behalf from the God who dwells on high, so that they might be spared.[58]

The Hebrew chronicles also reported the more immediate steps taken by French Jewry to avert the threatened catastrophe. This information is contained in the brief description of the passage of Peter the Hermit through Trèves.

---

[56]The absence of the emperor in Italy was prominently noted by the longest Hebrew chronicle—Neubauer and Stern, *Hebräische Berichte*, p. 3; Habermann, *Sefer Gezerot*, pp. 26-27.

[57]Note, for example, the role of the bishops in Spires, Worms, Mayence, and Cologne.

[58]Neubauer and Stern, *Hebräische Berichte*, p. 47; Habermann, *Sefer Gezerot*, p. 93.

When he came to Trèves—he and the multitude of men with him—to go forth on their pilgrimage to Jerusalem, he brought with him from France a letter from the Jews, indicating that, in all places where he would pass through Jewish communities, they should afford him provisions. He then would speak favorably on behalf of the Jews.[59]

Given the lack of destructive violence against the Jews in northern France, we can readily understand the lack of a political aftermath parallel to that which took place in Germany. Guido Kisch has carefully chronicled the evolution in Germany of safeguards designed to protect the vulnerable Jewish communities.[60] Jewish political status in France, however, underwent no significant development in the wake of the First Crusade. There had been, after all, no major calamity to arouse among the Jews themselves or among their baronial overlords a heightened sense of the urgent need for new protective devices.

Furthermore, French Jewry never viewed 1095–1096 as a watershed in its history, as did its German counterpart.[61] While the works of Rashi represent an early high point of French Jewish religious creativity, his successors did not see themselves as mere compilers of his legacy; they considered their efforts a continuation, not a collection. When, much later on, the sense of a chain of giant figures emerges, this series runs from Rashi through R. Samson of Sens, from the late eleventh through the early thirteenth centuries. The years of the First Crusade are in no sense construed as a major dividing line. Interestingly enough, when in 1171 French Jewry suffered what it considered its first major catastrophe, the calamity at Blois, it very movingly expressed the feelings of horror evoked by the utterly senseless death of over thirty Jews. If ever one might expect French Jewish recollection of the First Crusade, this would surely be the point. Yet significantly there is no recall whatsoever of 1096. When old memories are summoned up, they are recollections of a much earlier period. Thus, according to Ephraim of Bonn, R. Jacob Tam ordained that the twentieth of Sivan, the day of the catastrophe itself, "is fit to be set as a fast day for all our people. Indeed the gravity of this fast will exceed that of the fast of Gedaliah b. Aḥikam, for this is a veritable Day of Atonement."[62] The fateful year of the First Crusade in no way dominated the subsequent consciousness of northern French Jewry.

[59] Neubauer and Stern, *Hebräische Berichte*, p. 25; Habermann, *Sefer Gezerot,* pp. 52–53.

[60] Guido Kisch, *The Jews in Medieval Germany* (Chicago, 1949), pp. 129–45.

[61] On German views of 1096 as a decisive turning point in the history of Ashkenazic Jewry, see Joseph Hacker, "About the Persecutions during the First Crusade" (Hebrew), *Zion* 31 (1966): 225–31.

[62] Neubauer and Stern, *Hebräische Berichte*, p. 68; Habermann, *Sefer Gezerot*, p. 126.

Through the late tenth and on through the eleventh century, then, northern French Jewry continued to develop, benefiting from the general progress of western European civilization and making its own contribution to that progress. Already tightly allied with the powerful feudal barony, the Jews were involving themselves ever more heavily in the burgeoning urban commerce and had begun to develop viable institutions of self-government. By the end of the eleventh century, northern French Jewry was sufficiently mature to produce its first figure of renown, R. Solomon b. Isaac of Troyes. Relatively unscathed by the anti-Jewish outbreaks of the First Crusade, French Jewry proceeded into the twelfth century in a spirit of continued growth.

II

TWELFTH-CENTURY GROWTH AND

DEVELOPMENT

THE MAJOR EFFORTS expended during the First Crusade did not slow the rapid development of northern French civilization; in many ways the pace was in fact accelerated. During the twelfth century, population further increased, cities continued to expand, and trade and industry progressed. The strong principalities of the eleventh century grew larger and more powerful. The Angevin count turned king of England was considered by many the most formidable secular figure in western Christendom. Still obscured by some of their vassals, Louis VI and Louis VII quietly laid the foundation for the potent thirteenth-century Capetian monarchy. The burgeoning resources and confidence of the period are well-expressed in its religious and intellectual achievements. This age saw the birth of a majestic new architecture, intense monastic reform, and the intellectual vitality of the Parisian schools.[1]

---

[1] The period between 1096 and 1180 is covered by Auguste Longnon in Ernest Lavisse, *Histoire de France*, 9 vols. in 18 (Paris, 1900-1911), vol. 2, pt. 2, and vol. 3, pt. 1. The most detailed studies of the reigns of Louis VI and Louis VII are Achille Luchaire, *Louis VI le Gros* (Paris, 1890), and Marcel Pacaut, *Louis VII et son royaume* (Paris, 1964). For Champagne, see Henri d'Arbois de Jubainville, *Histoire des ducs et des comtes de Champagne*, 7 vols. in 8 (Paris, 1859-69). For Normandy, see Léopold Delisle, "Des revenus de la Normandie au XIIe siècle," *BEC* 10 (1848-49), 11 (1850), and 13 (1852); Charles Haskins, *Norman Institutions* (Cambridge, Mass., 1918); and Frederick Powicke, *The Loss of Normandy*, 2nd ed. (New York, 1961).

In this dynamic setting French Jewish life kept stride. The commercial needs of the vigorous urban centers made the Jews increasingly useful. Unshaken by the First-Crusade crisis that had disrupted German Jewish life, French Jewry still prospered. Its political and commercial alliance with the feudal barony deepened. The acknowledged genius of Rashi notwithstanding, the creative figures of the twelfth century, such as R. Samuel b. Meir, R. Jacob Tam, his brother, and R. Isaac of Dampierre, their nephew, were held in the highest esteem by their contemporaries and by succeeding generations.[2]

Evidence for Jewish life during this period remains vexingly sparse. Documentary sources do appear for the first time, helpfully augmenting the literary materials, both Jewish and Christian. Meagerness of data, however, does not imply a primitive state of development. The occasional glimpses available into twelfth-century Jewish life reveal ever more sophisticated political and economic ties between the Jews and the ruling authorities, deepening resentment in key sectors of Christian society, and increasingly advanced forms of Jewish self-government. The complexities of the early years of the reign of Philip Augustus can only be grasped against the background of the sparsely-documented preceding decades.

The paucity of documentary materials for this period renders impossible reconstruction of precise patterns of Jewish settlement. Many additional locales of Jewish residence are attested, however, including Bourges, Bray, Corbeil, Dampierre, Épernay, Étampes, Janville, Joigny, Loches, Melun, Montmorency, Pontoise, Ramerupt, Saint-Denis, Tonnerre, and Vitry. This list is clearly far from complete.[3]

An important document drawn up in the mid twelfth century affords insight into the major centers of this expanding Jewry.

---

[2] The best general treatment of twelfth-century northern French Jewry is by Salo Baron, *A Social and Religious History of the Jews*, 2nd ed., 14 vols. (New York, 1952–69), vol. 4. An interesting study of the fragmentary evidence for one community is Aryeh Grabois, "L'Abbaye de Saint-Denis et les Juifs sous l'abbatiat de Suger," *Annales* 24 (1969): 1187–95. Helpful material can be found in Louis Rabinowitz, *The Social Life of the Jews of Northern France in the XII–XIV Centuries* (London, 1938), and in Ephraim Urbach's depiction of major twelfth-century figures such as R. Jacob Tam in his *Ba'aley ha-Tosafot* (Jerusalem, 1955); on R. Tam specifically, compare Shalom Albeck, "Rabbenu Tam's Attitude to the Problems of his Time" (Hebrew), *Zion* 19 (1954): 104–41. The cultural history of the period is best treated in Urbach, *Ba'aley ha-Tosafot*, and in Samuel Poznanski's introductory essay to the commentaries of R. Eliezer of Beaugency.

[3] The evidence includes information on Jewish scholarly figures (Dampierre, Melun, Ramerupt, Vitry), details of the Blois incident of 1171 (Épernay, Janville, Loches, Pontoise), and random documentary materials (Bourges, Corbeil, Etampes, Montmorency, Saint-Denis, Tonnerre). The fragmentary state of the data makes it obvious that Jewish settlement was far wider.

Therefore have we taken counsel together: the elders of Troyes and its sages and those in its surrounding environs; the sages of Dijon and its environs; the leaders of Auxerre and Sens and its adjacent communities; the elders of Orléans and surrounding territories; our brethren the inhabitants of Châlons; the sages of the area of Reims; our masters in Paris and their neighbors; the scholars of Melun and Étampes. . . .[4]

The intense Jewish political activity in the wake of the Blois catastrophe of 1171 indicates that the Jewish communities of Paris and Troyes, each located in the capital city of a major principality, were, naturally enough, the two most important centers of Jewish political influence.[5]

Little evidence concerning the size of medieval northern French Jewish communities has survived, and few of these meager data antedate the thirteenth century. The only contemporary demographic estimate is the suggestion of Ephraim of Bonn that the Jewish community of Blois, prior to its decimation, consisted of four quorums of Jews.[6] This could mean forty adult males, giving a total population of approximately two hundred men, women, and children; it might indicate simply a settlement of forty or so Jews. There were probably a number of Jewish communities larger than that of Blois, for example, Paris, Troyes, Provins; there were also many settlements much smaller. Rabbinic sources of the twelfth century deal with a number of problems resulting from the minuscule size of many Jewish enclaves. One of the queries addressed to R. Jacob Tam concerned litigants who were forced to seek a court outside their own community, which was so small that almost every member was related and hence disqualified as a judge.[7] R. Isaac of Dampierre, a late–twelfth-century leader, even mentions Jews living alone in the midst of a completely non-Jewish town.[8]

During the twelfth century the Jewish population of northern France was in all probability, like the general population, increasing. As hamlets grew into substantial towns and new urban centers were founded, new Jewish settlements also developed. An echo of this spread is perhaps to be found in the charge leveled by Geoffroy of Courlon against King Louis VII: "Deceived by avarice and against the integrity of faith,

---

[4] Louis Finkelstein, *Jewish Self-Government in the Middle Ages* (New York, 1924), p. 153.

[5] Robert Chazan, "The Blois Incident of 1171: A Study in Jewish Intercommunal Organization," *PAAJR* 36 (1968): 22.

[6] Adolf Neubauer and Moritz Stern, eds., *Hebräische Berichte über die Judenverfolgungen während der Kreuzzüge* (Berlin, 1892), p. 66; Abraham Habermann, ed., *Sefer Gezerot Ashkenaz ve-Zarfat* (Jerusalem, 1945), p. 124.

[7] R. Jacob b. Meir, *Sefer ha-Yashar* (Berlin, 1898), p. 63.

[8] *Tosafot Eruvin*, 62b, s.v. R. Yohanan.

he [that is, Louis] gave the Jews certain privileges, e.g., leprosaria, new synagogues, and cemeteries."[9] These facilities probably reflect the establishment of new Jewish communities. Jewish population pressures are also revealed in the ongoing debate over the *herem ha-yishuv*, the power of any Jewish settlement to restrict the number of newcomers. Many of the major twelfth-century religious authorities felt it necessary to take a stand on the *herem ha-yishuv*.[10] This concern indicates an expanding Jewish population likely to outgrow old habitats and to found new ones.

The strong thrust towards establishment of new communities was a direct corollary of an increasing specialization in Jewish economic life. The more limited Jewish economic outlets became, the fewer Jews any urban agglomeration could absorb. The combination of population growth and economic specialization led inevitably to a steady proliferation of Jewish settlements.[11]

While evidence for Jewish agricultural activity continues and stray references to such professions as medicine can be found, the growing impression is one of preponderant Jewish involvement in commerce, especially in moneylending. Bernard of Clairvaux, in mid century, could already use the expression "iudaizare" as synonymous for usurious activities. The context of Bernard's comment was not an attack on the Jews or on Jewish moneylending. The observation was made in his letter stressing protection for the Jews during the Second Crusade. In a revealing digression, Bernard castigates Christian usurers: "I will not mention those Christian moneylenders, if they can be called Christian, who, where there are no Jews, act, I grieve to say, in a manner worse than any Jew." It is only the automatic association of Jew and money-lender that makes possible this totally irrelevant aside.[12] A more sympathetic contemporary of Bernard makes precisely the same observation, albeit in a far friendlier tone. In his *Dialogus inter Philosophum, Judaeum et Christianum*, Abelard has the Jew claim,

We can possess neither fields nor vines nor any land, since nothing can guarantee them against covert or overt attack. Therefore our sole resort is usury. It is only by practicing usury with non-Jews that we

[9] Gustave Julliot, ed., *Chronique de l'abbaye St.-Pierre-le-Vif de Sens par Geoffroy de Cour-lon* (Sens, 1876), p. 477.

[10] See, for example, the discussion by Albeck, "Rabbenu Tam's Attitude," pp. 133–34.

[11] A good summary of the relation of demographic spread and limited economy can be found in ibid., pp. 104–5.

[12] Bruno James, trans., *The Letters of St. Bernard of Clairvaux* (Chicago, 1953), p. 463.

can maintain our miserable livelihood. Yet through this we provoke bitter hatred on the part of those who consider themselves gravely burdened.[13]

Finally, a Jewish observer of the same period reinforces the impression. Ephraim of Bonn, the author of a Hebrew account of the Second Crusade, begins his description of the fate of French Jewry with reports on the death of one major French Jewish leader, R. Peter, and of the near-tragic assault on R. Jacob Tam, the outstanding scholar and communal leader of the period. He then observes:

> In the remaining communities of France, we have not heard that a single Jew was killed or forcibly converted. But they did lose much of their wealth. For the king of France commanded: "Anyone who has volunteered to journey to Jerusalem shall have his debt annulled if he be indebted to the Jews." Most of the loans extended by the Jews of France are by charter; hence they lost their money.[14]

The significance of financial losses stemming from the annulment of Crusader debts reflects the overwhelming importance of moneylending in Jewish economic life.

As noted earlier, the most rudimentary form of moneylending was the safeguarding of investments through deposit of a pledge. By its very nature, this type of lending leaves few records. Ephraim of Bonn does indicate that not all Jewish loans in mid-twelfth-century France were by charter; some, at least, were still issued against pawns. Whether such arrangements actually were in the minority is debatable.

According to Ephraim, Jewish moneylending by this time had proceeded to a more sophisticated level. Ephraim claims that "most of the loans extended by the Jews of France are by charter," that is, by documents carefully drawn up and guaranteed by governmental agencies.[15] Such procedures had numerous advantages for the Jewish creditors. Charters allowed greater flexibility, permitting the lender to move about unencumbered with profitless physical objects. They also made possible credit on a far larger scale. Loans could be extended against landed property, the most substantial wealth in medieval society. Properties worth significant sums could now serve as the collateral for large loans. Since such lands could not actually be controlled by the Jews, it was only through the promise of governmental support in case of de-

---

[13] *PL*, vol. 178, p. 1618.
[14] Neubauer and Stern, *Hebräische Berichte*, p. 64; Habermann, *Sefer Gezerot*, p. 121.
[15] Ibid.

fault that such arrangements could be made. The use of landed property or of property rights as security not only increased the size of the loans; it also afforded the lender the possibility of a continuous flow of income. A previously-cited responsum of Rashi shows a very early instance of Jews drawing revenue from landed property.[16] Abbot Suger of Saint-Denis supplies an early–twelfth-century instance of the same arrangement. In a description of the revenues of his abbey, Suger includes a portion of the taxes from the burg of Saint-Denis along with income from the village of Montlignon, both held for a time by a Jew of Montmorency as security for a loan.[17]

While advantageous from many points of view, lending based on governmental support exhibited one major flaw. It put the Jew further at the mercy of his baronial protectors. Were his feudal lord willing to come to some kind of accommodation with the debtor, there was little choice for the Jew but to accept. This was the situation, for example, of the Jew of Montmorency cited above. When the abbey of Saint-Denis wished eventually to redeem its lost revenue by repaying the original loan, it utilized the good offices of the lord of Montmorency in securing for itself highly favorable terms. The most radical manifestation of this danger came in the wake of the papal bull *Quantum praedecessores* issued by Pope Eugenius II on the eve of the Second Crusade. Armed with the papal annulment of interest, Louis VII, the staunchest secular backer of the Crusade, seems to have absolved Crusaders of much of their obligations to the Jews.[18] Loss of governmental support left the Jews no recourse whatsoever.

By the end of the reign of Louis VII, bureaucratization in the major principalities had proceeded to the point where specific agents were empowered to afford Jewish lenders the promised protection. Although extensive documentation comes only in the final two decades of the century, a charter of privileges granted the burghers of Étampes in 1179 indicates that governmental officials were already functioning on behalf of Jewish business interests. In this charter, provision is made for free

---

[16] See above, chapter 1.

[17] Albert Lecoy de la Marche, ed., *Oeuvres complètes de Suger* (Paris, 1867), p. 156.

[18] The papal bull stipulated that "all they that are burdened by debt and have, with pure heart, undertaken so holy a journey need not pay the interest past due, and if they themselves or others for them have been bound by oath and pledge, by reason of such interest, by apostolic authority we absolve them" (Otto of Freising, *The Deeds of Frederick Barbarossa*, trans. Charles Mierow [New York, 1953], p. 73). According to Ephraim of Bonn, who may be inaccurate as to the precise details, Louis VII ordered that "anyone who volunteered to go to Jerusalem shall have his debt annulled if he is indebted to the Jews" (Neubauer and Stern, *Hebräische Berichte*, p. 64; Habermann, *Sefer Gezerot*, p. 121). If Ephraim is accurate, then Louis went beyond the papal provisions.

access to the town market, and notice is specifically given that the *praepositus Judaeorum* shall not have the right to arrest anyone going to or from the market for nonpayment of debt.[19] The existence of a royally-appointed *praepositus Judaeorum* charged with responsibility for aiding the Jews in realizing the sums owed them indicates how advanced Jewish business techniques were and how deeply they depended on governmental support.

The political fortunes of twelfth-century French Jewry continued to rest primarily upon the feudal barony of northern France. The Jews looked to their overlords for protection and for business support; the price for such boons was, above all, significant contributions to the seigneural treasuries. There were, at the same time, other elements on the political scene striving to assert their rights over the Jews. The king of France, increasingly powerful as a feudal lord, was beginning to claim limited royal prerogatives, including some related to the Jews. The municipalities of northern France, demanding and acquiring greater jurisdiction over their own affairs, were often vexed by the presence within town boundaries of Jewish communities over which they could exercise no real control; efforts to gain some power over the Jews began during the twelfth century. The Church, while not descending directly into the political arena, could hardly remain aloof. As the French Church grew stronger and began to press on wide-ranging issues, ecclesiastical concern with the Jews developed. Finally, the populace at large could on occasion make its own rude and inarticulate attitudes deeply felt. The antipathy towards the Jews that had surfaced during the First Crusade continued to ferment within the popular ranks, crystallizing by the end of the century into a series of damaging stereotypes of alleged Jewish crimes.

As always during the Middle Ages, the foundation for Jewish political status lay in the mutually beneficial relationship between feudal overlord and Jew. In this relationship, the primary concern of the Jews was basic physical security. As had been the case prior to and down through the First Crusade, the political authorities of northern France were extremely effective in their protection of the Jews. The Second Crusade was in general far less destructive of Jewish life and property than had been the First; for French Jewry there are scarcely any reports of persecution. The Christian chronicles which recount Jewish suffering locate it exclusively in Germany. Ephraim of Bonn, the Jewish chron-

---

[19] *Ordonnances*, vol. 11, pp. 211-13.

icler, knows only of the death of one eminent French Jewish scholar, of a near-disastrous attack on R. Jacob Tam, and of substantial financial loss.[20]

During the period under consideration, the Jewish communities of northern France suffered but one major catastrophe—the Blois attack of 1171.[21] In the late spring, the Jews of Blois were accused of drowning an innocent Christian youth in the Loire. The charge had first been brought by a Christian servant whose horse had been frightened at the riverside by a Jew; it was never even substantiated by a corpus delecti. The accusation, an increasingly popular one at the time, was fed by the political intrigues at the court of Blois, particularly by the hatred that grew out of the count's fondness for the Jewess Polcelina. The Jews' attempt at bribing their way out of difficulty fell short, and, further incited by clerical pressures, the count had more than thirty Jews burned on the fateful day of May 26, 1171. It is significant that this major crisis was in no way occasioned by a breakdown in the ability of the authorities to protect their Jews. The disaster struck only at the point when a major baron himself became a persecutor, rather than a protector.

That the Jews' faith in baronial protection was in no way shaken by the events of May 1171 is indicated by their immediate and frantic efforts to secure enhanced seigneural assurances for the future.[22] In the days and weeks following the burning at Blois, the leadership of northern French Jewry undertook a coordinated campaign to approach key political figures and to elicit promises of physical safety. The following is a firsthand documentary account of the encounter between Parisian Jewry and King Louis VII:

> Today is a day of good tidings for his Jews from the great king [that is, Louis VII], who has beneficently inclined his heart towards us.
>
> We went to the king at Poissy to fall before his feet concerning this matter [that is, the Blois incident]. When we saw that he was favorably disposed, we said that we would like to speak with him pri-

---

[20] Neubauer and Stern, *Hebräische Berichte*, p. 64; Habermann, *Sefer Gezerot*, p. 121. There is an intriguing problem concerning three towns— בהם, סולרי, קנושון —in which large numbers of Jews perished. Various identifications for these three locales have been proposed, some in France and some elsewhere. In the absence of corroborative evidence, all this speculation must remain highly tentative.

[21] On this episode, see Shalom Spiegel, "In Monte Dominus Videbitur: The Martyrs of Blois and the Early Accusations of Ritual Murder," *The Mordecai M. Kaplan Jubilee Volume*, 2 vols. (New York, 1953), Hebrew volume, pp. 267–87.

[22] On these efforts, see Chazan, "The Blois Incident of 1171," p. 22.

vately. He responded: "Speak openly!" Then he himself called forth all his ministers stationed in the fortress and said to them: "Listen all of you to what Count Theobald has done—may he and his descendants be barren through the entire year! If he has acted properly, fine; if he has behaved improperly, may he be punished. For I too am frightened over what he has done. Now then, you Jews of my land, you have no cause for alarm over what that persecutor has done in his domain. For people have leveled the same accusation against the Jews of Pontoise and Janville, and, when the charges were brought before me, they were found false. . . . Therefore, be assured, all you Jews in my land, that I harbor no such suspicion. Even if a body be discovered in the city or in the countryside, I shall say nothing to the Jews in that regard. . . ." Now, thank the Lord, the king has drawn up a sealed charter to be sent throughout his domain—that the Jews might be at ease—to all his officials, enjoining they show respect for the Jews, protecting their lives and their property more zealously than heretofore.[23]

The king and the count of Champagne, who gave similar guarantees, were, it would seem, effective in providing the promised protection. The general impression is one of continued security, despite Jewish spread throughout the countryside of northern France and notwithstanding increasingly shrill verbal assaults and growing popular animosity.

During the twelfth century the responsibilities of the barony towards the Jews expanded into the economic sphere as well. As we have seen, the authorities became the ultimate guarantors for Jewish loans, with the threat of confiscation or imprisonment by baronial officials serving as the final prod towards repayment. Here, too, of course, the situation of dependence meant eventually that the Jews had no real recourse from an adverse decision taken by their protectors.

Clearly the extensive obligations undertaken on behalf of the Jews were not the expression of an abstract concern for justice or of a deep-seated attachment to the cause of the Jews. As political power rapidly consolidated and ready resources became paramount, the tax potential which the Jews represented made them an object of interest

---

[23]Neubauer and Stern, *Hebräische Berichte*, p. 34; Habermann, *Sefer Gezerot*, p. 145. In Neubauer and Stern, the meeting place is designated as Vassy, for which no evidence is adduced (see p. 149). For some unfathomable reason, I have earlier suggested Falaise (see "The Blois Incident of 1171," p. 22). The correct identification is almost certainly Poissy, which (1) corresponds closely to the Hebrew, (2) is quite near Paris, and (3) was a well-known royal residence during the period, the scene in fact of the birth of Louis IX in 1214; see Henri Gross, *Gallia Judaica* (Paris, 1897), p. 453.

to the most progressive and ambitious of the rulers of northern France. In the political sphere as in the economic, the Jews were extremely useful in furthering the new and more sophisticated order.

A number of sources leave the general impression of heavy exaction from the Jews. From the Christian side, Peter Abelard, in the *Dialogus*, has the Jewish protagonist emphasize strongly Jewish insecurity and the heavy price which the exposed Jews must pay for baronial protection.[24] In his more famous *Historia Calamitatum*, Abelard, depicting his unhappy experiences as abbot of St. Gildes de Rhuys in Brittany, describes the situation of the abbey as follows:

> The abbey itself a certain tyrant, the most powerful in that district, had for a long time kept in subjugation to himself. He takes advantage of the disorders there to convert to his own use the adjacent lands and to levy greater imposts on the monks than he would have on Jews subject to tribute.[25]

Jewish religious leaders, in their discussions of the legality of governmental taxation, reinforce the impression of new kinds of levies and of an increasingly heavy tax burden.[26]

Unfortunately, lack of records makes specific information on form and amounts of taxation unavailable. A grant of privileges to the municipality of Tonnerre does afford some insight, however. In this grant the count of Nevers included rights to revenue from the Jews, specifically 20 shillings per Jew, a further 5 shillings for heads of households, and ten percent of the Jews' wine and alms.[27] Other royal grants indicate that Jews were subject to tolls at the key bridge crossings of major French routes.[28] Taxation of the Jews took other forms as well, some undoubtedly connected with their moneylending business.

In addition to regular levies, Jews were always potentially or actually subject to many special exactions. One of Peter the Venerable's radical suggestions concerning the Jews was that their ill-gotten gains be taken from them in order to pay for the Second Crusade.[29] While there is no record of the implementation of Peter's suggestion, there is abundant

[24] *PL*, vol. 178, p. 1618.

[25] Joseph Muckle, trans., *The Story of Abelard's Adversities* (Toronto, 1954), p. 58.

[26] See Simon Schwarzfuchs, "De la condition des Juifs de France aux XIIe et XIIIe siècles," *REJ* 125 (1966): 226-29.

[27] *Ordonnances*, vol. 11, pp. 217-19.

[28] Léopold Delisle, ed., *Recueil des Actes de Henri II, roi d'Angleterre et duc de Normandie*, 3 vols. (Paris, 1909-27), vol. 1, p. 366, and vol. 2, p. 55.

[29] *RHF*, vol. 15, p. 642.

indication that crisis would often call forth a heavy price from endangered Jewish communities. In the tragedy of 1171, the community of Blois seems to have miscalculated and offered far too low a bribe—220 pounds—to secure its release; this miscalculation, coupled with clerical pressure, sealed its doom.[30] The Jews of the county, on the other hand, managed to save themselves by the payment of 1,000 pounds.[31] Champenois Jewry closed its account of successful negotiations with Count Henry by indicating that, despite the count's rejection of the malicious-murder charge, it gave liberally to halt the spread of the slander.[32] So ubiquitous was Jewish bribery in the face of danger that Ephraim of Bonn, recounting the vigorous intervention of Bernard of Clairvaux against anti-Jewish preaching during the Second Crusade, notes quizzically that "we have heard no report of his taking bribes for speaking out on behalf of the Jews."[33]

The terminology and ramifications of Jewish political status developed slowly. By the early twelfth century, the expression "Judeus meus" or "Judeus suus" was already in use.[34] The lack of documentary material obscures subsequent utilization of this important expression until it burst into prominence at the end of the century.

Transfer of rights over the Jews was already in evidence early in the twelfth century as well. There are instances of the royal grant of rights over the Jews of Saint-Denis (specified as *justicia* and *exactio*) to the famed abbey of that town.[35] Shortly afterwards, Louis VI granted the revenue from the Jews of Touraine to the renowned abbey of Saint Martin of Tours.[36]

The bureaucracy for handling Jewish affairs also began to crystallize during the reign of Louis VII. While we find the *praepositus Judaeorum* active only as a governmental agent for the protection of Jewish business interests, it seems most unlikely that his responsibilities ended there. The very title *praepositus* would seem to reflect a concern with revenue and probably a measure of judicial jurisdiction. The paucity of sources makes the precise range of his functions purely speculative, however.

---

[30] Neubauer and Stern, *Hebräische Berichte*, p. 67; Habermann, *Sefer Gezerot*, p. 125.

[31] Neubauer and Stern, *Hebräische Berichte*, p. 68; Habermann, *Sefer Gezerot*, p. 125.

[32] Neubauer and Stern, *Hebräische Berichte*, p. 35; Habermann, *Sefer Gezerot*, p. 146.

[33] Neubauer and Stern, *Hebräische Berichte*, p. 59; Habermann, *Sefer Gezerot*, p. 116.

[34] Lecoy de la Marche, *Oeuvres complètes de Suger*, p. 156.

[35] *Ordonnances*, vol. 4, p. 137.

[36] Luchaire, *Louis VI le Gros*, p. 131 (dated 1119); Auguste Longnon, *Études sur les actes de Louis VII* (Paris, 1885), p. 369 (a reference to the same transaction in a later act of Louis VII).

Although the barony exercised the most decisive influence over the destiny of the Jews, there were other forces with some impact on their fate. As indicated, a municipality could be granted rights over its Jewish inhabitants, as in the case of Tonnerre. This, to be sure, was a rather rare occurrence. While often generous towards the municipalities of northern France, the barons were generally closefisted with rights over Jews. This reflects both baronial awareness of the profit to be exacted from their Jewish subjects and strong Jewish desires to remain out of the grasp of the burghers, whom they feared and distrusted.

It is difficult to discern the development of royal authority over the Jews. The king, as one of the major barons of the north, controlled his share of Jews. Regalian rights, however, do not manifest themselves prominently at this early period. The only signs of royal prerogatives are related to those religious and moral areas in which the king could claim special powers. Thus, for example, Louis VII's letter of 1144 dealing with the problem of relapsed converts seems to extend beyond the royal domain itself and to reflect the general authority of the monarchy.[37] Louis was surely the prime secular proponent of the Second Crusade, and it is possible—although not certain—that his annulment of interest to the Crusaders, decreed in consonance with Eugenius II's papal bull, may have affected broad areas of the north beyond the royal domain. It is also possible that the alacrity with which the Jews hastened to the royal court after the Blois affair of 1171 may indicate recognition that the king, beyond his position as a major baron, exercised far-reaching moral and religious influence in the realm.

Although the municipalities and the throne represented but minor infringements upon the power of the barony over the Jews, not so was the case with the Church. The Church was a key factor on the medieval scene, a force often in conflict with the secular rulers and deeply distressed over problems flowing from Jewish presence and activities.

The traditional balance in ecclesiastical policy towards the Jews is expressed in the well-known *Constitutio pro Judeis*, the first promulgator of which was supposedly the early-twelfth-century pope, Calixtus II:

> Therefore, just as license ought not to be granted the Jews to presume to do in their synagogues more than the law permits them, just so ought they not to suffer curtailment in those (privileges) which have been conceded them.[38]

[37] *RHF*, vol. 16, p. 8.

[38] Solomon Grayzel, *The Church and the Jews in the XIIIth Century* (Philadelphia, 1933), pp. 92-95. The attribution of the first *Constitutio pro Judeis* is based on the list of previous

In a sense the Jewish hope during the Middle Ages was to maximize the protective aspect of this Church stance while minimizing its limitations.

During the twelfth century, there are a number of incidents of the activation of ecclesiastical protection for the Jews. The most important was the concerted effort of Bernard of Clairvaux to save the Jews of Christendom from a repetition of the slaughter accompanying the First Crusade. Bernard responded vigorously to the reports of anti-Jewish agitation forwarded by the archbishop of Mayence, included specific prohibition of persecution in a number of his calls to the Crusade, and finally journeyed in person to the Rhineland to halt the activities of the recalcitrant Cistercian monk Radulph. The Jewish chronicler Ephraim of Bonn expresses the deeply-felt Jewish appreciation for the intervention of the abbot of Clairvaux:

> The Lord heard our supplication, turned to us, and had mercy upon us in accord with the fullness of his pity and lovingkindness. He sent after the wicked one (i.e., Radulph), a proper monk, great and indeed the master to all monks, knowledgeable in their law and a man of understanding. His name was Bernard, the abbot of Clairvaux, in France. He too preached, as is their wont. . . . Were it not for the mercies of our Creator in sending us the aforementioned abbot and his epistles, Israel would have been left without remnant and vestige.[39]

Some years later, after the Blois crisis, the Jews of France again turned to a leading churchman for aid. While one thrust of Jewish activity aimed at securing repudiation of the malicious-murder charge by the key secular powers of northern France, there was also deep concern for the dignified burial of the victims and for the release of those still held captive. A skilled negotiator was chosen and the approach was made through the good offices of William of the White Hands, archbishop of Sens, bishop of Chartres, and brother of the count of Blois.[40]

Far more prominent, however, was the desire of the Church for limitation of the Jews. This took a number of important forms, some very old and some quite new. One of the oldest concerns of the Church

---

popes who supposedly made similar grants. For the possibility that the edict may have predated the twelfth century, see Robert Chazan, "1007–1012: Initial Crisis for Northern-European Jewry," *PAAJR* 38–39 (1970–71): 101–18.

[39] Neubauer and Stern, *Hebräische Berichte*, p. 59; Habermann, *Sefer Gezerot*, p. 116.

[40] Chazan, "The Blois Incident of 1171," pp. 22–23. It was unusual of course for one man to hold power over two sees as William did. For the special circumstances, see *Gallia Christiana*, 13 vols. (Paris, 1739–1877), vol. 8, pp. 1144–46, and vol. 12, pp. 50–53.

was for the potential influence of Jews on their Christian neighbors. During the twelfth century little concern was expressed over Jewish impact on heretical movements. Guibert of Nogent does paint a horrible portrait of Jewish involvement in the perversities of the family of the count of Soissons.

> In the end the count, to whom it could properly have been said "Thy father was an Amorrhite and thy mother a Cethite," not only became as bad as his parents, but did things much worse. He practiced the perfidy of the Jews and heretics to such an extent that he said blasphemous things about the Saviour, which through fear of the faithful the Jews did not dare to do. How evilly he "set his mouth against heaven" may be understood from that little work which I wrote against him at the request of Bernard the dean. Since such words may not be uttered by a Christian's lips and must bring the horror of detestation to pious ears, we have suppressed them. Although he supported the Jews, the Jews considered him insane, since he approved of their religion in word and publicly practiced ours.[41]

This description, however, is an isolated one and reflects no ongoing preoccupation with the problem.

More persistent is the concern with the potential influence of Jews on those Christians who came within the orbit of the Jewish home. That Jews used Christian domestic help is perfectly clear from extensive rabbinic discussion of some of the ritual problems arising from the presence and activities of such non-Jews.[42] It comes, therefore, as no surprise to find papal complaints addressed to Louis VII concerning the presence of Christian maids and servingmen in Jewish homes and exhortations to end such abuses.[43] Rigord, in describing the anti-Jewish program of the early 1180's, mentions specifically not only the issue of Christian servants but the consequent religious complications as well. "When they [that is, the Jews] had made a long sojourn there [that is, in Paris], they grew so rich that they claimed as their own almost half of the whole city, and had Christians in their houses as menservants and maidservants, who were open backsliders from the faith of Jesus Christ, and judaized with the Jews."[44]

---

[41] John Benton, ed., *Self and Society in Medieval France* (New York, 1970), p. 210.

[42] See, for example, Albeck, "Rabbenu Tam's Attitude," pp. 123-25.

[43] *RHF*, vol. 15, p. 968.

[44] Jacob Marcus, *The Jew in the Medieval World: A Source Book: 315-1791* (Cincinnati, 1938), p. 25, translation taken from James Robinson, *Readings in European History*, 2 vols. (Boston, 1906), vol. 1, pp. 426-27.

Equally unacceptable was the flourishing of Judaism in a way that might tarnish the luster of the ruling faith. As Peter the Venerable insisted, the Jews were to be preserved, but only in such a fashion as would make patently obvious their secondary status.[45] Thus, the building of new synagogues and other Jewish communal facilities was of concern to many churchmen, and old canonical precedents were invoked to oppose such projects. The same papal letter that complained of Christian servants in Jewish homes also deplored the construction of new synagogues.[46] In his rebuke of Louis VII for pro-Jewish activities, Geoffroy of Courlon singled out specifically the king's support for a wide-ranging extension of Jewish communal facilities.[47]

Most alarming of all was the growing possibility of church vessels falling into the possession of Jews as a result of mounting debts. By mid century Peter the Venerable already deplored the tendency, claiming rather absurdly that such sacred objects were purchased by Jews from thieves—pilferage from the churches of northern France could hardly have been so widespread.[48] However the Jews may have come by these vessels, it was deeply disturbing to see them in Jewish hands and to contemplate the possibilities of sacrilege.

Rigord, describing the beginning of the reign of Philip Augustus, saves his most potent venom for alleged Jewish sacrilege.

> Finally came the culmination of their wickedness. Certain ecclesiastical vessels consecrated to God—the chalices and crosses of gold and silver bearing the images of our Lord Jesus Christ crucified—had been pledged to the Jews by way of security when the need of the churches was pressing. These they used so vilely, in their impiety and scorn of the Christian religion, that from the cups in which the body and blood of our Lord Jesus Christ was consecrated they gave their children cakes soaked in wine. . . .[49]

A new element in Church concern with the Jews related to Jewish economic activity. While not mentioning usury, Peter the Venerable was troubled over Jewish economic success, accruing, he felt, from nefarious Jewish business practices.[50] By the end of the reign of

---

[45]*RHF*, vol. 15, p. 642.

[46]Ibid., p. 968.

[47]Julliot, *Chronique de l'abbaye St.-Pierre-le-Vif*, p. 477.

[48]*RHF*, vol. 15, p. 642.

[49]Marcus, *The Jew in the Medieval World*, p. 26.

[50]*RHF*, vol. 15, p. 642.

Louis VII, there was overt condemnation of Jewish usury, not only for related abuses such as possession and desecration of church vessels but as offensive in and of itself.

> When they had made a long sojourn there, they grew so rich that they claimed as their own almost half of the whole city, and had Christians in their houses as menservants and maidservants, who were open backsliders from the faith of Jesus Christ, and judaized with the Jews. And this was contrary to the decree of God and the law of the Church. And whereas the Lord had said by the mouth of Moses in Deuteronomy (23:20–21), "Thou shalt not lend upon usury to thy brother," but "to a stranger," the Jews in their wickedness understood by "stranger" every Christian, and they took from the Christians their money at usury. And so heavily burdened in this wise were citizens and soldiers and peasants in the suburbs, and in the various towns and villages, that many were constrained to part with their possessions. Others were bound under oath in houses of the Jews in Paris, held as if captives in prison.[51]

Although there is in these observations of Rigord reference to such traditional issues as Judaizing, there is also a direct condemnation of Jewish usury per se. This castigation is, on the one hand, theoretical, that is to say, a negation of the Jewish right to lend money at interest; at the same time it is a practical horror at the social results of Jewish lending—both Jewish wealth and Christian impoverishment. This new motif in Church thinking was destined to have the most profound impact on the fate of northern French Jewry.

While these specific concerns reflect primarily the developments in French economic life, the new avenues in which the Jews were moving, and perhaps increased Jewish wealth, the changing intellectual scene in the twelfth century had its own effect on ecclesiastical conceptions of Judaism and the Jews. In his superb study of the twelfth-century shift in Christian polemics against the Jews, Amos Funkenstein has shown convincingly two major developments.[52] The first was a growing rationalism, which could potentially have led to greater tolerance but which in fact led to enhanced impatience with the Jews. Increasingly it was assumed that the Jewish failure to acknowledge the truth of Christianity, now further buttressed by the new rationalism, reflected satanic perversity. At the same time the expanding horizons of knowledge

---

[51] Marcus, *The Jew in the Medieval World*, p. 25.

[52] Amos Funkenstein, "Changes in the Patterns of Christian Anti-Jewish Polemics in the 12th Century" (Hebrew), *Zion* 33 (1968): 125–44.

included a serious though slanted investigation of the religious literature of Judaism and Islam. In the process, the unsympathetic reading of rabbinic texts composed in an idiom highly alien to twelfth-century Europe reinforced the sense of Jewish irrationality and perhaps willful disbelief.

The key French figure in this shift was the influential abbot of Cluny, Peter the Venerable. The famed cleric's tone towards the Jews was unusually harsh. "You, you Jews, I say, do I address, who till this day do deny the Son of God—how long, poor wretches, will ye not believe the truth? How long will you fight against God? How long before your hearts of iron are softened?"[53] Thus Peter began his *Tractatus adversus Judeorum inveteratam duritiem.*

Peter the Venerable's major contribution was dissemination of the Talmudic lore of the Jews first introduced to western Europe by the Spanish convert, Petrus Alfonsi. Peter the Venerable, strongly aware of new frontiers in the campaign for the spread of his faith, brought rabbinic materials to the attention of the northern European Church.

> I lead out then a monstrous animal from its den, and show it as a laughing stock in the amphitheatre of the whole world, in the sight of all peoples. I bring forward, thou Jew, thou brute beast, in the sight of all men, thy book, yea, I say, that Thalmuth of thine, that thy precious collection of doctrine, which forsooth is to be preferred to the books of the Prophets and all Divinely approved opinions.[54]

There follows a collection of Talmudic *agadot*, designed to prove the ludicrous nature of Jewish belief.[55] The damage done by this viciously negative presentation of Jewish folk literature was substantial, extending over a number of centuries.

Related to this shift in Church concerns and attitudes was a marked upsurge in the popular hatred harbored against the Jews of northern France. While Jewish-Christian relations were rarely untroubled during the Middle Ages, the twelfth century was an especially active period in the gestation of deep-seated animosities. To be sure, this antipathy broke forth into physical violence only infrequently—a tribute to the power of the governing authorities—but it seriously endangered the Jews and exacerbated their already precarious position. Doubly disturb-

---

[53] *PL*, vol. 189, p. 507; translated in A. Lukyn Williams, *Adversus Judaeos* (Cambridge, 1935), p. 385.

[54] *PL*, vol. 189, p. 602; Williams, *Adversus Judaeos*, p. 388.

[55] On this, see Funkenstein, "Changes in the Pattern of Christian Anti-Jewish Polemics," pp. 137–41, and Ch. Merchavia, *Ha-Talmud be-Rei ha-Nazrut* (Jerusalem, 1970), pp. 128–52.

ing from the Jewish point of view was the fact that many of the most vicious canards were repeated or even initiated by leading ecclesiastical and secular figures of the period. When the abbot of Clairvaux, the abbot of Cluny, and the count of Blois lent their prestige to the spate of anti-Jewish slanders, the Jewish community could properly feel profoundly threatened.

The concern voiced by Church leadership over Jewish influence and economic activity and the stance taken by key ecclesiastics towards Jewish doctrine and belief certainly filtered down into the populace, although on the economic issues the animosity may have risen up from the masses as well. Popular views during this period are permeated with the notions of Jewish power, Jewish irrationality, and Jewish malevolence.

The suggestion of an alliance between the Jews and the omnipresent satanic forces evoked real fright and had a serious impact on Jewish-Christian relations. Guibert of Nogent expresses this view in his story of an evil monk.

> In a certain famous monastery, a monk had been brought up from childhood and had attained some knowledge in letters. Directed by his abbot to live in an outlying cell of the abbey, while he was staying there he fell ill of a disease. Because of this, to his sorrow, he had occasion for talking with a Jew skilled in medicine. Gathering boldness from their intimacy, they began to reveal their secrets to one another. Being curious about the black arts and aware that the Jew understood magic, the monk pressed him hard. The Jew consented and promised to be his mediator with the Devil. They agreed upon the time and place for a meeting. At last he was brought by his intermediary into the presence of the Devil, and through the other he asked to have a share in the teaching. That abominable ruler said that it could by no means be done unless he denied his Christianity and offered sacrifice to him.[56]

Perhaps the most pernicious and damaging set of popular motifs revolved about the Jews' alleged enmity towards Christian society. The notion of such Jewish hatred for Christendom had been traditional and had found powerful expression in the infamous First-Crusade battle cry with which the Rhineland Jewish communities had been attacked: "Behold we set forth on a long journey to seek the Holy Sepulcher and to take vengeance upon the Moslems. Yet the Jews dwell among us, those whose ancestors slew and crucified Jesus. Let us take vengeance upon

---

[56] Benton, *Self and Society in Medieval France*, p. 115.

them first. . . ."[57] The powerful Jewish response to First-Crusade attacks can only have heightened the Christian sense of the Jew as adversary.[58] In a classic case of vicious cycle, the conception of Jewish enmity led to assaults which evoked Jewish behavior that further ingrained the stereotype.

It is the supposed Jewish animosity against Christendom that lent credibility to Rigord's charge of Jewish defilement of sacred church vessels. This desecration, says Rigord, the Jews had committed "in their impiety and scorn of the Christian religion."[59]

The same conception of Jewish enmity led to the more serious charge of Jewish willingness, and in fact compulsion, to murder Christian neighbors, generally those innocent, weak, and defenseless. This allegation, found throughout northern Europe from the 1140's on, made an early appearance in France, where it soon began to develop the same significant additions and refinements which it was undergoing elsewhere.[60]

The accusation began in the simple form of a Jewish propensity for murder of Christian children. Prior to the incident at Blois the charge had already been made at Pontoise, at Janville, and at Épernay. The incident at Blois in early 1171 represented not the beginning but a culmination of this indictment in a dual sense. There was in this instance the flimsiest possible evidence—the testimony of a Christian servant unsupported by even the discovery of an unidentified corpse or the report of a missing child. Moreover, despite the shaky foundations of the allegation, it was dignified for the first time by acceptance on the part of a major figure in the political life of northern France.[61]

The earlier incident at Pontoise shows a second stage of development. In this case the murdered boy became a martyr to his Christian faith, his body being transported to Paris and transformed into an object of veneration at the Church of the Holy Innocents. Readiness to

---

[57] For reflections of this slogan, see *inter alia* the Hebrew chroniclers in Neubauer and Stern, *Hebräische Berichte*, pp. 1, 4, 36–37, 47, and in Habermann, *Sefer Gezerot*, pp. 24, 27, 72, 93, and Guibert of Nogent in Benton, *Self and Society in Medieval France*, pp. 134–35.

[58] The Jewish response to the onslaughts of 1095–96 has been widely discussed. For recent treatments, see Jacob Katz, *Exclusiveness and Tolerance: Studies in Jewish-Gentile Relations in Medieval and Modern Times* (London, 1961), pp. 82–92; idem, "Martyrdom in the Middle Ages and in 1648–49" (Hebrew), *Sefer Yovel le-Yitzhak Baer* (Jerusalem, 1960), pp. 318–20; and Gerson Cohen, "Messianic Postures of Ashkenazim and Sephardim," *Studies of the Leo Baeck Institute*, ed. Max Kreutzberger (New York, 1967), pp. 148–52.

[59] Marcus, *The Jew in the Medieval World*, p. 26.

[60] For the development of this motif, see Robert Chazan, "The Bray Incident of 1192: *Realpolitik* and Folk Slander," *PAAJR* 37 (1969): 10–14.

[61] Idem, "The Blois Incident of 1171," pp. 16–17.

see the supposed victims of Jewish assault as martyrs reflects clearly an assumed religious basis for the attacks. Jewish animosity is not viewed, then, as the expression of social or economic antipathy; it is seen as the fundamental hatred of the enemies of Christendom for the true faith.[62]

Such views led, by the close of the twelfth century, to a novel and destructive twist in the murder motif, namely, the contention that this religiously-based aggression was cultic in form as well. The Jews were charged with killing their neighbors by crucifixion out of a perverse compulsion to reenact the great historic sin of their corporate existence. This allegation, raised first in England, was brought to the continent by Philip Augustus's biographer, Rigord. The monk of Saint-Denis claims that his hero had become familiar with the accusation as a young lad.

> For he had heard many times from the children who had been raised with him in the royal palace—and had carefully committed to memory—that the Jews who dwelt in Paris were wont every year on Easter day, or during the sacred week of our Lord's Passion, to go down secretly into underground vaults and kill a Christian as a sort of sacrifice in contempt of the Christian religion. For a long time they had persisted in this wickedness, inspired by the devil, and in Philip's father's time many of them had been seized and burned with fire. St. Richard, whose body rests in the church of the Holy-Innocents-in-the-Fields in Paris, was thus put to death and crucified by the Jews, and through martyrdom went in blessedness to God. Wherefore many miracles have been wrought by the hand of God through the prayers and intercessions of St. Richard, to the glory of God, as we have heard.[63]

The twelfth century thus saw in northern France an upsurge in Church concern with specific aspects of Jewish economic and social life accompanied by deepening distrust and hatred of the Jews in broad segments of Christian society. Rather than abating, these tendencies accelerated during the ensuing century and played a major role in the deterioration of Jewish status that culminated in total expulsion.

These strong anti-Jewish pressures formed the final strand in the bonds that tied the Jews to the feudal barony. Despite hopes in many quarters for enhanced control over the Jews, the old alliance between the secular authorities and the Jews intensified during the twelfth century. This resulted from the new need for governmental support of

---

[62] Idem, "The Bray Incident of 1192," p. 11.
[63] Ibid., pp. 11-12.

Jewish business, from the increasing ecclesiastical clamor for limitation, and from the rising chorus of popular slanders. Reliance on the feudal lords was, in these circumstances, unavoidable; but it spawned its own set of dangers.

The Jewish community, during the twelfth century, continued to function as an independent self-governing body. This autonomy had for some time been recognized by the feudal authorities of northern France and had been anchored in a viable set of self-governing institutions. Since the communities of the twelfth century underwent no radical change in size or structure, there was no need for any thoroughgoing reform. There was progress in a number of directions, but it proceeded from previously-laid foundations.

Jews continued to settle in a distinct section of town, known usually as the Juiverie or the rue des Juifs. A rue des Juifs is attested early in the century in Rouen—it is mentioned in a Norman chronicle as the area out of which a devastating fire swept the city.[64] Some specific information on the location of the pre-1182 Juiveries of northern France is available in the documents that dispose of Jewish property in the wake of the expulsion by Philip Augustus. The most famous of these Jewish quarters was that of Paris, located in the center of the Île-de-la-Cité on the major trade route traversing the capital. From the number of Jewish houses confiscated by the king and granted to others, it seems that the Paris Juiverie was extensive.[65]

The Juiverie included a number of major facilities, especially a synagogue. Larger Jewish communities were normally equipped with cemeteries, usually placed some distance from the Jewish neighborhood, and occasionally a leprosarium or a communal oven. It will be recalled that Geoffroy of Courlon admonished Louis VII for granting the Jews rights to establish new synagogues, cemeteries, and leprosaria. We have earlier suggested that this expansion of facilities may well reflect the founding of new Jewish settlements.[66]

As a result of its physical separatism, the Jewish community of northern France exhibited remarkable cohesiveness. There were a number of additional factors that maximized intense solidarity. The small size of these Jewish settlements surely had an impact. The Jews of any

[64] Alexandre Heron, ed., *Deux chroniques de Rouen* (Rouen, 1900), p. 31.

[65] On the Paris Juiveries during the twelfth century, see Robert Anchel, "The Early History of the Jewish Quarter in Paris," *JSS* 2 (1940): 47–56, and Michel Roblin, *Les Juifs de Paris* (Paris, 1952), pp. 10–18.

[66] See above.

given town were certain to know one another intimately, many or even most being related by family ties. There was also a constant sense of pressure from non-Jewish society, making the Jewish community an oasis of physical and psychological security for its members. Cohesiveness was reinforced by the relative economic homogeneity among the Jews. While there were unquestionably differences in wealth, all the Jews were members of a broad urban trading class. In fact, the money-lending enterprise so widely pursued was particularly well-suited towards aiding the impoverished members of the group. Partnerships in which the wealthy afforded the capital and the poor provided the energy undoubtedly sustained many Jews who otherwise would have been forced to live on charity. Twelfth-century complaints rarely reflect serious social or economic cleavage within Jewish society.

In providing for its internal needs, the Jewish community had already developed extremely effective institutions. The Jewish courts were of decisive importance, of course, handling the major portion of litigation between Jew and Jew. These courts continued to fulfill the broad range of functions which they had arrogated to themselves early in their development. The Jewish courts judged civil cases, decided religious questions, and even levied fines for breach of communal regulations. Under certain circumstances, Jews were permitted to by-pass the Jewish courts and appear before the gentile authorities. This was permissible, first of all, if both parties agreed to the procedure. Where the defendant refused to appear before the Jewish tribunal, the plaintiff could unilaterally appeal to the non-Jewish courts.[67] The losing parties in litigation did on occasion seek redress before external powers—a breach severely condemned. For the Jew dissatisfied with the justice meted out by a particular Jewish court or apprehensive at the prospects of the decision to be reached, there was an alternative more moderate than turning to the non-Jewish world: it was possible in some cases to request a change of venue. The question was raised, towards the end of the twelfth century, before R. Isaac of Dampierre of a Jew who refused to appear in the Jewish court of R. Haim in Paris and insisted instead on appearing before R. Joseph in Orléans. R. Isaac sustained the refusal, although he did insist that the recalcitrant party pay the expenses involved.[68] A second request to R. Isaac, reflecting the same situation, has also been preserved. In this second instance the reason for the request is specified. The two litigants in this case were the *nadiv* R.

---

[67] Finkelstein, *Jewish Self-Government*, pp. 153–55 (Hebrew) and pp. 155–58 (English).

[68] Quoted by R. Meir of Rothenberg and cited by Urbach, *Ba'aley ha-Tosafot*, p. 199.

Eliezer and the *nadiv* R. Abraham, the head of the Jewish community of Troyes. R. Eliezer requested a court other than that of Troyes because of the influence of R. Abraham. Again the request was allowed.[69]

The Jewish community also boasted its philanthropic agency—the charity box, or communal fund (*kupah shel ẓedakah*). This communal fund was supported by contributions, especially by bequests. Its disbursements were varied. Some authorities (R. Isaac of Dampierre, for example) indicated that the number of poor in the small Jewish communities of northern France was low.[70] Given the kind of business cooperation already noted, this is not surprising. The communal charity box was also used for support of wayfarers. Most authorities generally took a liberal stand on the range of permitted uses for these communal funds. A vexing problem was the obligatory nature of contributions to these charity funds. R. Jacob Tam opposed the use of force; many of the other authorities permitted it.[71] With the growing burden of taxation, forced contributions to Jewish philanthropic agencies may have been increasingly necessary.

The Jews of northern France possessed a well-developed school system for both elementary and advanced education. There is a curious encomium to the Jewish school and the Jewish thirst for learning penned by a student of Abelard:

> If the Christians educate their sons, they do so not for God, but for gain, in order that the one brother, if he be a clerk, may help his father and mother and his other brothers. They say that a clerk will have no heir and whatever he has will be ours and the other brothers'. A black cloak and hood to go to church in, and his surplice, will be enough for him. But the Jews, out of zeal for God and love of the law, put as many sons as they have to letters, that each may understand God's law. . . . A Jew, however poor, if he had ten sons would put them all to letters, not for gain, as the Christians do, but for the understanding of God's law, and not only his sons, but his daughters.[72]

The major institutions of higher learning were centered in larger Jewish communities, such as Paris, Sens, and Troyes. They attracted students from all of northern Europe, a tribute both to the veneration of

---

[69] Ibid., p. 399. In this second responsum of R. Meir of Rothenberg, reference is made to three similar cases during the thirteenth century.

[70] Quoted by R. Isaac b. Moses of Vienna, *Or Zaru'a*, 4 vols. in 2 (Zhitomir, 1862–90), vol. 1, 9a, and cited by Albeck, "Rabbenu Tam's Attitude," p. 135.

[71] See *Or Zaru'a*, vol. 1, 7b, and Albeck, "Rabbenu Tam's Attitude," p. 135.

[72] Beryl Smalley, *The Study of the Bible in the Middle Ages*, 2nd ed. (Oxford, 1952), p. 78.

the earlier R. Solomon b. Isaac of Troyes and to the continued vitality of the schools and their outstanding teachers. The curriculum continued to revolve about Biblical and Talmudic studies. The former proceeded in a number of directions, including careful literal analysis of the text, development of the midrashic tendencies found in Rashi, and concern with the polemical issues raised in Scriptures.[73] Talmudic studies became increasingly dialectical, with the simple commentary of Rashi often serving as the starting point for reexamination of the text. Inconsistency between Talmudic law and contemporary practice also served as the goad for reanalysis of the classical sources.[74] There is substantial evidence for the impact of the Jewish scholarship of the period on Christian learning; relatively unexplored is the reverse impact of developments in Christian academic circles on their Jewish counterparts.[75] There are a number of striking parallels, but a full-scale investigation is required.

In enforcing its decision within the community, the leadership had essentially three sources of power at its disposal: religious authority, the social force of boycott, and appeal to the gentile government. In a sense, the second of the powers indicated, that of boycott, derived from the first; for, in essence, the boycott was the utilization of religious authority on the rest of the community, in cases where it had failed with an individual. Given the smallness and cohesiveness of most of the Jewish communities in medieval northern France, the boycott was a powerful weapon.

It was the appeal to secular authorities that was the final and most forceful alternative. Utilization of governmental support in the internal affairs of the Jewish community is revealed in a decree of R. Yom Tov of Joigny concerning a Jew who married a girl without the consent of her father or her relatives. According to R. Yom Tov, the Jewish community may force the offender to divorce the girl and may even use the power of the non-Jewish government in achieving that end.[76]

Similar permission for the utilization of governmental authority is indicated in the well-known ordinance of R. Jacob Tam and his older brother, R. Samuel b. Meir. The purpose of this edict was to eliminate

---

[73] See Samuel Poznanski's introductory essay to the commentaries of R. Eliezer of Beaugency.

[74] The most important study of this aspect of the intellectual life of the community is Urbach's *Ba'aley ha-Tosafot.*

[75] For the Jewish influence on Christian scholarship, see Smalley, *The Study of the Bible,* pp. 149–72.

[76] Urbach, *Ba'aley ha-Tosafot,* p. 126.

undesirable interference by the non-Jewish world in the affairs of the Jewish community. After the decrees prohibiting appeal by any individual Jew to the non-Jewish powers, the ordinance detailed the excommunication to be levied against the transgressor. To this excommunication one exception was made: "If one refuses to come to court and there are proper witnesses in regard to the matter and the plaintiff collects a claim through the power of Gentiles, our excommunication will not apply."[77] In other words, there could be legitimate instances of such appeal.

The same ordinance concludes with the following exhortation: "We, the undersigned, request all those that are in touch with the government to coerce through the power of Gentiles anyone who transgresses our commandments in order that the Scriptural injunction, 'to observe very much and to carry out' what they are commanded, may be fulfilled. And righteous action leads to peace."[78] Although it may seem contradictory to end an ordinance outlawing the use of gentile force in Jewish affairs with a call to marshal just such force, the contradiction is only superficial. What is prohibited is individual, unwarranted use of external intervention; what is encouraged is the enlisting by the community and its duly appointed leadership of gentile support.

As rich individual Jews came to the fore in the Jewish community, there was the dangerous possibility that these men of wealth might abuse private links to their overlords in order to circumvent the authority of the Jewish self-governing agencies. Undercutting the Jewish communal leadership was disastrous for Jewish self-government. Rashi, in the ordinance on taxation already mentioned, outlawed individual appeals by means of which the Jew might evade his communal responsibility.[79] A clear and decisive stand against such actions was taken in the ordinance of R. Tam and R. Samuel b. Meir noted above. The essentials of the ordinance are as follows:

1. We have voted, decreed, ordained and declared under the *ḥerem*, that no man or woman may bring a fellow-Jew before Gentile courts or exert compulsion on him through Gentiles, whether by a prince or a common man, a ruler or an inferior official, except by witnesses.

2. If the matter accidentally reaches the government or other Gentiles, and in that manner pressure is exerted on a Jew, we have decreed that the man who is aided by the Gentiles shall save his

---

[77] Finkelstein, *Jewish Self-Government*, p. 155 (Hebrew) and p. 158 (English).
[78] Ibid.
[79] Ibid., p. 149.

fellow from their hands, and shall secure him against the Gentiles who are aiding him so that the Jew may not be harmed or even be in apprehension because of the Gentiles, nor shall he lose his claim or his property. He shall see to it that his fellow shall be in no fear of them, and he shall make satisfaction to him and secure him in such a manner as the seven elders of the city will ordain. If there is no such board in his town, he shall act on the order of those of the nearest city in which such are to be found.

3. He shall not intimidate the "seven elders" through the power of the Gentiles. And because the masters of wicked tongue and informers do their deeds in darkness, we have decreed also excommunication for indirect action unless he satisfy him in accordance with the decision of the "seven elders" of the city.

4. It was further decreed that he should apply to them (to the "seven elders") on the first possible day, and that he should return the damage in accordance with all that they decree to him.

5. No man shall try to gain control over his neighbor through a king, prince, or judge, in order to punish or fine or coerce him, either in secular or religious matters, for there are some who play the part of saints and do not live up to ordinary standards.[80]

Again, this is not an absolute condemnation of the appeal to gentile powers. The ordinance ends with a plea for the aid of these authorities. It is a strong condemnation of an *illicit* appeal beyond the confines of the Jewish community.

In addition to the role that Jewish communal leaders played in controlling internal affairs, they continued to serve an indispensable function as liaison between the Jewish world and gentile society. From the point of view of the feudal barony, the major contribution of the Jewish self-governing apparatus lay in its ability to provide easily and cheaply substantial tax revenues. The arrangements for fair apportionment and rapid collection of these taxes were already well-established by the dawn of the twelfth century, and there is no sign of any significant change in this area. There are reflections, in both Jewish and non-Jewish sources, of an increasingly heavy tax burden, which probably began to strain both the resources and the patience of the Jewish community.

For the Jews, their leadership provided the most effective possible representation before the non-Jewish political powers. Suger describes,

---

[80] Ibid., pp. 153-54 (Hebrew) and pp. 155-57 (English).

for example, the representatives of Paris Jewry presenting themselves before Pope Innocent II during his visit to Saint-Denis.[81]

The one incident that lifts the curtain of obscurity from the political negotiations undertaken by the Jewish community is the Blois incident of 1171. The seriousness of the catastrophe prompted both a feverish whirl of Jewish activity and deep concern for information and memorialization. The fortuitous preservation of a set of four communal and personal letters in a late-twelfth-century Spires chronicle affords a rare glimpse into the Jewish community's ability to mobilize politically in self-defense.[82]

The Blois community itself seemingly depended at the outset upon the personal influence of the Jewess Polcelina, who had for some time been the object of Count Theobald's affections. This type of special power in courtly circles, whether flowing from an affair of the heart or of the purse (as was more usual), normally provided an effective tool for the Jewish communities. In Blois, Polcelina had unknowingly lost her leverage with the eroding of princely ardor. There is, nonetheless, sharp awareness on the part of her enemies of her potential power. After being taken prisoner she was accorded special treatment, probably out of fear that mistreatment of his former favorite might provoke Theobald. Only in one respect was she seriously limited, namely, from speaking to the count himself—tacit recognition of her possible sway over him.[83]

Other channels of influence functioned as well. According to the Orléans letter, Baruch b. David ha-Cohen and Isaac b. Judah, Jews of the county of Blois but not residents of the city itself, approached Theobald directly. He utilized them as intermediaries in approaching the imprisoned Jews to ascertain the ransom the Jews would be willing to pay for their release. A misestimate on the part of the Jews, coupled with the inflammatory appearance of an Augustinian canon, nullified this effort. However, Baruch b. David ha-Cohen was successful in rescuing the sacred objects of the Blois community and in protecting the remaining Jews living under the rule of Theobald. The price was a high one—1,000 pounds. It is not clear whether Baruch undertook these negotiations as a representative of the Jews of the county or by virtue of his own personal access to the comital court.[84]

---

[81] Suger, *Vie de Louis le Gros*, ed. Auguste Molinier (Paris, 1887), p. 120.

[82] On the letters, see Chazan, "The Blois Incident of 1171," pp. 17-21. On the Jewish communal activity, see ibid., pp. 21-26.

[83] Ibid., p. 21.

[84] Ibid.

The unprecedented acceptance of the malicious-murder charge at Blois deeply disquieted all of the Jewish communities of northern France. In its wake a major campaign of political negotiation was undertaken.

The most important figure in northern France was King Louis VII, and it was to him that the first efforts were directed. The representative leadership of the Jewish community of Paris (*kezinei Paris*) approached the king, asking to confer with him in private. The king, who already knew of the matter which had brought his Jews, insisted on a public sitting, to which he called all of his advisors. In this public meeting, he indicated explicitly his refusal to accept the increasingly popular slander, in the case of Blois as well as in the earlier cases in which tangible evidence of crime had existed. According to the Paris letter, the king ordered a charter prepared which would circulate throughout his realm, reassuring his Jews and ordering his officials to guard even more carefully these endangered subjects.[85]

The king was not the only ruler approached in northern France. The count of Champagne, a brother of Theobald of Blois, was, like Louis VII, both a prominent governmental figure and ruler over an important Jewish community. He too received a delegation of Jews and gave much the same response. The charge was not new to him. It had recently been sounded in the Champenois town of Épernay, and he had refused to accept it. So too did he reject the accusation of Blois, despite his own brother's actions. The effort to halt the spread of the slander would seem to have been successful, for the moment at least.[86]

Northern French Jewry, however, did not stop here. Although deeply concerned with insuring their own safety, the Jewish communities did not neglect their responsibilities to the remnants of Blois Jewry. Attempts had to be undertaken to salvage whatever possible. These negotiations had to be conducted in an altogether different manner; commissions of Jews would have been out of place. What was needed was a skilled negotiator, and for this sensitive undertaking the Jews chose Nathan b. R. Meshullam. Nathan was the scion of a distinguished Jewish family, the "Officiels." This clan, so well traced through a number of its generations by Zadoc Kahn, was prominent both within the Jewish community and in the non-Jewish world. Various members of the family are widely cited as disputing Biblical verses with prominent churchmen. Such a background of contact with the higher clergy

---

[85] Ibid., p. 22.
[86] Ibid.

made Nathan a fine choice to represent the Jews in this delicate matter, for it was obvious to the Jews that greatest leverage on the actions of Theobald of Blois could be exerted by his brother William, archbishop of Sens and bishop of Chartres. The Troyes letter, written prior to the reception of Nathan's account of his achievements, mentions two specific goals to the negotiations: burial of the deceased and redemption of captives. In his own letter detailing his accomplishments, Nathan fails to mention burial of the dead. He does indicate a number of other successes, including release of the captives, permission for youngsters forcibly converted to return to the Jewish fold, and a declaration by Theobald that the same charge would not be raised again. All the foregoing was accomplished through the mediation of William, with the sum of 120 pounds paid to him for his efforts and a further 100 pounds for the assent of his brother Theobald.[87]

The final stage in this political activity involved alerting the Jewish communities of the area to both the nature of the incident itself and to the vigorous and successful negotiations which followed in its wake. The Orléans community, which had been the first to hear of the tragedy and had firsthand information at its disposal, was assigned the onerous task of detailing the catastrophe. The major communities, Paris and Troyes, drew up letters describing their negotiating successes.[88]

In all this flurry of activity can be seen both the operation of the recognized representatives of the Jewish communities of northern France and the occasional intervention of one or another of the Jews with special connections in courtly circles. In this one instance, at least, these various kinds of negotiators were able to function in complete harmony.

If there is any major development in the machinery of Jewish self-government during the twelfth century, it is the ability of the Jewish communities spread across northern France, over a variety of principalities, to work together for their common benefit. The twelfth century saw the growing crystallization of ever larger and more powerful principalities. In an area where unification was very much in vogue, the always exposed Jewish minority had to follow suit.

Even during the pre-Crusade period, some intercommunal cooperation was called for, particularly by the problem of small communities unable to provide for themselves all the needed facilities. What resulted was a constellation of communities clustered about a major center

---

[87]Ibid., pp. 22–23.
[88]Ibid., pp. 18–19.

whose extensive institutions they could always utilize. The preamble to the important ordinance of R. Tam indicates a continuation of the same arrangements. R. Tam mentions "the elders of Troyes and its sages and those in its surrounding environs"; "the sages of Dijon and its environs"; "the leaders of Auxerre and Sens and its adjacent communities"; and "the elders of Orléans and surrounding territories. . . . "[89]

What was new in the twelfth century was the ability of these local groupings to function as a cohesive unit. This unity is again revealed most strikingly by the crisis of 1171. The foundation of Jewish cohesion lay in the system of communication that linked Jewish settlements. Immediately upon reception of eyewitness accounts of the execution—both Christian and Jewish—Orléans Jewry spread the unhappy news. Again, it was Orléans Jewry, with its comprehensive information, that composed the detailed report of the incident for its fellow communities. This report reached Ephraim of Bonn in Germany and the Jewish community of Spires, where it was fortunately preserved for the future. The Paris letter clearly passed through Troyes. It too obviously reached Spires, as did the letters of Nathan b. R. Meshullam and of the Troyes community.[90]

Tangible behind this communication is a central force, directing almost all of this activity. The focal point out of which the diversified response of northern French Jewry emanated seems to have been the towering figure of R. Jacob Tam. R. Tam, one of the well-known grandchildren of Rashi, has long been recognized for his outstanding contributions to the development of the Tosafist school. His position as a Jewish communal figure has also been long acknowledged. Nowhere, however, does his commanding role in Jewish affairs emerge with as much clarity and specificity as in the aftermath of Blois.

Most of the stages of Jewish response radiated from headquarters at Troyes. Although the approach of Parisian Jewry to Louis VII is nowhere linked to R. Tam, the audience with Henry of Champagne was undoubtedly carried out by Troyes Jewry and its great leader. The entire approach to William, archbishop of Sens and bishop of Chartres, reflects the hand of Jacob Tam. The Troyes letter, written prior to Nathan's letter, details the goals of the negotiations, specifying in fact the exact sums of money to be offered. At the successful close of his mission, Nathan immediately communicated the results to R. Tam.

The circular letter drawn up by Orléans Jewry to inform the Jewish communities of the details of the disaster was composed at the behest

---

[89] Finkelstein, *Jewish Self-Government*, p. 153 (Hebrew) and p. 155 (English).
[90] Chazan, "The Blois Incident of 1171," pp. 17-21, 24.

of R. Tam. The institution of an annual commemoration fast, mentioned in the Orléans letter, is specifically attributed by Ephraim of Bonn to the dictate of Jacob b. Meir. The other ritual commemorations enumerated in the Troyes letter must also have been initiated by R. Tam.[91]

The Jewish drive towards coordinated activity, spurred by the growing political consolidation of northern France, at this point managed to draw together Jews from a number of discrete principalities. The Orléans community, so responsive to the directives of R. Tam of Champagne, was not subject to the same political authority but was under the control of the king of France. Indeed Ephraim of Bonn records that all of northwestern European Jewry accepted the annual fast ordained by R. Tam of Troyes.[92]

The same network of communication and the same far-reaching authority exercised by key religious leaders were also effective under peaceful circumstances. A number of important ordinances were widely adopted as a result of extensive intercommunal action.[93] The most well known of these ordinances was the prohibition of the unauthorized private use of governmental authority in Jewish affairs. The technique for the acceptance of this document is revealed in the following heading:

> This is the document called *Zaz ha-Mateh*, that was decreed by R. Samuel b. R. Meir and R. Jacob b. R. Meir and their brother R. Isaac, the descendants of the great guide Rashi. They sent [this document] throughout the entire dispersion in the kingdom of France and Lotharingia and Germany and much of Spain. The great and the illustrious all signed this letter and levied excommunication on its transgressors and their descendants forever.[94]

A more detailed list of assenting communities has also been preserved:

> Therefore have we taken counsel together: the elders of Troyes and its sages and those in its surrounding environs; the sages of Dijon and its environs; the leaders of Auxerre and Sens and its adjacent communities; the elders of Orléans and surrounding territories; our brethren the inhabitants of Châlons; the sages of the area of Reims; our masters in Paris and their neighbors; the scholars of Melun and Étampes; the inhabitants of Normandy and Brittany and Anjou and

---

[91]Ibid., pp. 24-25.
[92]Ibid., p. 25.
[93]Ibid., pp. 26-30.
[94]Finkelstein, *Jewish Self-Government*, p. 159. The translation has been modified slightly.

Poitou; the greatest of our generation, the inhabitants of Lotharingia. Of those listed here, some have assented, but the reaction of others we have not heard—for the matter was urgent. Therefore we have depended on the fact that we know them to be great authorities who accede to their inferiors. For the law is a just one, and were it not so stipulated, it would be worthy of stipulation.[95]

The communities mentioned stretch from imperial lands through Burgundy, Champagne, the royal domain, and on into Angevin territories in the west—a remarkable degree of unity.

The most explicit indication of the mechanism for the achievement of joint consent to important enactments stems from an ordinance concerning disposition of dowry. The ordinance was promulgated by the key communities of Troyes and Reims, and from there its authority spread widely.

This principle we have accepted upon ourselves, the inhabitants of Troyes and Reims. We then sent messengers to those neighboring communities within the radius of one day's travel, and they responded favorably. We then decreed all the foregoing for ourselves, for those who had joined us, and for our descendants; [indeed we decreed this] for all of the inhabitants of France, Anjou, Poitou, Normandy, and those inhabiting areas within a day or two's travel time of these communities—that they and their descendants observe this decree.[96]

This impressive unity in a still fragmented northern France suffered from one major shortcoming: it lacked the crucial quality of stable continuity. Mechanisms for joint effort existed, but activation of these mechanisms was normally effected only through the authority of an outstanding personality. It is by no means accidental that all the important instances of intercommunal cooperation in twelfth-century French Jewish history are linked with the name of R. Jacob Tam. The power exercised by R. Tam was the result of a unique combination of wealth, political influence, prodigious scholarship, and religious prestige. Such an individual could fuse the shaky bonds linking the independent Jewish communities of northern France into a strong chain of concerted action. Obviously, such individuals were rare—and without them French Jewry had to slip back into a pattern of disorganization.

[95] Ibid., p. 153 (Hebrew) and p. 155 (English).
[96] Ibid., pp. 164–65 (Hebrew) and p. 167 (English).

The twelfth century thus reveals a Jewish community that exhibited many of the major characteristics of Christian life of that period: expansion; growing business sophistication, where the Jews in some senses pioneered; vigorous intellectual creativity. Yet these decades saw a number of ominous signals that boded ill for the future of northern French Jewry. As a result of the business advances of the times, the Jews were thrown ever more firmly into the alliance with the feudal rulers; increasing ecclesiastical agitation and heightened popular animosity deepened these ties. The alliance which now afforded both physical safety and business stability left the Jews very little political mobility, a development fraught with serious dangers.

Only against this background can the unexpected outbursts of the early 1180's be fully understood. Philip Augustus may have been moved by the impetuousness of his youth. However, he also reflected the twelfth-century legacy of anti-Jewish animus and Jewish political vulnerability.

III

PHILIP AUGUSTUS—

EXPULSION, EXPLOITATION, AND

ECCLESIASTICAL PRESSURE

O N NOVEMBER 1, 1179, Philip, son of Louis VII, was crowned co-regent of France. Louis, who had long delayed elevating Philip to the throne, was now gravely ill; his young son had become in reality the new king. Unbeknown to the participants in the ceremonies at Reims, Philip's would be one of the longest and most significant reigns in the history of France. During the more than five decades of his rule, royal control was extended far beyond the narrow confines of 1179. Equally important, with the defeat of John in 1204 and the victory at Bouvines in 1214, the French monarch suddenly took his place among the great powers of Christendom. No longer was he a weak king surrounded by potent vassals; he was now the major political authority in France and one of the key rulers in all of Europe. A capable administrator, Philip Augustus built the governmental machinery necessary for controlling and exploiting his expanding domains. He successfully undertook the task of transforming his chief city, Paris, into a splendid political and intellectual center of northwestern Europe.[1]

---

[1] The most detailed treatment of the important reign of Philip Augustus is the four-volume study by Alexander Cartellieri, *Philipp II August, König von Frankreich*, 4 vols. in 5 (Leipzig, 1899–1922). Also useful are Achille Luchaire's study of Philip Augustus in Ernest Lavisse's

Certainly the Jews of northern France could never have anticipated that his efforts would so decisively affect the history of their community. By his death in 1223, the majority of the Jewish communities of the area had fallen under direct royal rule. Those Jews still living in the domains of independent barons, for example, the Jews of Champagne, had already felt the harsh hand of Philip Augustus and were ever more tightly bound by royal policy. The first major expulsion had taken place; the most serious single slaughter in the history of northern French Jewry had been perpetrated by the king himself; the relatively positive baronial policies had given way to careful governmental exploitation of Jewish business; the antipathetic Church views which had been gathering momentum during the twelfth century had strongly made their mark on Jewish life.[2]

In late 1179 all this lay ahead. The onset of change, however, was not long in coming.

At the very inception of his reign, the young sovereign, surrounded by baronial cliques striving to bend him to their wills, undertook vigorous independent action aimed at replenishing his financial resources. On February 16, 1180, a Sabbath day, royal agents arrested the Jews at worship and confiscated their precious goods.[3] The precise technique of this seizure is unclear, but a Hebrew source gives us some insight. R. Ḥaim ha-Cohen, dealing with some of the problems caused by the incident, considered Jewish wine unsullied by gentile use, even though "the officials were in the Jews' homes, with key in hand, searching."[4] Curiously, the most detailed source for Philip Augustus's early anti-Jewish

---

Histoire de France, 9 vols. in 18 (Paris, 1900–1911), vol. 3, pt. 1, and his *Social France at the Time of Philip Augustus*, trans. E. B. Krehbiel (New York, 1912). For Champagne, see Henri d'Arbois de Jubainville, *Histoire des ducs et des comtes de Champagne*, 7 vols. in 8 (Paris, 1859–69). On Normandy, see especially Frederick Powicke, *The Loss of Normandy*, 2nd ed. (New York, 1961). For recent studies on the cultural climate midway through the reign of Philip Augustus, see *The Year 1200*, 2 vols. (New York, 1970).

[2] The best treatments of Jewish life between 1180 and 1223 are those of Georg Caro, *Sozial- und Wirtschaftsgeschichte der Juden im Mittelalter und der Neuzeit*, 2 vols. (Frankfort, 1908–20), vol. 1, and Salo Baron, *A Social and Religious History of the Jews*, 2nd ed., 14 vols. (New York, 1952–69), vols. 4 and 10. In *The English Jewry under Angevin Kings* (London, 1960), H. G. Richardson devotes an important chapter to late-twelfth-century Norman Jewry. The development of Jewish political status has been carefully analyzed by Gavin Langmuir in " 'Judei Nostri' and the Beginning of Capetian Legislation," *Traditio* 16 (1960): 203–69. The most useful work for the cultural history of the period is Ephraim Urbach, *Ba'aley ha-Tosafot* (Jerusalem, 1955).

[3] Jacob Marcus, *The Jew in the Medieval World: A Source Book: 315–1791* (Cincinnati, 1938), p. 25; Ralph of Diceto, *Opera historica*, ed. William Stubbs, 2 vols. (London, 1876), vol. 2, p. 4.

[4] Urbach, *Ba'aley ha-Tosafot*, p. 108, citing Mordechai b. Hillel.

actions, his biographer, Rigord, leaves the impression of a simple confiscation. According to the English historian Ralph of Diceto, however, the Jewish valuables were held until redeemed by a ransom payment of 15,000 marks, a very substantial sum of money.[5]

The king's next move took place sometime shortly thereafter and was a far cleverer ploy. By this time Louis VII had died and his heir was deeply involved in battling a dangerous alliance of feudal barons headed by the counts of Flanders and Champagne. Still badly in need of funds, the young monarch contrived to replenish his coffers, to win popular sympathy, and to ingratiate himself with reform elements in the Church. Prodded by an important royal advisor, the monk Bernard of Coudray, Philip ordered the remission of all debts owed the Jews, with one-fifth of the total to be paid into the royal treasury.[6] While documentary records for the early years of the reign are still sparse, mention survives of an agreement between King Philip and the abbot of Château-Landon. The abbot was to pay 44 pounds and thereby be free of all obligations to the king accruing from the provisions set for Jewish debts.[7] This is, in all probability, an arrangement concerning final payment of the required twenty percent.

In April 1182, still enmeshed in his battle against the Flanders-Champagne coalition, Philip Augustus took the most radical step against the Jews yet taken in feudal northern Europe. He announced that the Jews must leave the royal domain by the Feast of Saint John the Baptist, on June 24. According to Rigord, the Jews fell back upon precisely the techniques generally employed in such circumstances: "they sought to win with gifts and golden promises the great of the land—counts, barons, archbishops, bishops—that through their influence and advice, and through the promise of infinite wealth, they might turn the king's mind from his firm intention."[8] In this instance, however, the time-honored technique failed.

This step, like the preceding two, served first of all the financial need of the king. The arrangement described by Rigord was the following:

> The king gave them leave to sell each his movable goods before the time fixed, that is, the Feast of St. John the Baptist. But their real

[5] Ralph of Diceto, *Opera historica*, vol. 2, p. 4.

[6] Marcus, *The Jew in the Medieval World*, pp. 25–26.

[7] H.-François Delaborde, ed., *Recueil des actes de Philippe Auguste, roi de France*, 3 vols. (Paris, 1916–66), vol. 1, doc. no. 62.

[8] Marcus, *The Jew in the Medieval World*, pp. 26–27.

estate, that is, houses, fields, vineyards, barns, winepresses, and such like, he reserved for himself and his successors, the kings of the French.[9]

A number of documents disposing of some of the property taken over by the king have survived. The profit to the royal treasury must have been considerable.[10]

One particular class of confiscated property is singled out for special mention by Rigord. The synagogues of the Jews were not kept by the king; rather they were donated to the Church in order that they might be transformed into Christian places of worship. Rigord notes specifically the conversion of the synagogues at Orléans and Étampes into churches.[11] Documentary sources inform us also of the gift of the synagogue in Paris to the bishop of that city.[12] Thus, in addition to immediate economic benefit, the king had once more assured himself the approbation of many in ecclesiastical circles.

Indeed, while Rigord cannot be used as a reflection of the mind of the young monarch, he does provide an accurate gauge of the reaction to the king's actions among some churchmen; this response can only be described as unmitigated joy. Rigord chronicles the king's campaign in great detail. It is, for the monk of Saint-Denis, the major achievement of the first years of the reign. Expulsion clearly improved relations with those circles represented by Bernard of Coudray and Rigord.

What gave the young king the right to undertake these unprecedented actions against the Jews? The royal view itself is unavailable. Those documents surviving are simply transactions involving confiscated Jewish properties, without any establishment of legal fundamentals. It is interesting to note that the term "Judeus noster" is invoked on occasion.[13] The term, already familiar in the early twelfth century and widely used all through the thirteenth, certainly implies the Jew's deep dependency on his baronial overlord. Guillaume le Breton, the chronicler of the last years of the reign of Philip Augustus, finds the legal basis for the expulsion in this status of political dependency. In his poetic rendition of annulment of Jewish debts by Philip Augustus and

---

[9] Ibid., p. 26.

[10] See, for example, Delaborde, *Recueil des actes de Philippe Auguste*, vol. 1, doc. nos. 86, 94, 133, 134, 166, 223.

[11] H.-François Delaborde, ed., *Oeuvres de Rigord et de Guillaume le Breton, historiens de Philippe-Auguste*, 2 vols. (Paris, 1882–85), vol. 1, pp. 30–32. Compare Delaborde, *Recueil des actes de Philippe Auguste*, vol. 1, doc. no. 99.

[12] Ibid., vol. 1, doc. no. 90.

[13] Ibid., vol. 1, doc. no. 134.

royal seizure of one-fifth, Guillaume claims that the king, had he wished, could have taken all, since these funds fell into the category of property and chattel of royal serfs.[14] Whether the theory of Jewish political dependence was already widely accepted is questionable. The Jewish leaders of northern French Jewry, who debated the baronial right to limit Jewish movement and to confiscate the goods of tax-evading Jews, seem to know nothing of this far more radical claim to authority.

Rigord, who is the major source for the early years of the reign, takes quite a different tack. Again it must be emphasized that Rigord does not necessarily present the royal conception of these events; he does however reflect the attitudes of certain segments of French society at the time. Rigord sees the right to expel as rooted not in the political status of Jewish dependency but rather in the royal right—indeed obligation—to safeguard the religious purity of the realm.[15] Rigord goes to great lengths to delineate a reasonable basis for each of the actions undertaken by the king. Each of these alleged Jewish crimes can be related to pre-1180 anti-Jewish sentiment; each is viewed as a reflection of the perversity and perfidy of the Jews; taken together they are seen by Rigord as justifying the vigorous action initiated by the "rex Christianissimus." The three charges leveled by Rigord are: (1) malicious murder, an allegation whose development during the 1160's and 1170's has been traced; (2) usury, which is seen by Rigord as in itself a perversion of Biblical injunction and as a contributing factor toward the spectacle of economic oppression and toward the religious scandal of Judaizing on the part of Christians employed in the homes of wealthy Jews; and (3) the unspeakable desecrations committed by the Jews on religious articles that came into their possession as deposits for loans. It is the obligation of the royal authority—and Rigord emphasizes in his account the actions of Philip Augustus as monarch—to care for the religious state of his realm. Earlier, Louis VII had taken royal action when confronted with evidence of Judaizing on the part of newly-converted Christians; now, according to Rigord, Louis's son set himself the task of purging his realm of sin.

It is unfortunate that we have no direct insight into the king's own views. We do not know whether he shared Rigord's attitudes or whether he cynically exploited them. What is clear is that anti-Jewish sentiments

---

[14] Delaborde, *Oeuvres de Rigord et de Guillaume le Breton*, vol. 2, p. 22.

[15] Marcus, *The Jew in the Medieval World*, pp. 24–27.

provided the fertile soil out of which the king's campaign could spring, with immediate economic benefit and enhanced royal prestige as tangible gains.

Rigord's claim that the expulsion was royal in scope as well as rationale is obviously incorrect. A number of contemporary historians restrict it to Philip's domain only.[16] More telling is royal documentation itself. In a charter dealing with the former synagogue of Étampes, Philip Augustus uses the expression "Judeis a terris nostris fugatis."[17] Given the limited size of the royal lands during the early years of Philip's reign, only a fraction of northern French Jewry was affected. Evidence reveals expulsion from Paris, Bourges, Corbeil, Étampes, Melun, and Orléans. The flourishing Jewish communities in the baronies surrounding the royal domain were, as far as can be discerned, untouched. There is abundant record of Jewish life in the Angevin lands of the west; there are scattered references to continued Jewish presence in Auxerre, Bray, Provins, and Soissons in the east.

The fate of the expelled is not reflected in the surviving sources. It is, of course, easy to speculate that their normal response would be to move into adjacent Jewish communities. This would not have necessitated journeying great distances. The reduced size of the royal domain not only minimized the number of expellees; it also made relocation far easier. Short trips would bring them into safe territories, in the midst of Jewish communities with whom they shared a common vernacular, similar economic pursuits, and a like way of life. The influx of settlers must have strained the resources of the Jewish communities which served as refuges. As noted, population growth was a problem for the twelfth-century Jewish communities, with their limited economic outlets. Demographic expansion, resulting from an influx of expellees, was a serious matter. Jewish lenders were not prohibited, however, from plying their trade in the royal domain throughout the period of banishment. Philip's order of September 1198 for the enforcement of debts owed Champenois Jews indicates this clearly.[18] The possibility of lending in royal territories may have eased somewhat the economic hardships resulting from the expulsion.

Despite the absence of Jews from royal lands during the remainder of the 1180's and most of the 1190's, Philip Augustus continued to affect Jewish fate in France. In March 1188, as part of his preparations for the

---

[16] Note, for example, Robert of Auxerre in *RHF*, vol. 18, p. 251, and Albert of Trois-Fontaines in ibid., p. 746.

[17] Delaborde, *Recueil des actes de Philippe Auguste*, vol. 1, doc. no. 99.

[18] Ibid., vol. 2, doc. no. 583.

Crusade, Philip Augustus enacted an important ordinance concerning debts owed to Crusaders. The precedent for concern with debts owed by those taking the Cross lay in the famed bull of Pope Eugenius, *Quantum praedecessores*.[19] Philip Augustus's measure, however, was somewhat different from the earlier papal proclamation. The pope's annulment of interest on debts owed by the Crusaders was not enacted by the French monarch. What was stipulated was, rather, an end to the accumulation of interest and a carefully arranged period for repaying the principal and the interest already accrued.[20] There were, of course, no Jews in the royal domain at this juncture. However, Jewish money-lending was being carried on in royal territory. More important, it seems likely that this edict was intended as royal legislation, applicable to the entire kingdom rather than to the domain only. From both points of view, then, the measure probably had a significant effect on the Jews of northern France, their absence from the king's own lands notwithstanding.

The second instance of royal impact on northern French Jewry was the vicious and Machiavellian incident at the Champenois town of Bray-sur-Seine, the bloodiest single attack in the history of medieval northern French Jewry.[21] Philip Augustus had shown very little enthusiasm for crusading, tarrying only briefly in the East. By December 1191 he had returned to France and had celebrated Christmas at Fontainebleau. The following March, sojourning at Saint-Germain-en-Laye, the monarch heard reports of Jewish involvement in the death of one of his vassals at Bray-sur-Seine.[22] The precise details of the incident are blurred. It involved allegations of murder leveled against the king's vassal by the Jews of Champagne, as well as Jewish involvement in his eventual punishment.[23] Once more, Rigord presents the monarch in his now familiar guise of "most Christian king," setting out immediately to redress the unspeakable insult to the ruling faith. Philip traversed quickly the distance between Saint-Germain and Bray. He surrounded the town, captured its Jews, and executed eighty or more.

[19] See above, chapter 2.

[20] Delaborde, *Recueil des actes de Philippe Auguste*, vol. 1, doc. no. 228. James Brundage, *Medieval Canon Law and the Crusader* (Madison, 1969), p. 181, fails to note the extent to which the royal stance fell short of the earlier papal exhortation.

[21] On this catastrophe, see Robert Chazan, "The Bray Incident of 1192: *Realpolitik* and Folk Slander," *PAAJR* 37 (1969): 1–18.

[22] On the place and date of this incident, see ibid., pp. 2–5.

[23] On the various renditions of the events leading up to the king's intervention, see ibid., pp. 5–7.

Disregarding Rigord's continued attempt to emphasize royal dignity and prerogatives, it is possible to discern in this incident cold-blooded political cunning.[24] Philip Augustus was, in all probability, acting not as monarch but simply as an aggrieved overlord. The Hebrew source for the incident notes that the slain Christian was the king's vassal. Marching beyond his own domain to enforce feudal obligations is well-known as one of the methods consistently exploited by Philip Augustus to expand royal presence and power. In this instance, the circumstances were uniquely propitious. The count of Champagne, Henry II, was still in the East fighting in the Crusade that the king had so quickly abandoned. Henry's large and important county was left under the temporary rule of his mother, Mary—a situation always fraught with danger. Philip thus grasped the opportunity afforded by the obligations of feudal law and the temporary political weakness in neighboring Champagne to begin to make royal power more deeply felt there. This was but the opening salvo in the royal campaign for control of the key border fortress of Bray-sur-Seine. The Jews of northern France, however, were in no position to appreciate the legal and political adroitness of the young monarch; for them the incident was the costliest and ugliest they had yet suffered.

During the years between 1182 and 1198, while Jewish settlement in the royal domain remained prohibited, Jewish presence continued—and in fact was probably augmented—in the baronies, large and small, surrounding the king's own territories. The two major areas of settlement were the county of Champagne in the east and the Angevin lands in the west.

While materials for the history of Champenois Jewry at the end of the twelfth century remain sparse, records for Norman and Angevin Jewish life begin to multiply during the years immediately prior to Philip Augustus's takeover in 1204.[25] Since the data all stem from the copious governmental archives, certain facets of Jewish life emerge with comparative clarity, while others remain totally obscure.

The aspect of Jewish economic enterprise highlighted in the Angevin documentation is, of course, moneylending, particularly lending which involved substantial sums of money and governmental support. While no loan instruments themselves are preserved, they are frequently men-

---

[24] Ibid., pp. 7–9.

[25] Note again the valuable study by Richardson on the Jews of Normandy during this period in his *The English Jewry under Angevin Kings*.

tioned, usually in royal charters acquitting certain individuals of their obligation to repay debts and ordering that the documents in the possession of the Jewish creditor be returned.[26] The securing of loans through the presentation of guarantors was also a common practice, again often revealed in quittance charters.[27]

As noted earlier, lending carried on in cooperation with the governmental authorities involved a number of significant benefits for the Jews. The major disadvantage was the possibility of adverse governmental action. This danger is amply documented in the Angevin materials, with charters of quittance highly prominent. Related also is the practice of coercing the Jews into extending badly needed credit. In some instances it was the duke himself who was the recipient of such forced loans; in other cases it was a key figure to whom the duke wished to grant an important favor.[28] Both these practices indicate that the negative features inhering in Jewish dependence on governmental business aid had already become obvious in Angevin lands by the end of the twelfth century.

While it was possible for barons other than the duke to possess Jews, almost all of the Jews in Angevin territory probably belonged directly to him.[29] The relationship of Jew to overlord was articulated in an unusually precise manner. There survive, first of all, charters extended to individual Jews. In 1199, for example, Deusaie of Bernay was given a special grant of ducal protection and a promise of freedom from all tallages in return for an annual payment of five marks.[30] Likewise, in 1204 Duke John wrote the seneschals of Normandy and the custodians of the Jews, ordering special protection for a Jew named Morrell.[31] In the latter document, the price for such security is not spelled out.

The nexus between ducal authority and individual Jews is revealed also in a radically different kind of document, one that elaborates not on the government's responsibilities but rather on those of the Jews. In 1199, Dieudonné of Verneuil, one of the wealthiest Norman Jews, was forced to deposit substantial securities to reinforce his promise not to

---

[26] See, for example, Amédée Léchaudé d'Anisy, ed., *Grands rôles des echiquiers de Normandie*, 2 vols. (Paris, 1845–52), vol. 1, pp. 110, 114, 116, 124.

[27] Ibid., pp. 110, 114, 124.

[28] Ibid., p. 114; Thomas Duffy Hardy, ed., *Rotuli de oblatis et finibus in Turri Londinensi asservati* (London, 1835), p. 71; idem, *Rotuli litterarum patentium in Turri Londinensi asservati* (London, 1835), p. 25.

[29] Note the royal grant of a Jew to William Marshall in idem, *Rotuli chartarum in Turri Londinensi asservati* (London, 1837), p. 75.

[30] Ibid., p. 27.

[31] Hardy, *Rotuli litterarum patentium*, p. 73.

leave ducal territory.[32] This concern for restricting the movement of well-to-do Jews became increasingly prominent during the ensuing decade.

The most striking example of the articulated political position of the Jews of Normandy and Anjou comes in the broad charter of 1201.[33] This charter is the only one of its type for northern France prior to that of 1315. Such a grant of rights, so distinctly at variance with standard practice in northern France, must probably be seen as a reflection of the somewhat different situation in England. Whatever the explanation for this unique document, its contents are highly interesting. The provisions granted to the Jews fall into four major categories: (1) protection of life and limb; (2) safeguarding of property; (3) protection of business; and (4) regulation of judicial proceedings. Little is said of protection of Jewish life and limb. There is simply the order to royal officials "to guard and defend and protect" the Jews. No specific penalties are enumerated, as is so often done in German charters. Safeguarding Jewish property takes a number of forms, beginning with an affirmation of the Jews' right to hold that property which they now honorably possess. Further stipulations assure the Jews the right to pass their property on to their heirs, the right to move freely with their goods throughout royal and ducal territory, and freedom from customs and tolls. Jewish moneylending is protected from a number of limitations sometimes imposed upon it. Specifically Jews may purchase or accept, most probably as pledges, "all things which may be brought to them, except those which belong to the state and bloodstained cloth." Striking is the absence of a class of goods always mentioned in thirteenth-century ordinances on Jewish moneylending—Jews are not overtly prohibited from accepting Church vessels and ornaments.

The largest number of clauses in the charter deal with matters related to judicial procedure. The concerns exhibited include both the protection of the Jewish litigant and the reaffirmation of royal-ducal jurisdiction over the Jews. Perhaps the key provision is that which restricts litigation involving the Jews to the ducal courts. This stipulation undoubtedly served the purposes of both the Jews and the duke, affording the best possible guarantee of a fair hearing for the former and a strong reiteration of the political prerogatives of the latter. Other significant clauses include provision for mixed witnesses in cases involving contention between Jew and Christian and certification of the acceptability of

[32] Idem, *Rotuli de oblatis et finibus*, p. 73.
[33] Idem, *Rotuli chartarum*, p. 93.

writs held by the Jews for litigation. Since opposition to the use of such writs was occasionally voiced during the period, emphasis on their validity was far from superfluous.

The government's concern for the Jews was in no way disinterested. The protections promised in 1201 were almost certainly paid for by the recipients of the charter. More important, they reflect the duke's self-interest on a broader scale—the Jews represented a source of substantial revenue for a dangerously strapped government. Possibilities for exploiting Jewish business, with which the authorities were deeply involved, have already been noted. More profitable yet was direct taxation levied upon the Jews. H. G. Richardson has analyzed meticulously the extant data and has concluded "that the Jews of Normandy were taxed no more frequently than every two or three years and that in the fifteen years between Richard's accession and John's expulsion from the duchy not more than six or seven taxes are likely to have been imposed."[34] While such taxation is mild when compared to the levies in England, the total income from the Norman and Angevin Jewish communities was in all probability not insubstantial. Above all, it was revenue that could be raised in a variety of ways—through direct taxation, through a multiplicity of fines, and through interference in Jewish lending operations.

Jewish affairs were well organized, far better than in the neighboring Capetian lands. Evidence for the diverse activities of the Norman "keeper of the Jews" is contained in the documentation on the most prominent of these officials, Richard of Villequier. Richard was involved with taxation of the Jews; he was also deeply enmeshed in Jewish economic affairs. His business concerns ranged from enforcement of Jewish debts, a major boon to the Jews, to quittance of such debts, an important liability.[35]

Unfortunately there are practically no sources for internal aspects of the life of Norman and Angevin Jewry. These Jewries are mentioned in a number of the major ordinances of R. Jacob Tam, although specific communities and leaders are not singled out.[36] The level of development of these communities must remain obscure for the present.

By 1204, Norman and Angevin Jewry had fallen under Capetian control. This change of authority was destined to bring with it, however, no major alteration of Jewish status. Philip Augustus, whether

---

[34] Richardson, *English Jewry under Angevin Kings*, p. 203.
[35] Ibid., pp. 206–8.
[36] See above, chapter 2.

influenced by the Angevin model or not, was himself moving inex-
orably towards a more tightly centralized monarchy, with a concomitant concern for enhanced control and exploitation of his Jews.

In 1199, an errant arrow cut short the dynamic career of Richard,
king of England and duke of Normandy. With the demise of this worthy adversary, the fate of the Angevin lands in western France was
sealed—his successor was simply no match for the crafty and experi-
enced Philip Augustus. By the end of the first decade of the thirteenth
century, the French monarch was, for the first time, master of most of
northern France. Direct royal control now extended westward over the
vast Norman and Angevin territories. In the east, the death of the count
of Champagne had left his widow regent for their posthumous son, a
regency that was to last some twenty years. For a shrewd political
manipulator like Philip Augustus, such an arrangement offered inesti-
mable possibilities for the expansion of royal authority.[37] With the
return of the Jews to the Île-de-France in 1198, the absorption of
Norman Jewry into the royal domain in 1204, and the growing royal
influence over Blanche of Champagne, the fate of all of northern
French Jewry became ever more firmly conditioned by the attitudes
and actions of the king of France.

In his rehearsal of the events of 1198, Rigord, who had featured so
prominently the anti-Jewish programs of 1180 through 1182, grumbles
plaintively that "King Philip, against the advice of all men and his own
edict, returned the Jews to Paris."[38] Actually, the very same anti-Jewish
agitation that had either directly instigated the expulsion of 1182 or at
least facilitated it now led to the recall of the Jews to the royal domain.
The reforming ideals of late-twelfth-century Parisian academic circles
were not limited to the schools; there was every endeavor to bring them
to the populace at large through the preaching of gifted clerics.[39] One
of the most successful of these preaching efforts was that conducted by
Fulk of Neuilly between 1195 and 1200. Aimed primarily at the twin
evils of usury and prostitution, Fulk's campaign spilled over against the
Jews.

In those days, moreover, the Jews were troubled with serious plun-
dering and affliction. For since the lord Fulk demanded the complete

---

[37] Powicke, *The Loss of Normandy*; Arbois de Jubainville, *Histoire des ducs et des comtes de Champagne.*

[38] Delaborde, *Oeuvres de Rigord et de Guillaume le Breton*, vol. 1, p. 141.

[39] On these influential ecclesiastical circles, see John Baldwin, *Masters, Princes and Merchants: The Social Views of Peter the Chanter and His Circle*, 2 vols. (Princeton, 1969).

extirpation of sins and the implanting of virtues and utterly abhorred usurers, he detested the Jews in all ways, because many of us were weakened by infinite and heavy usuries. Hence through his instigation, and through the efforts of the bishops, it was brought to pass that half of all debts owed to the Jews were to be repudiated and half were to be paid at decreed terms. But some of the barons commanded that they be expelled from their lands; however the expelled were received and returned by the king. Truly that detracted no little from the king's reputation, when those whom he had expelled a long time back he admitted again.[40]

The movement stirred up by Fulk was thus utilized by the king to reverse his earlier policies concerning the Jews. It has been widely suggested that the mature Philip Augustus realized that, while profiting handsomely from the expulsion, he had stripped himself of an important flow of steady revenue; now the time was ripe for recouping his loss.

The return began in July, and important steps were taken a few months later to stabilize the status of the king's new Jews. With the treaties of September 1198, a new stage in the regulation of Jewish affairs began. On that date the king and the count of Champagne came to a series of agreements.

Let all whom the present letter reaches know that we have conceded that we shall retain in our land none of the Jews of our most beloved and faithful nephew, Theobald count of Troyes, unless with the verbal consent of that count; and that none of our Jews will be permitted to lend money to anyone nor to seize anyone or anything in the land of the aforesaid count unless with the verbal assent of the aforesaid count. The same Count Theobald conceded to us that he will retain none of our Jews in his land, unless with our verbal consent; and that none of his Jews will be permitted to lend money to anyone nor to seize anyone or anything in our land, unless with our verbal consent.[41]

The count, for his part, swore essentially the same thing. To this was added the king's order to the bailiffs and provosts of the royal domain to enforce the debts owed to Theobald's Jews.[42]

---

[40] *RHF*, vol. 18, p. 263. On Fulk, see also Milton Gutsch, "A Twelfth Century Preacher— Fulk of Neuilly," *The Crusades and Other Historical Essays Presented to Dana C. Munro*, ed. L. J. Paetow (New York, 1928).

[41] Delaborde, *Recueil des actes de Philippe Auguste*, vol. 2, doc. no. 582. The count's version can be found in *Layettes*, vol. 1, doc. no. 479.

[42] Delaborde, *Recueil des actes de Philippe Auguste*, vol. 2, doc. no. 583.

These well-known treaties require fresh analysis. What were the advantages to each of the signers, major holders of Jews in northern France? For the king, the agreements represented, first of all, a recognition of his newly-acquired title to a number of Jews. Equally important, the prohibition of lending by Champenois Jews in the royal domain—unless granted special royal permission—meant the building of a viable economic outlet for the newly-settled royal Jews, incentive for the enticement of new Jewish residents, and finally a safeguard for royal profit from those Jews who did occupy the king's lands.[43] For the count, on the other hand, the agreements meant that, should the king aggressively seek new royal Jews, as he was likely to do, the search would draw Jews from areas other than Champagne. Each of the parties then had much to gain; the only losers were the Jews themselves, who suffered diminution of both political and economic rights. The agreements of 1198 were only the beginning. Such treaties abound during the first two decades of the thirteenth century, eventually giving way to the more general *stabilimenta* of 1223 and 1230.[44]

The agreements of September 1198, struck so soon after return of the Jews to the royal domain, offered clear indication that the status of northern French Jewry was in a state of flux. The major developments of the remaining decades of the reign of Philip Augustus were conditioned by the increasing financial needs of the monarch, by the growing stabilization of Capetian administration, and by accelerating Church pressures for royal sanctions against certain aspects of Jewish life. For the Jews of the expanded royal domain, and indeed of the major baronies as well, the result was enhanced regulation, limitation, and exploitation.

The first years of the new century saw the feverish efforts of the Capetian king to humble his weak Angevin rival; his successes are well known. The struggle with John, however, dragged on for a decade and a half, culminating only in the major French triumph at Bouvines. Throughout this period the economic needs of both thrones were desperate, and the Jews represented one of the few resources that could be taxed almost without limit.

[43]Caro, *Sozial- und Wirtschaftsgeschichte der Juden*, p. 362, and Baron, *A Social and Religious History of the Jews*, vol. 4, pp. 62–63, suggest that these treaties were a royal effort "to secure the forcible return of those Jewish exiles from the royal possessions who had found new homes in the adjacent provinces." This seems unlikely. Recognition of a sixteen-year-old claim to Jews who had been willfully banished by the king himself is highly doubtful. Our analysis has shown that the treaties held tangible advantages for Philip Augustus, without postulating a forced return.

[44]On this development, see Langmuir, " 'Judei Nostri' and the Beginning of Capetian Legislation."

The first prerequisite for effective exploitation of the Jews was demographic stabilization. We have seen Philip Augustus concerned with this issue immediately upon recall of the Jews. The effort to restrict "his" Jews proceeded beyond the treaties reached with neighboring barons. There was a strong drive to bind the Jews directly. Dating from shortly after the conquest of Normandy, a list survives of Norman Jews who deposited substantial pledges and swore to remain in royal territory.[45] A more extended Jewish declaration to remain in the domain of Blanche of Champagne comes from the wealthy Jew Cresselin of Provins. According to a document drawn up by the royal chancery, Cresselin had promised that

> he would transfer to the aforesaid countess and her heirs all the debts owed to him, if he were to flee or to remove himself to the domain of another. Beyond this, he gave the same countess hostages as proof that he would not flee her or her heirs. If he were to do that, the countess or her heirs could take and hold his debts as their own and seize his hostages.[46]

The rabbis of the period discussed this new baronial drive towards limitation of Jewish movement and were decidedly opposed. Analyzing the religious validity of such oaths taken by Jews, R. Isaac of Dampierre, a late-twelfth-century authority, states:

> And thus is the practice when the oppressors force the Jews living under their rule to swear that they will not leave for another town. They are permitted to swear generally that they will not leave and silently add "today." Even if he [the Jew] states explicitly that he will not leave forever, he may add silently any qualification.[47]

The related issue of confiscation of the property of fleeing Jews also came in for rabbinic objection.[48] Objections notwithstanding, rigorous limitation of the Jews became the accepted norm.

The limitations on Jewish movement could always be suspended with the assent of the barons involved. In June 1219, for example, Walter, seigneur of Vignory, promised safeguards for certain Champenois Jews who had come to live in his domain. These Jews continued to belong to the countess of Champagne and were only free to make the move with

---

[45] Léopold Delisle, ed., *Catalogue des actes de Philippe Auguste* (Paris, 1856), p. 508.

[46] Delaborde, *Recueil des actes de Philippe Auguste*, vol. 2, doc. no. 776.

[47] *Tosafot Bava Kamma*, 113a, s.v. Nodrim.

[48] Ibid., 58a, s.v. I Nammi. R. Isaac of Dampierre claims that in adjacent areas the legal status of the Jews allowed them free movement.

permission from both the countess and the lord of Vignory.[49] Despite such exceptions, the new emphasis on the right to limit Jewish movement unquestionably constricted Jewish economic and personal freedom and enhanced the developing notion of Jewish political subjugation.

Along with limitation of Jewish movement came regularization of lending procedures, designed to limit abuses and to provide accurate information on the Jewish economic situation. The apparatus for such regularization had existed in Normandy for some time; it was introduced into the rest of the royal domain during the first two decades of the thirteenth century. In the joint legislation of 1206, signed by Philip Augustus, Blanche of Champagne, and Guy of Dampierre, provision was made for selecting two burghers in each city who would have custody of the seal used for validating Jewish loans and one special scribe who would write the loan documents.[50] A later ordinance, enacted sometime between 1206 and 1219, further stipulated that the two burghers entrusted with the seal would henceforth bear the additional responsibility of retaining a copy of the loan document.[51] Philip Augustus's third important ordinance concerning the Jews, the edict of February 1219, did not add any further regulations for Jewish lending practices in the old royal domain. It did order that in Normandy both the debt and the *assignamentum* from which the debt would be paid should be enrolled before the bailiff and his court.[52] The success of these efforts is best indicated by the rather extensive statistics on Jewish loans compiled by royal officials at the end of the first decade of the thirteenth century.[53] Such detailed information presupposed fairly successful enforcement of the new regulations for recording Jewish loan arrangements.

The evidence for governmental exploitation of Jewish business is relatively sparse, since full tax records are available only from the end of the century. From the fragmentary data we can discover only some of the major types of taxes imposed upon the Jews and a few instances of unusually heavy imposition. The governmental budget of 1202–1203 preserves random record of the revenue derived from the Jews. Jewish lending operations were a double source of income—some from the writing of the loan instrument and some from the affixing of

---

[49] Solomon Grayzel, *The Church and the Jews in the XIIIth Century* (Philadelphia, 1933), p. 353.

[50] Delaborde, *Recueil des actes de Philippe Auguste*, vol. 2, doc. no. 955.

[51] *Ordonnances*, vol. 11, p. 315.

[52] Ibid., vol. 1, pp. 35–37.

[53] *RHF*, vol. 24, p. 277.

the royal seal.[54] There is also an interesting item registered as "pro vino."[55] This seems to be a standard early tax on Jewish wine, noted also prior to the reign of Philip Augustus.[56]

A special impost levied in 1222 provides unusual information on the normal categories of taxation imposed on the Jews. In order to facilitate payment of this heavy fine, Blanche of Champagne and her son Theobald ordered that all standard Jewish revenues were to be turned over to the Jewish community for the five-year period during which the fine was to be paid. We thus learn that the Jews of Champagne paid a *cens*, a tax upon settling in the county, a tax on the seals used for registering their debts, a toll for cleaning causeways, as well as an inheritance tax and a tax upon departure from the county.[57]

In a period of rapidly escalating governmental expenditures, the Jews were particularly useful for the special tax burdens to which they could be subjected. In May 1222, the count of Champagne and his mother, badly in need of funds, imposed a special fine of 70,000 pounds on their Jews, to be paid over the ensuing five years.[58] As noted, during this special period, all the normal taxes paid by the Jews were to be directed to the Jewish community officials, to aid them in their onerous task of meeting the heavy yearly installments. Some of the strain of meeting this special burden is reflected in a comital document, dated October 1222, confirming the agreement between the Jewish community of Champagne and one of its wealthiest members as to his precise obligation.[59]

During the period 1198–1223, the heaviest single exaction from the Jewish community of northern France came in 1210. The paucity of evidence for this incident has led to its general neglect; yet there can be little doubt as to the broad outlines of the affair. Again the financial needs of the crown led Philip Augustus to exploit his Jews, just as John Lackland was despoiling his. Philip laid the groundwork for his maneuvers carefully, renewing, in May 1210, nonretention treaties with the countess of Champagne, the count of Nevers, and the count of Saint-

---

[54] Nicolas Brussel, *Nouvel examen de l'usage des fiefs en France*, 2 vols. (Paris, 1750), vol. 2, pp. CLIII b, CLXXVI a, CLXXVIII a, CXCVII a, CXCIX b, CCIII a, reprinted at the end of Ferdinand Lot and Robert Fawtier, *Le premier budget de la monarchie française* (Paris, 1932).

[55] Ibid., p. CLI a.

[56] See above, chapter 2.

[57] Grayzel, *The Church and the Jews in the XIIIth Century*, pp. 353–54.

[58] Ibid.

[59] Ulysse Robert, "Catalogue des actes relatifs aux Juifs pendant le moyen âge," *REJ* 3 (1881), doc. no. 14.

Pol.[60] This enabled the monarch to proceed without fear of a large-scale defection of Jews to neighboring territories. There followed, later the same year, a mass arrest of the Jews. How many were detained is unclear, but a list of Jews held prisoner in the Châtelet includes some of the wealthiest members of the community.[61] The major focus of royal cupidity was the realization of Jewish loans. An extensive list of debts owed the Jews probably served as the guideline for exploitation of these funds.[62] The financial crisis of 1210 seriously affected northern French Jewry. The evidence for a major migration, in 1211, of both English and French Jews to Palestine is undoubtedly related to the heavy exactions of John and Philip.[63]

While regulation of Jewish affairs and exploitation of Jewish resources became increasingly serious problems during the first decades of the thirteenth century, these were not the only major pressures felt by the Jewish communities of northern France. The reforming Church circles of Paris, already active at the close of the twelfth century, continued to press programs that in many ways impinged on the Jews. With the rise to the papacy of Innocent III, formerly a capable and vigorous member of the Paris circles, these programs gained important new support.

The concerns voiced relating to the Jews were many and varied, but the major preoccupation was Jewish moneylending. Opposition to Jewish usury ranged from demands for elimination of specific abuses to an outright negation of the Jews' right to lend at interest.

One of the peripheral issues related to Jewish moneylending was the schools for Jewish children, "where they teach them their doctrines which are contrary to the true fundamentals of learning, and where they instruct them so that they may write down the debts due to their parents which these obtain through usury."[64] Another minor concern was the tithes, which the churches lost as property fell into the hands of Jews through unpaid obligations.[65] Far more serious was the matter of Jewish wealth acquired through usury and the power it gave the Jews over Christians in their employ. Papal letters and Church synods affirm and reaffirm the prohibition of Christian servants in Jewish houses,

---

[60]Delaborde, *Recueil des actes de Philippe Auguste*, vol. 3, doc. no. 1127; *Layettes*, vol. 1, doc. nos. 922, 923.

[61]Delisle, *Catalogue des actes de Philippe Auguste*, pp. 508-9.

[62]*RHF*, vol. 24, p. 277.

[63]See fuller discussion below.

[64]Grayzel, *The Church and the Jews in the XIIIth Century*, pp. 306-7.

[65]Ibid., pp. 124-25, 308-9.

seemingly with relatively little impact on widespread practice.[66] Another serious problem was the depositing of ecclesiastical goods with Jewish creditors, raising possibilities for blasphemous mishandling.[67]

Church leaders were deeply disturbed over the matter of debts owed Jews by Crusaders. The papal bull concerning the Second Crusade, *Quantum praedecessores*, had ordered the remission of all past interest owed by Crusaders. While Jewish creditors had not been singled out, French Jewry seems to have suffered significant financial loss as the result of Louis VII's enforcement of remission.[68] On the eve of the Third Crusade, Philip Augustus had failed to decree a remission of past usury but had imposed a two-year period of grace during which obligations were to be paid without the accrual of additional interest.[69] At the end of the twelfth century and the beginning of the thirteenth, Pope Innocent III vigorously demanded remission of past usury for Crusaders, based on the earlier precedent. This insistence occasioned stiff objection in baronial circles, as evidenced by a letter from the duke of Burgundy to the king.[70] By 1208 the pope had intensified his demands, urging both the remission of past usury and a moratorium on payment of the principal.[71] Finally, among the decrees of the IV Lateran Council was the provision that:

> ... the secular powers shall compel the Jews to remit their usury, and until the Jews have done so they shall be denied commercial intercourse with Christians, the latter being forced to do so under pain of excommunication. Moreover, for those who are unable at the present time to pay their debts to the Jews, the princes shall procure the needed moratorium, so that, until their death or return be definitely established, they shall not suffer any inconvenience of accruing interest. The Jews shall be compelled to count into the capital the income from the gage, minus the cost of maintenance, which it will yield in the meantime.[72]

This threefold demand thereafter became the classical formulation of Church policy concerning Crusader debts.

---

[66] Ibid., pp. 106–7, 114–17, 300–301, 306–7; Delaborde, *Recueil des actes de Philippe Auguste*, vol. 2, doc. no. 900.

[67] Grayzel, *The Church and the Jews in the XIIIth Century*, pp. 106–7, 300–301.

[68] See above, chapter 2.

[69] See above.

[70] *Layettes*, vol. 1, doc. no. 768.

[71] Grayzel, *The Church and the Jews in the XIIIth Century*, pp. 132–33.

[72] Ibid., pp. 312–13.

All was far from smooth, however, when it came to enlisting secular support for this policy. The objections of the duke of Burgundy have already been noted. The ordinance of 1206, decreed for the royal domain and Champagne, did not satisfy Church demands on the Crusader issue. All that Philip Augustus and Blanche of Champagne provided was a steady two pennies per pound per week accrual of interest, which seems only to have protected the Crusaders from the danger of continual compounding of interest.[73] In early 1217, Blanche of Champagne complained to Pope Honorius III that the archbishop of Sens and his suffragans "refused to permit to her the very same privileges with regard to crusaders and the Jews, who live in the territory of this Countess, which they permitted to Philip, king of France with regard to the Jews who live in his domain."[74] Unfortunately the papal reply, dated June 21, 1219, speaks only of unspecified excesses by the archbishop of Sens, without clarifying in any way the special privileges supposedly awarded Philip Augustus.[75] We can only speculate as to whether the king and the Church had come to some official compromise on their positions.

In the IV Lateran Council, anti-usury sentiment took a new turn, expressing itself in a condemnation of excessive Jewish usury. The well-known pronouncement on this issue emphasizes the strong campaign against Christian usurers and the concomitant increase in Jewish lending.

> The more the Christian religion refrains from the exaction of usury, the more does the Jewish perfidy become used to this practice, so that in a short time the Jews exhaust the financial strength of the Christians. Therefore, in our desire to protect the Christians in this matter, that they should not be excessively oppressed by the Jews, we order by a decree of this Synod, that when in the future a Jew, under any pretext, extorts heavy and immoderate usury from a Christian, all relationship with Christians shall therefore be denied him until he shall have made sufficient amends for his exorbitant exactions. The Christians, moreover, if need be, shall be compelled by ecclesiastical punishment without appeal, to abstain from such commerce. We also impose this upon the princes, not to be aroused against the Christians because of this, but rather to try to keep the Jews from this practice.[76]

---

[73] Delaborde, *Recueil des actes de Philippe Auguste*, vol. 2, doc. no. 955.

[74] Grayzel, *The Church and the Jews in the XIIIth Century*, pp. 144–45.

[75] Ibid., pp. 150–53.

[76] Ibid., pp. 306–7.

The growing opposition to Jewish usury was generally pragmatic, pointing to resultant abuses such as impoverishment of the Christian lower classes, unseemly wealth on the part of the Jews, resultant influence over the behavior of servants hired with these riches, and misuse of ecclesiastical objects acquired through lending. Such charges are prominent in the condemnation of the Jews by Rigord and are adduced by him as part of the justification for the king's program of despoliation and expulsion.[77]

There developed, at the same time, a theoretical assault on the fundamental right of the Jews to lend at interest. This attack began with the crucial passage in the book of Deuteronomy.

> You shall not deduct interest from loans to your countryman, whether in money or food or anything else that can be deducted as interest. You may deduct interest from loans to foreigners, but not from loans to your countryman.[78]

Robert de Courçon, a key member of the Paris circle of influential theologians, proposed that in fact Christians did not fall into the category of "foreigners"; rather they were to be viewed as "sojourners" whom the Jews were enjoined not to injure or oppress.[79] The same attitude is reflected in the following observation by Rigord: "And whereas the Lord has said by the mouth of Moses in Deuteronomy, 'Thou shalt not lend upon usury to thy brother,' but 'to a foreigner,' the Jews in their wickedness understood by 'foreigner' every Christian, and they took from the Christians their money at usury."[80]

The Jews of the period seem to have been alert to this new repudiation of their right to usury from the Christians. R. Moses of Paris, a late-twelfth-century scholar, is reported to have opposed the following view:

> Perhaps the rebellious contend that they are our brethren, since it is written: "You shall not abhor an Edomite, for he is your kinsman" (Deut. 23:8). R. Moses of Paris replied that the prophet Obadiah removed the quality of brotherhood, when he said: "When foreigners trooped in by his gates and parcelled out Jerusalem by lot, you yourselves were of one mind with them" (Obad. 11). There he spoke

---

[77]See above.

[78]Deuteronomy 23: 20-21. The translation is taken from the new Jewish Publication Society version.

[79]Georges Lefèvre, ed., *Le Traité "De Usura" de Robert de Courçon* (Lille, 1902), p. 7.

[80]Marcus, *The Jew in the Medieval World*, p. 25. I have modified the translation slightly.

of Edom, as is written at the beginning of the book: "Thus the Lord God has said concerning Edom" (Obad. 1).[81]

Church leadership active in the struggle against Jewish usury was well aware that the level of Jewish moneylending could only be diminished with the continued cooperation of the barony and that the barons in fact profited greatly from Jewish interest. While the Church often spoke in terms of its own resources, especially the decree of excommunication against those doing business with Jewish usurers, it generally recognized that an effective campaign against Jewish usury would have to enlist the support of the Jews' protectors. While such rulers as Philip Augustus, the countess of Champagne, and the duke of Burgundy were sharp in their opposition to Church demands, the major legislation of the reign of Philip Augustus definitely shows the growing impact of Church objection to Jewish usury, grounded in both theological and social concerns.

The legislation of 1206, aimed partially at more effective control and exploitation of Jewish lending, also imposed some important limitations on this lending.[82] This restriction took two major forms. First, the rate of interest was fixed at approximately 43 percent per annum. Second, the earliest time for reckoning interest was set at one year, in an effort to outlaw the compounding of interest before the first year of the debt had elapsed. While the establishment of a legal interest rate of 43 percent is the most widely-known provision of this ordinance, the clause on compounding of interest was probably equally significant from the viewpoint of the Jewish creditor.

In addition to these two important provisions, two further issues of concern to Church circles were mentioned. The problem of usury owed by Crusaders was treated in a manner far from satisfactory from the ecclesiastical point of view. Instead of remission of past usury and a moratorium on the repayment of the principal, there was simply the order that such debts were to run at a steady two pennies per pound per week, eliminating only the burden of compounded interest. More acceptable was the provision that there could be no lending against ecclesiastical goods, a matter which had aroused great indignation.

---

[81] Judah Rosenthal, ed., *Sepher Joseph Hamekane* (Jerusalem, 1970), p. 61. On the general issue of Christian brotherhood and its legal implications, see idem, "The Law of Usury Relating to non-Jews" (Hebrew), *Talpioth* 5 (1953–54): 139–52, and Gerson Cohen, "Esau as Symbol in Early Medieval Thought," *Jewish Medieval and Renaissance Studies*, ed. A. Altmann (Cambridge, Mass., 1967), pp. 44–45.

[82] Delaborde, *Recueil des actes de Philippe Auguste*, vol. 2, doc. no. 955.

The next important legislation on Jewish lending, promulgated between 1206 and 1219, added a serious new restriction. Henceforth interest was not to run beyond one year, meaning that compound interest was now completely outlawed.[83] There could be no compounding within the first year as a result of the legislation of 1206, and now there could be no interest whatsoever after the first year. It is significant that this ordinance ended with a warning to royal officials to enforce promptly Jewish debts. This order is directly related to the restriction of interest to one year; since long-term debts were henceforth profitless, any delay in repayment meant pure financial loss to the Jew.

In 1219, legislation concerning Jewish usury took an important new turn.[84] Heretofore such legislation had attacked only excessive profit from usury and certain specific abuses. Now the government exhibited a concern for entire segments of the population, prohibiting Jews from lending to all those who supported themselves by their own labor, without benefit of accumulated property or capital. Jews were similarly barred from lending to monks or canons, unless they had written permission from their superiors. There is a strenuous effort here to protect the poorer classes from the depredations of Jewish creditors. There was even an attempt to safeguard the wealthier class from the loss of family property through mounting obligations. In all loan agreements, which could involve henceforth only the propertied class, provision was to be made for an *assignamentum*, or assigned income, from which the loan would eventually be repaid.

The ills which this law was designed to cure are revealed by the stipulations made for loans contracted prior to the new regulation. No Christian was to be imprisoned for nonpayment (as the poorer elements would have been); nor was anyone to be forced to sell his property (as would have been the case for the wealthier). The impoverished were to have a three-year period during which to discharge their obligations. The propertied were to assign two-thirds of their income to their creditors until the obligation was met.[85]

---

[83] *Ordonnances*, vol. 11, p. 315. Note in this regard the agreement drawn up in 1194 in favor of the burghers of Auxerre, stipulating that the Jews could draw interest on their loans for no more than two years (Maximilien Quantin, ed., *Cartulaire général de l'Yonne*, 2 vols. [Auxerre, 1854], vol. 2, p. 461).

[84] *Ordonnances*, vol. 1, pp. 35–37.

[85] These new provisions were not always observed. Note, for example, the sale of lands in Normandy in 1222 to pay debts owed to the Jews (Lucien Musset, "Morel de Falaise, brasseur d'affaires du XIIIe siècle," *Bulletin de la Société des Antiquaires de Normandie* 50 [1946–48]: 308). For further instances of such disregard, see below, chapter 4.

All of this legislation undoubtedly represents major progress on the part of the Church in its efforts to stamp out the ills stemming from Jewish usury. Despite his strength and independent mind, even the powerful Philip Augustus was deeply influenced by these new ecclesiastical pressures.

In the years between 1198 and 1223, the Jews of northern France may well have continued the demographic growth and spread noted in the earlier periods. As documentation becomes more plentiful, we glean solid evidence for the first time of Jewish settlements in specific minor towns, a tendency not new to the early thirteenth century, but perhaps still on the increase.[86]

Certainly the demographic instability signaled by the expulsion of 1182 from the royal domain was far from ended with recall in 1198. That return itself was occasioned by a series of local expulsions stirred up by the preaching of Fulk of Neuilly.[87] The order of expulsion issued by the count of Auxerre in 1201, at the instigation of the local bishop, may well have been part of the aftermath of Fulk's preaching.[88] Also notable during this period are specific grants to certain locales of the right to exclude Jews. Such privileges were extended to Saint-Spires of Corbeil and to the town of Liquiel.[89]

The end of the first decade of the new century saw a significant voluntary movement of Jews. The report preserved in the sixteenth-century *Shevet Yehudah* has long intrigued Jewish historians. According to this account, "in the year 4971 the Lord aroused the rabbis of France and of England to make their way to Jerusalem. Indeed they counted more than three hundred. The king honored them greatly, and they built for themselves synagogues and houses of study."[90] Some contemporary corroboration for this late account does exist, including a report by the son of the great Maimonides concerning R. Joseph b. Baruch of Clisson and his brother, who visited Egypt on their way to Jerusalem, and mention by the Spanish poet Alharizi of his visit with

---

[86] See the material in Robert Chazan, "Jewish Settlement in Northern France, 1096–1306," *REJ* 128 (1969): 60–65.

[87] See above.

[88] Maximilien Quantin, *Histoire anecdotique des rues d'Auxerre* (Auxerre, 1870), pp. 259–60.

[89] Émile Coüard-Luys, ed., *Cartulaire de Saint-Spire de Corbeil* (Rambouillet, 1882), p. 50; *Layettes*, vol. 1, doc. no. 1159.

[90] Solomon ibn Verga, *Shevet Yehudah*, ed. Azriel Shoḥet (Jerusalem, 1947), p. 147.

the same northern French rabbis in Jerusalem.[91] The wave of immigrants to Palestine was divided into southern and northern French components. The northern French pilgrims, who included the famous R. Samson of Sens, were stimulated not by the curious philosophic and religious programs often suggested but by the immediate problems stemming from the wide-ranging royal confiscation of 1210.[92] The late tradition of an emigration from both France and England reflects serious attacks on Jewish economic life in both countries.

Jewish economic life revolved primarily about moneylending, as had been the case already in the mid-twelfth century. Rigord, like Bernard of Clairvaux, Peter Abelard, and Ephraim of Bonn, notes explicitly the central role of Jewish moneylending, although Rigord's generally hostile bent towards the Jews makes his testimony suspect.[93] During this period, however, a new type of evidence makes its appearance. It is highly significant that the treaties exchanged between Philip Augustus and Theobald of Champagne in 1198 deal with the Jews exclusively as usurers.[94] This is the only vocation mentioned and a major preoccupation of the agreements. Further, each of the three major legislative acts of Philip Augustus concerning the Jews dealt almost exclusively with Jewish lending.[95] There were certainly other economic outlets available to the Jews; their major occupation, however, unquestionably lay in usury.

Lending against pledges continued to be a normal procedure, although, as always, such dealings have left very little in the way of tangible evidence. Such lending is reflected in the prohibition of Jewish acceptance of Church objects as pledges for loans in two of the three ordinances of Philip Augustus. The ordinance of 1219 in fact expands the category of prohibited pledges. In addition to Church items and stained garments, which were assumed to imply violence and wrongdoing, this edict outlaws the acceptance of certain basic tools indispensable to the work of the farmer and the craftsman.[96]

---

[91] R. Abraham b. Moses, "Milḥamot ha-Shem," *Koveẓ Teshuvot ha-Rambam*, 3 vols. (Leipzig, 1859), vol. 3, 16b; Judah Alharizi, *Taḥkemoni*, ed. Paul de Lagarde (Gottingen, 1883), p. 168.

[92] On the supposed philosophic and religious motivations, see Samuel Krauss, "L'émigration de 300 rabbins en Palestine en l'an 1211," *REJ* 82 (1926): 333–43; on the confiscation of 1210, see above.

[93] Marcus, *The Jew in the Medieval World*, p. 25.

[94] Delaborde, *Recueil des actes de Philippe Auguste*, vol. 2, doc. no. 582; *Layettes*, vol. 1, doc. no. 479.

[95] Delaborde, *Recueil des actes de Philippe Auguste*, vol. 2, doc. no. 955; *Ordonnances*, vol. 1, pp. 35–37, and vol. 11, p. 315.

[96] Ibid.

While lending assured by governmental charters was prevalent prior to Philip Augustus, it is from his reign that we possess the most detailed information on practice and procedures. In view of the widespread use of these charters and of the stabilization of techniques through Capetian legislation, it is striking that no loan charter as such has survived. The thorough disappearance of these charters is due undoubtedly to the inclination of the debtor to destroy such materials after the loan had been repaid and to the very specific developments of the reigns of Louis VIII and Louis IX.[97]

The procedures for loans by charter were increasingly standardized during the reign of Philip Augustus. The ordinance of 1206 stipulates the appointment in every town of one special scribe for Jewish loan charters.[98] In 1219, provision was made for the retention of copies of the loan documents.[99] On each charter a seal was to be affixed. This seal was to be entrusted to two of the most upright citizens of each town. The ordinance of 1206 enjoined new seals for Jewish loans, designed to replace those already in use in the royal domain and in Champagne.[100] While none of these new seals have survived, we do possess two examples of those in use prior to 1206.[101] Interestingly, neither of these seals is affixed to a Jewish loan contract. One is found on a deed attesting sale of property to the abbey of Saint-Denis in order to repay debts owed to Jews.[102] The second is appended to a document ceding to the abbey of Saint-Victor property held in gage by the Jews.[103] Clearly, the use of the seal was not limited to the loan instrument itself. A second interesting aspect of these seals is their uniformity. Although one is for the Jews of Pontoise and the other for the Jews of Paris, the design is exactly the same in both cases. This suggests that one royal seal may have been utilized throughout the kingdom. In a charter of 1203, the seal for the Jews of Provins, in the county of Champagne, is mentioned. Although the original document still exists, the seal has been lost.[104] It is quite possible that the design of this seal

---

[97] See below, chapter 4.

[98] Delaborde, *Recueil des actes de Philippe Auguste*, vol. 2, doc. no. 955.

[99] *Ordonnances*, vol. 1, pp. 35–37.

[100] Delaborde, *Recueil des actes de Philippe Auguste*, vol. 2, doc. no. 955.

[101] Louis Claude Douet d'Arcq, ed., *Collection de sceaux*, 2 vols. (Paris, 1863–67), seal nos. 4495, 4496.

[102] Adolf Neubauer, "Documents inédits—XI–XII," *REJ* 9 (1884): 63.

[103] Ibid., p. 64.

[104] Michel Veissière, *Une Communauté canoniale au Moyen Age, Saint-Quiriac-de-Provins* (Provins, 1961), pp. 289–90.

might have revealed the joint regulation of Jewish loans by the king of France and the count of Champagne even before the important ordinance of 1206. This possibility, however, is relegated to the realm of conjecture by the loss of the Provins seal.

These documents and seals were a source of royal profit from the Jews during the early thirteenth century. In the rolls for 1202–1203, the most complete financial record available for these years, the taxes levied on Jewish charters and seals are indicated a number of times.[105]

A complaint by Innocent III in 1205 reflects the seriousness with which these loan contracts were treated. Having been drawn up and attested carefully, they obviously carried great weight in litigation. Thus, the pope complains:

> Moreover, although the same council (i.e., III Lateran) decided to admit Christian evidence against Jews in lawsuits that arise between the two, since they use Jewish witnesses against Christians, and although it decreed that whoever preferred the Jews to the Christians in this matter should be anathematized, yet they have to this day been given the preference in the French realm to such an extent that Christian witnesses are not believed against them, while they are admitted to testimony against Christians. Thus, if the Christians to whom they have loaned money on usury, bring Christian witnesses about the facts in the case (the Jews) are given more credence because of the document which the indiscreet debtor had left with them through negligence or carelessness, than are the Christians through the witnesses produced.[106]

Although the papal logic here is questionable, the importance of the loan instruments in court proceedings is not.

The loan charter was, of course, worthless except insofar as it assured the creditor powerful governmental backing for his claims. In his letter of January 17, 1208, Innocent III complained to the count of Nevers of comital support for Jewish usury.[107] The late–twelfth-century moralist, Guiot of Provins, bitterly criticizes the lords who sustain Jewish moneylenders, claiming that the severest punishment will be meted out to these erring Christians.[108] Numerous documents of the period indicate that the objections of Innocent III, Guiot of Provins, and others were far from groundless. Clearly there was significant governmental support.

---

[105] See above.

[106] Grayzel, *The Church and the Jews in the XIIIth Century*, pp. 106–7.

[107] Ibid., pp. 126–27.

[108] John Orr, ed., *Les oeuvres de Guiot de Provins, poète lyrique et satirique* (Manchester, 1915), p. 26.

In September 1198, as part of his complex agreement with Count Theobald, Philip Augustus ordered his bailiffs and provosts to enforce debts owed to the Jews of the count of Champagne.[109] In February 1216, the seigneur of Bourbon promised to enforce debts owed to the Jews of the same count.[110] In September 1218, Philip Augustus repeated his order of twenty years earlier.[111] The king's second important edict concerning Jewish moneylending, issued sometime between 1206 and 1219, ended with the exhortation to all duly empowered authorities to facilitate immediately the repayment of Jewish loans.[112]

A royal official, the *praepositus Judaeorum*, or provost for Jewish affairs, continued to exercise prime responsibility for the enforcement of Jewish loans. In 1204, the abbot of Saint-Germain ordered the provost for Jewish affairs to pay the Jews of Pontoise 143 pounds owed by a certain Batella, who had sold some of his possessions to the abbey in order to pay these debts.[113] During the same year, the abbot of Saint-Denis made a similar request, indicating that Batella had sold further possessions to his abbey for the same reason.[114] In the second instance the provost is identified as Robert de Baan. In both cases he is clearly involved in the process of enforcing Jewish loans. In fact the provost for Jewish affairs seems to have operated as a sort of clearing house for Jewish loans, accepting moneys from those ready to discharge their obligation and transferring funds to the Jewish creditors.

Even with governmental support, the moneys owed to the Jews had to be produced from some source. In many cases the borrower simply lacked the necessary funds to repay his debt. Where the impoverished debtor possessed land, he could of course sell or be forced to sell his lands in order to pay his debts. Such sales are well attested in thirteenth-century documentary sources. Richardson, in his study of English Jewry, discusses at length the impact of Jewish lending on land transfer in England.[115] Jewish lending in France seems to have had the same results, although perhaps on a more limited scale. The pressures on Christian lenders to sell landed inheritance aroused ire in Church circles, as reflected, for example, in the complaints of Rigord.[116] The

---

[109] Delaborde, *Recueil des actes de Philippe Auguste*, vol. 2, doc. no. 582.

[110] Grayzel, *The Church and the Jews in the XIIIth Century*, p. 352.

[111] Ibid.

[112] *Ordonnances*, vol. 11, p. 315.

[113] Germaine Lebel, ed., *Catalogue des actes de l'Abbaye de Saint-Denis relatifs à la province ecclésiastique de Sens de 1151 à 1356* (Paris, 1935), p. 30.

[114] Neubauer, "Documents inédits—XI–XII," p. 63.

[115] Richardson, *The English Jewry under Angevin Kings*, pp. 92–108.

[116] Marcus, *The Jew in the Medieval World*, p. 25.

Capetian government responded to ecclesiastical demands by prohibiting in 1219 the forced sale of property for the payment of Jewish loans.[117]

In the ordinance forbidding such sale, the method specified for the repayment of Jewish debts was the assigning of income to the Jewish creditor over a fixed period of time. *Assignamenta* included such diverse revenues as income from the fairs of Champagne, the bread tax on the city of Paris, and annual levies from minor monasteries.[118] The problems in collecting such revenues are mirrored in the proviso that, where collection is impeded, the normal interest rate begins once more and continues to accrue until payment from the *assignamentum* resumes.[119] It was no easy matter to realize the promised revenue, and the safeguards provided for the Jewish creditor seem to have been of limited value. Ultimately, the effectiveness of these measures depended on baronial will.

In extreme cases, the debtor unable to meet his obligations could be imprisoned. Such imprisonment figures in Rigord's condemnation of Jewish usury.[120] Among the reform measures legislated in 1219 was the outlawing henceforth of any such imprisonment.[121]

An additional safeguard for the creditor was the specifying of certain individuals as surety for the loan. These guarantors were liable to the same penalties as the original borrowers. The protections afforded to French debtors in 1219 were extended to the guarantors as well. They too could no longer be forced to sell their property nor be imprisoned, as had been the case heretofore.[122]

Through the early years of Philip Augustus's reign, we find no official limitations on the rate of interest to be charged on loans. In their joint legislation of 1206, however, Philip Augustus and Blanche of Champagne stipulated a maximum rate of two pennies per pound per week. This was equal to approximately 43 percent interest per year.[123] This seems to have been a standard legal rate in northern Europe during the period. In 1233, the king of England decreed this same maximum

---

[117] *Ordonnances*, vol. 1, pp. 35-37.

[118] Arbois de Jubainville, *Histoire des ducs et des comtes de Champagne*, vol. 5, doc. no. 610; Adolphe Dutilleux, "Recueil des principales chartes de l'abbaye de Joyenval," *Mémoires de la Société historique et archéologique de Pontoise et du Vexin* 13 (1890): 78-79; Maximilien Quantin, ed., *Recueil de pièces pour faire suite au Cartulaire général de l'Yonne* (Auxerre, 1873), doc. no. 13.

[119] *Ordonnances*, vol. 1, pp. 35-37.

[120] Marcus, *The Jew in the Medieval World*, p. 25.

[121] *Ordonnances*, vol. 1, pp. 35-37.

[122] Ibid.

[123] Delaborde, *Recueil des actes de Philippe Auguste*, vol. 2, doc. no. 955.

rate of two pennies per pound per week for English Jewry.[124] There is, however, some variety in such legislation. In August 1223, Countess Mathilda of Nevers, in a charter to the residents of Auxerre, limited Jewish usury to three pennies per pound per week, equal to 65 percent per annum.[125]

Jewish profit from moneylending was substantially enhanced by the compounding of interest. When loans were unpaid over a long period of time, with interest regularly compounded, profits soared. Thus, for example, a loan of 1,700 pounds made by the Champenois Jew Valin in 1196 resulted in a total debt of 9,825 pounds by 1207.[126] One of the major thrusts of Capetian legislation on Jewish moneylending was progressive limitation of compound interest. This began in 1206 with the prohibition of compounding within the first year of the loan and ended with the subsequent outlawing of interest beyond the first year.[127]

The range of debtors borrowing from the Jews extended from the top to the bottom of French society. We find numerous instances of Jewish loans to the nobility of northern France—for example, the count of Champagne, the duke of Burgundy, and the countess of Hainaut.[128] The Jewish creditor in such cases usually "belonged" to a different baron. Thus, in the case of the large debt incurred by the count of Champagne in the 1220's the lenders are royal Jews.[129] The reason for this is quite clear: the Jewish creditor would need the backing of a powerful lord in order to assure himself the collection of such a debt. This, of course, was the attraction, for the wealthy Jews, of "belonging" to the greatest French magnates.

The clergy also was heavily indebted to Jewish moneylenders. Certain institutions, seemingly poorly run, were regularly slipping more deeply into debt. Two examples of this were Saint-Loup of Troyes and

---

[124] Richardson, *The English Jewry under Angevin Kings*, p. 294. Note the same interest rate decreed for the Lombards in fourteenth-century Bruges (Raymond de Roover, *Money, Banking and Credit in Mediaeval Bruges* [Cambridge, Mass., 1966], p. 104).

[125] Jean Lebeuf, *Mémoires concernant l'histoire civile et ecclésiastique du diocèse d'Auxerre*, 2nd ed., 4 vols. (Auxerre, 1848–55), vol. 4, pp. 89–90. We might note also the legal rate of four pennies per pound per week in Burgundy during the fourteenth century and the rate of eight pennies per pound in Austria during the thirteenth. See Léon Gauthier, "Les Juifs dans les deux Bourgognes," *REJ* 49 (1904): 244, and Marcus, *The Jew in the Medieval World*, p. 32.

[126] Luchaire, *Social France at the Time of Philip Augustus*, p. 230.

[127] See above.

[128] Louis Chantereau-Lefebvre, *Traité des fiefs et de leur origine*, 2 vols. (Paris, 1662), vol. 2, pp. 125–26; Arbois de Jubainville, *Histoire des ducs et des comtes de Champagne*, vol. 5, doc. nos. 1452, 1503, 1584.

[129] Arbois de Jubainville, *Histoire des ducs et des comtes de Champagne*, doc. nos. 1452, 1503, 1584.

Saint-Rémy of Sens.[130] Individual clerics also were among the Jews' most common customers. Ecclesiastical leadership was much disturbed over such lending—a concern which was eventually reflected in royal legislation. By 1219, Philip Augustus had ordered that no monk or canon was to borrow from a Jew without the permission of his superior.[131]

Finally, of course, the ordinary townsfolk and peasants borrowed from the Jews. These small debtors rarely leave traces. The reform of 1219 included an attempt by the monarchy to keep the poorer classes from dealing with Jewish moneylenders.[132] This was a measure which must have been extremely difficult to enforce; we may well surmise that the poor continued to make their way to the Jewish usurers.

Governmental support of Jewish usury and the resultant documentation make it possible to gain a brief glimpse of some of the most successful Jewish businessmen of the reign of Philip Augustus. The list of debts owed royal Jews compiled in 1210 shows a number of wealthy individuals, headed by Moses of Sens, Dieudonné and Élie of Bray, and Dieudonné of Verneuil.[133]

There is strikingly little information on Moses of Sens, despite his position as the richest of the royal Jews. Aside from his appearances in the lists stemming from 1210, the only mention available is a document describing an exchange of land at Gonesse for a house in Paris by his wife.[134] This Jewess was the widow of Samuel of Bray, also known as Samuel of Gonesse. After the death of the wealthy Samuel, she then married Moses. This perhaps reflects the close relationships among the Jewish financial elite.

The brothers Dieudonné and Élie of Bray are far better known.[135] The earliest dated document relating to the transactions of the two brothers—transfer of a house to the abbey of Saint-Victor—includes, on the back, some Hebrew notations identifying the two parties as יצחק ר' הק' בן מתתיהו and יצחק ר' הק' בן אליאב. It seems certain, as Gross long ago deduced, that Isaac, the father of the financiers,

---

[130] Charles Lalore, ed., *Collection de principaux cartulaires du diocèse de Troyes*, 7 vols. (Paris, 1875–90), vol. 2, pp. 205–6, 230, 248–49, 250–52, 266–67, 271–72; Arbois de Jubainville, *Histoire des ducs et des comtes de Champagne*, vol. 5, doc. no. 560; Quantin, *Recueil de pièces*, doc. no. 13.

[131] *Ordonnances*, vol. 1, pp. 35–37.

[132] Ibid.

[133] *RHF*, vol. 24, p. 277*.

[134] Ibid., pp. 277–78*; Delisle, *Catalogue des actes de Philippe Auguste*, p. 508.

[135] Chazan, "The Bray Incident of 1192," pp. 15–17.

perished in the attack on Bray.[136] This document has affixed to it the seal of the Jews of Paris, significant in reflecting the community to which Dieudonné and Élie belonged. They continue to be identified as Parisian Jews down through the 1220's.[137] Whether the brothers were among those youngsters saved by Philip Augustus—which would put them in their mid twenties by the time of their first dated transaction—remains a matter of conjecture. Somehow they did escape the fate of their townsmen and of their own father.

The business affairs of Dieudonné and Élie were varied. They lent money to high-ranking nobles and churchmen, which often involved them in further dealings, such as the acquisition and disposition of landed property and tax rights.[138] The most remarkable set of loans for which evidence remains are those to the count of Champagne, Theobald IV. Obligations of 720 pounds (October 1222), 5,500 pounds (shortly thereafter), and 10,500 pounds (February 1224) are attested. Such large loans made to a powerful baron imply royal backing, and this is indeed the case. Our information for the 1224 obligation has survived in the form of royal attestation of this large debt made by Louis VIII, along with a schedule for its liquidation.[139]

Striking here are the utilitarian instincts of both king and Jew. The same Philip Augustus who had attacked and destroyed the Jewish community of Bray did not hesitate to support the lending operations of the remnant of this community. At the same time, Dieudonné and Élie did not recoil from aligning themselves with that same monarch "who had remained steadfast in his wickedness from beginning to end,"[140] responsible for the destruction of their community and the death of their own father.

Dieudonné of Verneuil was the wealthiest of the Norman Jews of this period. It is interesting to recall the great concern on the part of the duke of Normandy to ensure that Dieudonné remain in Normandy.[141] The attraction to royal territory seems to have been strong.

---

[136] Neubauer, "Documents inédits—XI–XII," pp. 63–64; Henri Gross, *Gallia Judaica* (Paris, 1897), p. 123.

[137] *Layettes*, vol. 1, doc. no. 1580.

[138] Neubauer, "Documents inédits—XI–XII," pp. 63–64; Dutilleux, "Recueil des principales chartes de l'abbaye de Joyenval," pp. 78–79.

[139] Arbois de Jubainville, *Histoire des ducs et des comtes de Champagne*, vol. 5, doc. nos. 1452, 1503, 1584.

[140] Ephraim of Bonn's designation for Philip Augustus—Adolf Neubauer and Moritz Stern, eds., *Hebräische Berichte über die Judenverfolgungen während der Kreuzzüge* (Berlin, 1892), p. 70; Abraham Habermann, ed., *Sefer Gezerot Ashkenaz ve-Zarfat* (Jerusalem, 1945), p. 128.

[141] Richardson, *The English Jewry under Angevin Kings*, p. 202; see above.

Curiously, after the royal conquest of Normandy, Dieudonné does seem to have shifted the focus of his activities to the royal domain. In the list of prisoners held in the Châtelet in 1210, Dieudonné is listed among the Jews of Francia.[142]

One of the most prominent Jewish families of Champagne was that of Valin of Troyes. Valin himself was a well-to-do moneylender in the first years of the thirteenth century. He appears as the creditor of the church of Saint-Rémy of Sens, of the abbey of Saint-Bénigne of Dijon, of the church of Saint-Loup of Troyes, and of the duke of Burgundy.[143] In each case, the countess of Champagne strongly supported her Jew. Valin seems to have died sometime before June 1210, on which date one of his sons, Baudin, promised to pay the countess moneys owed her by his late father.[144]

With the death of Valin, the financial activities of his family did not cease however. He had four sons—Baudin, Jacob, Sonet, and Haquin. After his demise, Baudin and Haquin transferred into the domain of the count of Nevers. Jacob and Sonet remained active in Champagne for some time.[145] In October 1222, the count of Champagne ratified the agreement reached by Jacob and the Jewish community of Troyes on the amount he was to contribute to the special tax of 70,000 pounds. In this connection Jacob is referred to as *magister*, or rabbi.[146]

Cresselin of Provins was sufficiently important to the countess of Champagne to occasion a special agreement between her and Philip Augustus. This agreement included the promise of Cresselin not to leave Champagne and the vow of Philip Augustus not to interfere. Clearly this was a Jew of considerable wealth and importance.[147]

We have very little information on the workings of the institutions of Jewish self-government during the reign of Philip Augustus. The local organization in all probability changed very little. It does seem likely that the intensified governmental exploitation of Jewish wealth placed heavy new tax burdens on the Jewish community. We find, for example, the Jewish community of Champagne responsible for raising the 70,000 pounds which the count had levied upon his Jews. The tension

---

[142] Delisle, *Catalogue des actes de Philippe Auguste*, p. 508.

[143] Arbois de Jubainville, *Histoire des ducs et des comtes de Champagne*, vol. 5, doc. nos. 560, 610, 677; Lalore, *Collection de principaux cartulaires*, vol. 1, p. 255.

[144] Grayzel, *The Church and the Jews in the XIIIth Century*, pp. 351–52.

[145] Chantereau-Lefebvre, *Traité des fiefs*, vol. 2, p. 121.

[146] Arbois de Jubainville, *Histoire des ducs et des comtes de Champagne*, vol. 5, doc. no. 1447.

[147] Delaborde, *Recueil des actes de Philippe Auguste*, vol. 2, doc. no. 776; see above.

involved in meeting the heavy obligation necessitated special governmental ratification of the arrangements made between the Jewish community and one of its wealthiest members.[148]

The major change in Jewish self-government was the disappearance of the centralizing force generated by R. Jacob Tam. While R. Tam was succeeded by very worthy intellectual heirs, beginning with his nephew R. Isaac of Dampierre, none of these intellectual and religious leaders was able to provide the same thrust towards unification as R. Tam.[149] The Jewish communities fell back into the earlier pattern of decentralization. Lack of broad unity was undoubtedly a serious weakness during the reign of Philip Augustus.

The intellectual level of French Jewry remained high throughout this period. The mantle of R. Jacob Tam passed to his nephew R. Isaac of Dampierre, then on to R. Samson of Sens and R. Judah Sire Leon. The major academies continued to be located in the great centers of Champagne and the Île-de-France, such as Troyes, Sens, Orléans, and Paris. The academies of the royal domain were of course disrupted by the expulsion of 1182. After 1198, however, they revived quickly, and during the early years of the new century Paris was once more a focal point for Jewish study.[150] During the late twelfth and early thirteenth centuries, the academies of northern France continued to serve as the major institutions of advanced Jewish learning for all of northern European Jewry. The best students in German Jewry made their way westward to study with the heirs to the legacy of Rashi and R. Tam.

It is interesting to note in these academies a growing concentration on Talmudic studies. The flourishing period of Biblical exegesis seems to have ended, with the great masters of the late twelfth and thirteenth centuries primarily concerned with the legal curriculum. The philosophic interests of surrounding Christian society and even the developing mystical-moral movement in German Jewry seems to have had little impact on the spiritual life of northern French Jewry.[151]

The community's preeminence in the area of Talmudic studies, however, gave it a place of great honor even beyond the boundaries of northern European Jewry. During the reign of Philip Augustus, at a

[148] Grayzel, *The Church and the Jews in the XIIIth Century*, pp. 352–54; Arbois de Jubainville, *Histoire des ducs et des comtes de Champagne*, vol. 5, doc. no. 1447.

[149] Urbach, *Ba'aley ha-Tosafot*, pp. 195–283.

[150] Ibid.

[151] On the achievements in legal studies, see ibid. On the state of Biblical studies, see Poznanski's introduction to the commentaries of R. Eliezer of Beaugency. The recent study of Ashkenazic pietism reveals almost no mystical activity in northern French Jewry (Joseph Dan, *Torat ha-Sod shel Ḥasidut Ashkenaz* [Jerusalem, 1968]).

time when important lines of communication were being laid between northern and southern France, we find, not coincidentally, the first evidence of substantial contact between the Jewries of southern Europe and northern France.

The issue which brought the scholarly leadership of the two Jewries into contact was the first flare-up of opposition to the writings of Maimonides. A Toledan Jew, R. Meir Abulafia, wrote to Lunel criticizing some of the philosophic doctrines of the great north African sage. One of the key Jewish leaders in Lunel returned a stinging reply, eliciting a second letter from his Toledan adversary.[152] At this point, with the differences sharply drawn within the southern European communities, R. Meir decided to submit the entire matter to the arbitration of the renowned scholars of the north. In a long missive addressed to a series of specific northern French authorities, R. Meir detailed the dispute and pleaded for their decision. The addressees are R. Solomon of Rouen, R. Samson of Sens and his brother R. Isaac the Younger of Dampierre, R. Samson of Corbeil, R. David of Château-Thierry, R. Abraham of Touques, and R. Eliezer of Bourges. The lines of communication were sufficiently well developed so that major figures in the north were known in the south.[153]

The reverence for these northern scholars is surely reflected in the very decision to submit the argument to their consideration. It is overtly articulated in the terms with which R. Meir addresses his colleagues:

Indeed you are a people
To whom learning is sweet;
In your presence,
The gold of justice cannot be dimmed.
Your scales are just
And your weights are just;
Your heart has not waxed proud
Nor have your eyes become haughty.
You do not remove your eyes
From either the humble or the mighty;
You hear the case

---

[152] The materials on this dispute were published by Yehiel Brill, ed., *Ketab al-Rasil* (Paris, 1871). For an overview, see Yitzhak Baer, *A History of the Jews in Christian Spain*, 2 vols. (Philadelphia, 1961–66), vol. 1, pp. 100–101.

[153] Brill, *Ketab al-Rasil*, p. 4. It is interesting to note, in contrast, that Abraham ibn Daud, writing a few decades earlier, knew only of R. Jacob Tam (see Abraham ibn Daud, *Sefer ha-Qabbalah*, ed. Gerson Cohen [Philadephia, 1967], p. 66 [Hebrew text] and p. 89 [English text]).

Of small and great alike.
They are the guardians of Torah,
Presenting before the Lord pure offering;
They turn night into day,
Making darkness and light alike.
Our teachers, the sages of France and its elders,
Its sapphires and its pearls,
Its judges and leaders, its scholars and scribes,
Its kings and officers, its warriors and heroes—
May He who preserves truth forever
Preserve both the small and the great among them.[154]

While much of this is simply formal rhetoric, there can be no gainsaying the profound sense of respect for northern erudition.

Unfortunately for R. Meir of Toledo, flattery achieved little. The only response from northern France that has survived is that of R. Samson of Sens. R. Samson begins his epistle with the image of the ram falling before the onslaught of the he-goat, indicating that R. Moses b. Maimon and his aide R. Aaron of Lunel had been defeated by the assault of R. Meir. He then quotes the verse "And there was none that could deliver the ram out of his hand," specifying that this refers to the French who were unable to assist the stricken ram, since they had concluded also that there would be bodily restoration at the end of days.[155] R. Samson then proceeds to a close scrutiny of some of the specifics of the dispute, falling far short of the broad castigation for which R. Meir had hoped.[156] The correspondence between R. Meir and R. Samson continued, with disappointment on the part of the former and increasing petulance on the part of both manifest.[157] Reflected in this incident nonetheless is a growing awareness in the south of northern achievements and, at the same time, a forced confrontation in the north with some of the philosophic issues deeply disturbing the Mediterranean Jewries.

Looking back over the long and brilliant reign of Philip Augustus, we can certainly see in it an important stage in the history of northern French Jewry. The older laissez-faire tradition had come to an end. The vigor and vibrance of the age had produced for the Jews the twin

---

[154] Brill, *Ketab al-Rasil*, pp. 3-4.
[155] Ibid., pp. 107-8.
[156] Ibid., pp. 108-37.
[157] Ibid., pp. 138-52.

dangers of heightened governmental exploitation and increasingly effective ecclesiastical pressure. Royal policy showed enhanced concern with utilization of the Jews for its own fiscal purposes, while constantly giving ground on a series of Church demands for greater regulation of Jewish affairs. If even the powerful and secularly-oriented Philip Augustus had been unable to withstand ecclesiastical prodding, the Jews could only look forward with trepidation to the reigns of Louis VIII, Blanche of Castille, and their pious offspring, Louis IX.

IV

LOUIS IX—THE VICTORY OF THE CHURCH

THE MID THIRTEENTH CENTURY, particularly the reign of Louis IX, represents a high-water mark in the history of medieval France. It was a period of continued growth, to be sure; but, above all else, it was a time of stabilization and consolidation. The vast territorial gains of the reign of Philip Augustus were solidified and the bureaucracy necessary for effectively administering the expanded royal holdings was developed. In all of this achievement two major figures dominated—Blanche of Castille and Louis IX. It was Blanche whose tenacity and vision enabled the Capetian dynasty to survive one of its most serious crises—the sudden death, in his prime, of Louis VIII. Marshaling the royal resources as regent for her young son, Blanche preserved the monarchy and handed it over to Louis in a stronger state than she had found it. Never really laying down the reins of government, Blanche continued to conduct the affairs of state alongside her son. It was Louis IX, however, who set the tone of this period, not only through his accomplishments but through the force of his personality. Louis represented to medieval France, and indeed to medieval Christendom at large, the ideal figure of the Christian king. His concerns were peace, justice, and the religious purity of his realm. His ultimate goal was the fulfillment, as private person and as king, of the duties imposed by a life of Christian virtue. Despite the fiascos of the two Crusades in which he was involved, his French subjects and their descendants looked back longingly to the happy days of Saint Louis.[1]

With the growing power of the Capetian monarchy, the fate of the Jews of France was bound ever more firmly to the views and policies of the king. The nature of Louis IX's conception of Christian virtue and of the Christian kingdom made it impossible for the Jews to share in the general sense of well-being associated with his reign. For French Jewry, the middle four decades of the century were the beginning of a decline from which it was never to recover. This deterioration can be attributed to the increasing expendability of the Jews in a society with a growing Christian urban middle class, to the dangers of excessive political dependence on the highest secular powers in the state, and to the adverse ecclesiastical programs to which the saintly king of France was so deeply devoted. The last factor may perhaps be counted as the decisive one in the rash of unfavorable actions which punctuated the period from 1223 to 1270. The long reign of the most pious of French kings witnessed a series of profound catastrophes for the once proud French Jewish community; by the end of this reign, French Jewry had lost the vigor, strength, and intellectual prowess that had been its pride since the late eleventh century.[2]

The personal piety of Louis IX, as well as that of his mother, was legendary in medieval Christendom. His entourage was heavily flavored with ecclesiastical personnel, often devoted members of the new and

---

[1] The reigns of Louis VIII and Louis IX are covered by Achille Luchaire and Charles-Victor Langlois in Ernest Lavisse, *Histoire de France*, 9 vols. in 18 (Paris, 1900–1911), vol. 3, pt. 2, and vol. 3, pt. 1. The standard study of Louis VIII is Charles Petit-Dutaillis, *Étude sur la vie et le règne de Louis VIII (1187–1226)* (Paris, 1894). There is no comprehensive study of the reign of Saint Louis. Useful are Élie Berger, *Histoire de Blanche de Castille, reine de France* (Paris, 1895), and idem, "Les dernières années de saint Louis," *Layettes*, vol. 4. For Champagne, see Henri d'Arbois de Jubainville, *Histoire des ducs et des comtes de Champagne*, 7 vols. in 8 (Paris, 1859–69). For Normandy, see Joseph Strayer, *The Administration of Normandy under Saint Louis* (Cambridge, Mass., 1932). Helpful for understanding some of the influences on Louis's attitudes and policies towards the Jews is Lester Little, "Saint Louis' Involvement with the Friars," *Church History* 33 (1964): 125–48.

[2] The most useful general treatments of Jewish life during this period are again Georg Caro, *Sozial- und Wirtschaftsgeschichte der Juden im Mittelalter und der Neuzeit*, 2 vols. (Frankfort, 1908–20), vol. 1, and Salo Baron, *A Social and Religious History of the Jews*, 2nd ed., 14 vols. (New York, 1952–69), vol. 10. The seven-hundredth anniversary of the death of Louis IX occasioned a wide variety of commemorative notices, including some observations on Louis and the Jews. A serious response to some of the superficialities expressed can be found in Gérard Nahon, "Les ordonnances de Saint Louis sur les Juifs," *Les nouveaux cahiers* 6 (1970): 18–35. On Jewish political status down through the early years of Louis IX, see Gavin Langmuir, " 'Judei Nostri' and the Beginning of Capetian Legislation," *Traditio* 16 (1960): 203–69; on aspects of Jewish economic life, see Gérard Nahon, "Le credit et les Juifs dans la France du XIIIe siècle," *Annales* 24 (1969): 1121–48; on cultural developments, see Ephraim Urbach, *Ba'aley ha-Tosafot* (Jerusalem, 1955).

influential Dominican and Franciscan orders; his major goal as ruler was a political realm that would encourage the widest possible fulfillment of Christian ideals; in his personal behavior he was a model of fervent commitment to Christian virtue. Louis's praises were already widely sung during his own lifetime. Pious accounts of his deeds abound.[3] Even John of Joinville, Louis's devoted seneschal and the first nonclerical biographer of the Capetian monarchy, was so deeply impressed with his subject's piety that he devoted the first part of his study to a hagiographic portrait of his saintly hero.[4]

Louis's faithful seneschal records a dramatic expression of the monarch's personal feelings towards the Jews:

> The King told me also that there was once a great debate at the monastery of Cluny between clerks and Jews. There was a knight present who had been charitably fed at the monastery by the Abbot for the love of God. He asked the Abbot to allow him to be the first to speak, and rather unwillingly his request was granted. He stood up, then, and, leaning on his crutch, he asked them to bring the most learned of the clerks and the greatest master of the Jews. This they did; and he asked but one question, which he put so: "Master," said the knight, "I want to know whether you believe that the Virgin Mary, who bore God in her womb and in her arms, gave birth a virgin, and whether she is indeed the Mother of God."
>
> The Jew answered that he believed no such thing. Then the knight told him that it was indeed the act of a fool to enter her church and her house when he neither believed in her nor loved her. "And I can assure you," he added, "that you shall pay for your folly." He raised his crutch and struck the Jew on the side of the head, felling him to the ground. The Jews all fled, taking with them their wounded master; and that was the end of the debate.
>
> Then the Abbot came up to the knight and told him that he had been foolish; the knight answered that the Abbot had been a great deal more foolish to arrange the debate, for before it was finished there would have been a great many good Christians who would have gone away with their faith impaired, having been deceived by the Jews' arguments. "I agree myself," said the King, "that no one who is not a very learned clerk should argue with them. A layman, as soon

---

[3]Most of the sources for Saint Louis are listed in Auguste Molinier, *Les sources de l'histoire de France des origines aux guerres d'Italie*, 6 vols. (Paris, 1901-6), vol. 3, source nos. 2538-2759. A striking number of the literary records are hagiographic recollections.

[4]John of Joinville, *The Life of St. Louis*, trans. René Hague (New York, 1955), pp. 26-40.

as he hears the Christian faith maligned, should defend it only by the sword, with a good thrust in the belly, as far as the sword will go."[5]

A number of observations must be made concerning this recollection. It should be noted, first of all, that it falls in Book I of Joinville's account, in that section where Louis's biographer set out to tell how the king "ordered himself at all times by the will of God and of the Church, and for the well-being of his kingdom."[6] It is not simply a random observation; it has been adduced to highlight a major facet of the devout king's personality. More specifically, it is placed in that section which deals with the need for firm adherence to true faith and adamant rejection of doubt and disbelief; it is, significantly enough, preceded by a story of Simon de Montfort's rebuff to Albigensian heretics. The association of heresy and Judaism was dangerous for an already-exposed Jewish minority. Finally, the disparity between the royal injunction to defend the Christian faith "only by the sword, with a good thrust in the belly, as far as the sword will go" and the temperate monarch normally devoted to the calm proceedings of justice and the extirpation of violence in the settlement of disputes is striking. Royal hatred of disbelief, Judaism included, was extreme.

Louis's biographers preserve a second recollection of direct royal expression on the issue of the Jews. While less flamboyant, this second statement is in many ways even more noteworthy. In the biography of Louis written by William of Chartres, the chronicler describes the king's anti-usury campaign and objections to it on the part of royal advisors. The first objection was that society needed moneylending, which might better be carried on by Jews, who are damned anyway, rather than by Christians. Further, it was claimed that the Jews were actually more benign than their Christian counterparts. To this, the king replied:

Matters relating to Christians who lend money and to their usury seem to be the concern of the prelates of the churches. To me, however, pertain matters relative to the Jews—who are subjected to me by the yoke of servitude—that they might not oppress Christians through usury and that they not be permitted, under the shelter of my protection, to engage in such pursuits and to infect my land with their poison. Let those prelates do what pertains to them concerning those subject Christians, and I must do what pertains to me concerning the Jews. Let them abandon usury or they shall leave my land completely, in order that it no longer be polluted with their filth.[7]

[5] Ibid., pp. 35–36.
[6] Ibid., p. 23.
[7] *RHF*, vol. 20, p. 34.

This recollection reflects far more than the personal animosity depicted by Joinville. Striking here is the view, expressed earlier by Rigord, that the king had, above all, a moral and religious responsibility for the impact of "his" Jews upon Christian society.[8] Dereliction of duty is conceived not as a matter of political ineptness or incompetence but as a grave moral and religious sin. To be sure, the king was, in general, accountable for the religious well-being of his realm. The Jews were special, however, in being present only through his consent and protection. This made them a far more serious responsibility resting on the soul of a truly Christian monarch. What follows quite logically is the royal conclusion that "his" Jews must either abide by the program which he decreed a moral necessity or face the consequences of withdrawal of royal consent and protection. It is out of this conception of total responsibility for the behavior of the Jews that the disastrous programs of Saint Louis emerged.[9]

While the reign of Louis IX saw a number of major anti-Jewish decrees, the two decisive campaigns involved attacks on the foundations of Jewish economic existence, moneylending, and on the cornerstone of Jewish spiritual survival, the study of Oral Law. It was the success of these campaigns that made the pious monarch's reign so catastrophic for medieval French Jewry.

Even Louis's vigorously secular grandfather, Philip Augustus, had been unable to totally withstand ecclesiastical pressures and had instituted a number of reforms designed to curb the abuses stemming from Jewish moneylending.[10] These included, for example, limitation on interest rate, prohibition of compound interest, and outlawing of lending to certain classes in Christian society. The ordinance of 1223, enacted under the leadership of Louis VIII, represents a new response to the anti-usury pressures; rather than limiting abuses, it was designed to eliminate governmental enforcement of Jewish claims to usurious profit.

The ordinance of 1223, enacted less than four months after the death of Philip Augustus, was promulgated "with the will and assent of the archbishops, bishops, counts, barons, and knights of the French kingdom, those who hold Jews and those who do not." The clauses

---

[8] See above, chapter 3.

[9] It is significant to note the tradition that introduced into Louis's famed instructions to his son a warning to hold the Jews in great contempt (see H.-François Delaborde, "Le texte primitif des enseignements de Saint Louis à son fils," *BEC* 73 [1912]: 246, n. 9).

[10] See above, chapter 3.

dealing with Jewish lending were specifically sworn to by a number of the barons present. Unfortunately the first and most important of these provisions is somewhat ambiguous.

(1) No Jews' debts shall accumulate interest from this November 8 and further. Neither we nor our barons shall henceforth cause to be returned to the Jews usury which accrues from this November 8 and further.

(2) All debts which are owed the Jews are to be terminated in nine payments within three years by being returned to the lords to whom the Jews are subservient. . . .

(3) It is to be known that we and our barons have decreed and ordained concerning the status of the Jews that none of us shall be able to receive and retain Jews of another; and this is to be understood both for those who have sworn to the ordinance as well as those who have not.

(4) The Jews henceforth shall not have seals for sealing their debts.

(5) The Jews must have enrolled, by the authority of the lords to whom they are subservient, all their debts prior to the coming Feast of the Purification of the Virgin Mary; debts not then enrolled in the prescribed manner shall not henceforth be repaid to the Jews nor returned to them. Moreover, if the Jews exhibit loan documents more than five years old, we order that they be considered invalid and that the loans contained therein need not be returned.[11]

The crucial ambiguity lies in the opening sentence of the ordinance. Is the order prohibiting usury intended to cover all Jewish loans, past and future, or only those loans already contracted? In other words, is this order simply an attempt to clear up past obligations owed the Jews or is it a major new departure in Capetian policy?[12] On a number of counts it seems clear that the prohibition is intended to cover all Jewish loans. In the first place, the framers of the law knew know to indicate past debts in a later clause by using the expression "debita universa que debentur Judeis." The categorical "nullum debitum Judeorum" would seem to have been consciously introduced as a more inclusive designation. More important, the subsequent legislation of the 1220's bears out this interpretation. In 1227, an ordinance was decreed stipulating once more a three-year payment arrangement, this time for debts contracted

---

[11] *Layettes*, vol. 2, doc. no. 1610.

[12] For some of the interpretations of this ambiguous clause, see Langmuir, " 'Judei Nostri' and the Beginning of Capetian Legislation," p. 215, n. 54.

between 1223 and 1227, provided that letters be available indicating that the moneys in question were principal and not usury. The basis for such a provision was probably the edict of 1223.[13] Finally, the ordinance of 1228, which deals with a series of chronologically ordered loan arrangements, repeats almost verbatim the key opening sentence of 1223 in a context which unquestionably refers to future loans.[14]

Having accepted the broader interpretation of this first sentence, we should proceed immediately to one major qualification. This order was not intended as a total prohibition of Jewish usury. The second sentence of the opening clause clarifies royal intentions. The decree was intended primarily as a withdrawal of governmental support for Jewish usury. There were instances where loans could be enforced without governmental aid through the depositing of pawns, and such cases seem to fall outside the purview of the new law. The major practical device for the execution of this enactment is specified in the fourth clause; it is the abolition of the seals heretofore used for validating and enforcing Jewish loans.

The ordinance of 1223 thus consists of three major items: (1) prohibition of all future governmental enforcement of Jewish usury; (2) provisions for the liquidation of all debts owed as of November 8, 1223, with no attempt to distinguish between principal and interest;[15] and (3) a nonretention clause designed to ensure that this bold new legislation would not result in an uncontrolled shift of Jewish population.[16] The final clauses of the ordinance are simply further elaboration on the two opening themes.

In gauging the impact of this striking departure in Capetian legislation, a number of factors must be taken into account. In the first place, as noted, there were still usurious arrangements unfettered by the new restrictions. Equally important, a number of powerful northern French barons did not ratify the usury provisions of the treaty, although there was constant royal pressure for such agreement, leading subsequently to ratification by the Countess of Nevers.[17] Other major holders of Jews,

---

[13] Edmond Martène and Ursin Durand, eds., *Veterum scriptorum et monumentorum historicorum, dogmaticorum, moralium, amplissima collectio*, 9 vols. (Paris, 1724–33), vol. 1, p. 1294. On the dating, see Caro, *Sozial- und Wirtschaftsgeschichte der Juden*, vol. 1, p. 507.

[14] Martène and Durand, *Veterum scriptorum et monumentorum*, vol. 1, p. 1223.

[15] The provisions for the liquidation of prior obligations are reminiscent of the legislation of Philip Augustus enacted on the eve of the Third Crusade (see above, chapter 3).

[16] On this nonretention clause, see Langmuir, " 'Judei Nostri' and the Beginning of Capetian Legislation," pp. 217–21, and Robert Chazan, "Jewish Settlement in Northern France, 1096–1306," *REJ* 128 (1969): 52.

[17] *Layettes*, vol. 2, doc. no. 1615.

however, most significantly Theobald of Champagne, remained aloof. The advantages to the Jews of leaving those territories where the new limitations had gone into effect for areas such as Champagne are clearly indicated by a set of agreements dating from 1223 and 1224.[18]

On December 31, 1223, accord on a number of matters was achieved by William of Dampierre and Theobald of Champagne. The provisions of the treaty included a series of transactions involving Jewish families. William turned over to Theobald the wives and children of those Jews who had left his territory for Champagne. In return, Theobald granted a delay in the payment of debts owed by William and his subjects to these Jews.[19] Again, on May 1, 1224, a long agreement was signed between William and Theobald, and again there were a number of clauses dealing with Jews. Two Jewish families were turned over to the count of Champagne. Both the count and William were absolved of all debts owed to these Jews; in addition, William was to hold all immovable possessions owned in his territories by the aforesaid Jews.[20] Unfortunately, most of the Jews who made the move from Dampierre to Champagne were not named in these documents. The only ones specifically mentioned are Cochin, a Jew of Saint-Dizier, and his two sons. This Cochin is known from a document of June 1210, in which a number of the wealthiest Jews of Dampierre pledged themselves as surety to an agreement drawn up between Blanche of Champagne and her Jew Baudin.[21] The Jews in transit were thus of some prominence. The proximity of these transfers to the ordinance of 1223 raises the suspicion that these Jews, probably all important moneylenders, may have sought to escape the harshness of the 1223 decree in effect in Dampierre by moving on to Champagne, where the same decree was not being implemented. Their weapon for achieving such a transfer is clear—absolution of debts already owed to them. They must have concluded that the temporary loss would be more than offset by the ultimate gain. Assuredly, the evidence is only circumstantial, but the proximity of these moves to November 8, 1223, seems more than coincidental. In fact, one may well wonder if the decline of the once flourishing center of Dampierre is not related to the events under discussion.

There were, then, major loopholes in this new anti-usury legislation. Such leeway notwithstanding, the edict was treated seriously by the

---

[18] Chazan, "Jewish Settlement in Northern France, 1096–1306," p. 53.

[19] *Layettes*, vol. 2, doc. no. 1619.

[20] Ibid., doc. no. 1648.

[21] Solomon Grayzel, *The Church and the Jews in the XIIIth Century* (Philadelphia, 1933), pp. 351–52.

government. We have already indicated the efforts to attract new signers. The provisions for enrollment of debts and for annulment of antiquated documents were promulgated by the Exchequer of Normandy, and in one interesting instance the abbot of Bec was absolved of responsibility for a loan not properly enrolled.[22]

By late 1226 the three-year period stipulated for payment of debts contracted prior to November 8, 1223, had elapsed. The first royal reaction was to consider the matter closed and to prohibit any further enforcement of these debts.[23] Shortly thereafter, however, the Jews seem to have been successful in convincing the authorities of the inequity or of the impracticality of such a stand. A second order was given for the enforcement of those pre-1223 obligations as yet unpaid.[24] In this second ordinance, mention is also made of the fact that some royal documents concerning post-1223 obligations to the Jews had been issued; such documents were to be honored. We can only surmise that this was a reference to nonusurious contracts.

The legislation of 1227, known only from a later reference to it, seems to have introduced no major innovation.[25] The intention seems only to have been the liquidation of all obligations contracted between 1223 and 1227. The assumption was that such loans were, in any event, nonusurious. Once more a three-year period for the repayment of all outstanding moneys was decreed. It is possible that the Jews may have been encountering increasing difficulties in realizing sums owed them; this being the case, the government's new edict would have been to the Jews' advantage.

The ordinance of 1228 was intended to deal with some of the problems resulting from the new governmental stand; it too introduced no substantive innovations.[26] The act is rather simply arranged; it deals with pre-1223 loans, loans contracted between 1223 and 1227, those contracted between 1227 and 1228, and future lending. Concerning the pre-1223 agreements, it only stipulates adherence to the ordinance of the late Louis VIII. The repayment arrangements for the 1223-1227 obligations are repeated, with one major clarification: in instances where the loan instrument is vague in the distinction between principal

[22] Léopold Delisle, "Recueil des jugements de l'Echiquier de Normandie," *Notices et extraits des manuscrits de la Bibliothèque nationale* 20,2 (1862), doc. nos. 394, 395.

[23] Reflected in the edict of 1227 (Martène and Durand, *Veterum scriptorum et monumentorum*, vol. 1, p. 1294).

[24] Ibid.

[25] Ibid., pp. 1222–23.

[26] Ibid.

and interest and where contention thus arises, provision is made for the introduction of evidence by either the debtor or the creditor as to the precise amount of the principal. In the case of the Christian borrower, the witnesses must be uninvolved in the transaction. In the case of the Jewish lender, the witnesses must be uninvolved in a different sense; that is, they must be members of the majority Christian community, thus not suspect of an underlying sympathy for the creditor. Two chosen officials in each town with a significant Jewish population were to receive such testimony and to decide the issue in instances of conflicting reports.[27] Loans contracted between 1227 and 1228 were to be repaid in accord with the written convention between creditor and debtor, with the articulated understanding that such obligations be nonusurious. Finally, for the future, the principle, already enunciated in 1223, prohibiting governmental support for Jewish usury was repeated. An important provision was added for administrative purposes. Henceforth three rescripts of every Jewish loan contract were to be made— one copy to be deposited with the authorities, one with the borrower, and the third with the lender.[28] It is somewhat ironic that the most sophisticated procedures for recording Jewish debts were pressed into service at precisely the point when Jewish lending was in a state of governmentally-induced decline.

The next major innovation in the royal attack on Jewish moneylending came in 1230. In that year another large gathering of French barons produced a new *stabilimentum*. The loan provision in this ordinance is brief and to the point, henceforth outlawing governmental enforcement of debts owed to the Jews: "... statuimus quod nos et barones nostri Judeis nulla debita de cetero contrahenda faciemus haberi."[29] Completing the major clauses are the anticipated prohibition of retaining the Jews of another and the usual arrangements for a three-year liquidation of debts already owed.[30]

While not the concluding step in the campaign against Jewish lending, this enactment represents the final statement on government involvement in Jewish financial affairs. It is for this reason that this provision was repeated by Louis in his great reform ordinance of

---

[27] Ibid.

[28] Ibid., p. 1223.

[29] *Layettes*, vol. 2, doc. no. 2083.

[30] For interesting speculation on some of the difficulties related to collection of loans in the wake of the 1230 legislation, see Aryeh Grabois, "Du credit juif à Paris au temps de saint Louis," *REJ* 129 (1970): 5-22.

1254.[31] Although the royal position on Jewish lending became even harsher after 1230, the *stabilimentum* of that year remained in force as the authoritative expression of the non-involvement of the French authorities in Jewish business affairs.

With regard to techniques for the liquidation of debts already owed, the Jews were enjoined to present their loan documents prior to the subsequent November 1. Fragments of governmental records from 1232 and 1233 indicate that the old technique of enrolling Jewish debts and having them collected by governmental agents was again instituted.[32]

The year 1234 witnessed the promulgation of another royal ordinance concerning Jewish usury. The opening provision of this decree is problematic, beginning as follows:

> It is to be known that the lord King of the French, for the salvation of his soul and the soul of his father and those of all his predecessors, acquits of a third part of the entire debt which they owed to the Jews all Christians who were indebted to the Jews when they were recently seized and their debts enrolled. . . .[33]

This seems simply a reduction of the debts owed the Jews out of fear that, despite all the precautions of the late 1220's, the sum involved may still have included usury. Related evidence, however, leads to the suspicion that this part of the royal order is concerned with debts taken over by the government. In a letter of 1237 to Louis IX, Pope Gregory IX extends the following dispensation:

> On your behalf we have been told that, since you have received no small sum of money from the Jews of your Kingdom and from their Christian debtors and in the latter's name, and since this money acquired by the Jews bears the stigma of usury, you desire to bring satisfaction for the said money for fear lest the sin of it be imputed to you and you be punished for it. Wherefore, you humbly pray us that, in view of the fact that many from whom the said Jews have extorted usury can no longer be discovered, and that you want to send the money, which you are bound to restore to them, as a subsidy to the Empire of Constantinople, we shall, in the benignity of the Apostolic Throne, take the trouble to grant to Your Serene Highness permission to do this, so that, by doing it, the matter may redound to your salvation in the sight of God, and that because of

---

[31] *Ordonnances*, vol. 1, pp. 73-74.

[32] *Layettes*, vol. 5, doc. nos. 371, 372, 373.

[33] *Ordonnances*, vol. 1, pp. 54-55.

the great amount of such assistance you may be free from the obligation of repayment. Therefore, inclined to your prayers, we grant to you by these letters, the authority asked for.[34]

Moreover, the first two provisions of the 1234 decree were reenacted in September 1248. In 1248 the reference is surely to confiscated debts; in all likelihood such was the case in 1234 as well.[35]

We have suggested that earlier confiscations were generally associated with some religiously respectable Christian enterprise or at least with some allegedly reproachable Jewish behavior. In this instance, it is possible that the confiscation was related to the beginning of papal efforts to rouse a new Crusade. Although the agreement struck between Frederick II and the Moslems was not due to lapse until 1239, by late 1234 Pope Gregory IX was already setting in motion the machinery for a new assault.[36] The royal confiscation of the early 1230's, like that of the 1240's, may well have been related to the incipient Crusade.

The second half of the ordinance of 1234 dealt with those facets of Jewish lending still permitted. Thus far the entire thrust of Louis's enactments had been directed toward the elimination of governmental involvement in Jewish business and the moral stigma resulting therefrom. Jewish lending against pledges, which necessitated no governmental intervention, had not been affected by the spate of legislation beginning in 1223. Now, in 1234, the monarchy turned its attention to pawnbroking, ordering that henceforth all pawns deposited with the Jews must be transferred in the presence of honorable and trustworthy witnesses.[37] While in no sense a limitation of Jewish pawnbroking, this provision did represent an important extension of governmental regulation.

The Exchequer of Normandy, on September 29, 1235, recorded the final royal step in the drive against Jewish lending. Having utterly removed his government from involvement with Jewish business, Louis now addressed himself to the Jews, ordering that henceforth all Jews were to live by their own labor or by nonusurious business dealings; for the first time, Jewish usury was directly outlawed.[38]

During the preceding half-century, strong antipathy to Jewish usury had developed in ecclesiastical circles, capped by the view that Jewish

[34] Grayzel, *The Church and the Jews in the XIIIth Century*, pp. 232–35.

[35] Delisle, "Recueil des jugements de l'Echiquier de Normandie," doc. no. 735.

[36] On the period between 1229 and 1239, see Steven Runciman, *A History of the Crusades*, 3 vols. (Cambridge, 1951–54), vol. 3, pp. 195–217.

[37] *Ordonnances*, vol. 1, p. 55.

[38] Delisle, "Recueil des jugements de l'Echiquier de Normandie," doc. no. 581.

exaction of interest from Christians was a transgression of Biblical law and hence illicit.[39] On the eve of Louis's prohibition, the first such royal order in medieval Europe, Pope Gregory IX wrote of the Jews' sufferings in northern France and pleaded eloquently on their behalf. The pontiff proclaimed that the Jews were not to be despoiled or expelled without good cause; those held captive were to be released, at which time they were "to observe the legitimate contracts and agreements which are made with them, though without the exaction of any usury."[40] The papal view—expressed in a sympathetic letter of protection—goes far beyond the IV Lateran Council stance of 1215; it is a striking prelude to the prohibition of 1235.

The impact of these new views on the ruling class is reflected in the order issued by Archembaud of Bourbon, in May 1234, prohibiting the Jews of his domain from usury. Archembaud mentions explicitly consulting with the king and obtaining his assent; moreover, the language of his prohibition is almost the same as that which the king was to use a year later.

> I, Archembaud lord of Bourbon, make known to all whom the present document reaches that, with the will and assent of my beloved lord Louis the illustrious king of France, for my salvation and that of my predecessors, I will and order that all Jews who wish to remain henceforth on my land, must live by their own labor and by honest business, abstaining completely from usurious exactions.[41]

In 1235, Louis himself followed suit.

The one major question remaining concerns the mode of enforcement of the new royal decree. All the earlier measures involved limitations on governmental involvement; since they were royal edicts dealing with governmental actions, enforcement was not an issue. Now the authorities turned to the Jews, banning directly Jewish usury. How was the edict to be enforced? The decree itself makes no reference whatsoever to penalities. The usury prohibition is simply stated along with a series of demands, most of which were items of longstanding ecclesiastical concern. No mention is made of the means of enforcement of these provisions; this omission is all the more noteworthy in the face of the explicitness of Archembaud of Bourbon, who threatened expulsion for those unwilling to accept his decree. It is also significant that Louis's second decree against usury is most explicit on the issue of

---

[39] See above, chapter 3.

[40] Grayzel, *The Church and the Jews in the XIIIth Century*, pp. 202–3.

[41] *Layettes*, vol. 2, doc. no. 2284.

penalities: "Those Jews unwilling to abide by this are to be expelled; those who transgress are to be properly punished."[42] While some expulsion did take place in the early 1250's on the basis of this clause, it is striking that no penalty clause was inserted in the ordinance of 1235 and that no information on any expulsion during the 1230's has survived.[43] This leads strongly to the conclusion that the royal edict was a pious expression of ideals, not inteneded in 1235 as a piece of realistic legislation.

Looking back over the period from 1223 through 1235, then, we see a pattern of steady pressure on Jewish lending—first through slow withdrawal of the governmental backing upon which the most profitable types of Jewish business were based; then through the imposition of controls on those aspects of Jewish lending heretofore unrestricted; and finally culminating in the outright order to the Jews to end all usurious practice, although without clear articulation of the penalties to be imposed for noncompliance. This legislative campaign was heightened by the practical step of confiscation of Jewish goods and of Jewish debts sometime during 1234.

Thus far we have focused on the royal campaign. There are a number of signs that Louis's efforts stimulated emulation on the part of many of the barons of northern France—sometimes for similarly pious motives, sometimes merely for economic gain. Archembaud of Bourbon preceded by a year the royal edict outlawing Jewish usury altogether; in fact his decree had included a heavy penalty for noncompliance lacking in the royal ban.[44] The king's confiscation of 1234 was imitated by the most important of the baronial possessors of Jews, the count of Champagne. Indication of this confiscation is contained in a papal letter dated November 29, 1238, permitting the count of Champagne to use moneys taken from the Jews for the Crusades.[45]

An explicit condemnation of the baronial excesses related to the royal campaign comes in a papal letter of April 6, 1233, detailing some of the anguished complaints of French Jewry and railing at the injustices perpetrated.

> Although the perfidy of the Jews is to be condemned, nevertheless their relation with Christians is useful and, in a way, necessary; for they bear the image of our Savior, and were created by the Creator

---

[42] *Ordonnances*, vol. 1, p. 75.

[43] On the expulsion of the early 1250's, see below.

[44] *Layettes*, vol. 2, doc. no. 2284.

[45] Grayzel, *The Church and the Jews in the XIIIth Century*, pp. 236-37.

of all mankind. They are therefore not to be destroyed, God forbid, by His own creatures, especially by believers in Christ, for no matter how perverse their midway position may be, their fathers were made friends of God, and also their remnant shall be saved.

But certain Christians of the French Kingdom, heeding this circumstance not at all, persecute and afflict the said Jews with many kinds of oppressions and with many unbearable burdens. Cruelly raging in their midst, and longing for their property, they torture them horribly by means of hunger and of thirst, by the privations of prison and by intolerable tortures of the body. Indeed, we have heard that recently in certain parts of the same kingdom it was enacted by means of a certain device, that after postponing for a period of four years the payments of the debts which Christians owed them, they agreed to pay them in annual instalments, not bound to pay anything above the principal, though all this was contrary to the contracts into which they had publicly entered. At the end of the four years, however, the Jews were seized and were kept for so long under custody in prison, until having pooled all the debts which were due them from the Christians, they gave the Lord of the place whatever security he thought proper that within a stated period of time they would not demand any payment of their debts whether these were being paid or not. Whence, some of the Jews, unable to pay what security was considered sufficient in their case, perished miserably, it is said, through hunger, thirst, and privation of prisons, and to the moment some are held in chains. Certain ones of these lords rage among these Jews with such cruelty, that unless they pay them what they ask, they tear their finger-nails and extract their teeth, and inflict upon them other kinds of inhuman torments. Some nobles of the kingdom, boldly intending to exterminate the Jews, are said to have vowed that they would not suffer the agreements entered upon, or to be entered upon, between Jews and Christians, to be held valid.

Wherefore, since the Jews, driven out from their lands by these lords because they cannot satisfy their greed, are being killed, robbed, or suffer other damage and injury to person and property at the hands of others who see them thus driven out by their own lords, and since there is no one who would afford them proper protection, or see to it that justice is shown them, they fled to the protection of the Apostolic Throne, begging us humbly to deign to take them under apostolic supervision in view of the fact that with regard to the matters in which they seem annoying to Christians they are ready, according to their agreement, to live among themselves as prescribed by legal and canonical regulations: that they will take no usury nor anything else in order to cover up their usury, nor do anything insulting to the Christian Faith. Wherefore, since we are, by the duty which the Apostolic Office lays upon us, under obligation alike to wise and foolish, we order that, if this be so, you shall pronounce the oaths, made in the heat of passion rather than in the the coolness of judgment, not at all binding, and that you make every effort carefully, in our name, to warn all the faithful Christians in your dioceses and to induce them, not to harm the Jews in their persons, nor to dare rob them of their property, nor, for the sake of plunder, to drive them from their lands, without some reasonable cause or clear guilt on their part, but rather to permit them to live in pursuance of their laws and their former status, as long as they do not presume to insult the Christian Faith. After the captive Jews have been restored to their former liberty, they are to observe the legitimate contracts and agreements which are made with them, though without the exaction of any usury. Such kindliness must be shown to Jews by Christians, as we hope might be shown to Christians who live in pagan lands.[46]

The papal account is certainly confused. The following elements, however, are discernible: (1) postponement of obligations owed the Jews, with payments spread over a period of years; (2) emphasis on the responsibility to pay principal only; (3) imprisonment and torture; (4) confiscation of Jewish funds; (5) a decision to hold agreements, past and future, invalid; and (6) expulsion. A number of these items have been seen in the royal campaign itself. Others are cruelties that go far beyond royal action; such, for example, is the refusal to recognize past obligations and the final step of expulsion. Royal activities were not isolated; others responded in similar or more extreme fashion, their actions losing on occasion the measured regularity associated with Blanche and Louis and degenerating into vicious exploitation and physical attack.

The theoretical foundations for this intensified assault on Jewish usury had been laid earlier. Reference has already been made to ecclesiastical views which negated the Jewish right to lend money at interest.[47] A number of Hebrew sources composed during the reign of Louis IX reveal the Jews contesting precisely these views.

The important polemical work *Sepher Joseph Hamekane* reflects some of the Christian criticism of Jewish usury. The objections include an emphasis on the broad negation of usury in Psalms 15, seemingly effacing the distinction between "countrymen" and "foreigners" in

[46]Ibid., pp. 200–203.
[47]See above, chapter 3.

Deuteronomy 23. To this the Jewish polemicist replies, "King David was the pupil of Moses and lacked the authority to disagree with his teacher and to add or detract from his teachings. Indeed Moses our Teacher said: 'You may deduct interest from loans to foreigners, but not from loans to your countryman.' "[48]

The more radical allegation that Christians are in fact included in the category of "countryman" is presented as well. To rebut this contention, the author cites an earlier sage's reference to the prophet Obadiah, who speaks explicitly of the Edomites (that is, Christendom in medieval Hebrew terminology) as foreigners.[49] While these Jewish efforts at rebuttal are of great historical interest, they obviously had no impact whatsoever on the royal and baronial programs.

With the outlawing of Jewish usury in 1235, the first stage of the royal anti-usury campaign came to a close. The next serious concern flared up in the late 1240's. During the intervening decade, however, a few items of interest may be noted. There is a curious decree by the Exchequer of Normandy in April 1239 ordering that the Jews not be paid for any claimed obligation nor even for any pledges held by them except for such pledges as were held at the time of their capture.[50] Is this the capture and confiscation of 1234 or a second such incident?

During this period, government records attesting debts owed the Jews almost completely disappear. While documents witnessing such obligations abound for the first decades of the thirteenth century, they are practically nonexistent from the early 1230's down through the end of the reign of Saint Louis. This is again indicative of the effective withdrawal of governmental support of Jewish lending.

Nonetheless, the royal inquiries into the state of the realm in 1247 and 1248 make it evident that many of the abuses attacked in the late 1220's and early 1230's had not been totally extirpated. While complaints concerning the Jews range over a broad spectrum of issues, the majority were related to moneylending. The utilitization of this material is complicated by the lack of specific dating in many instances;

---

[48] Judah Rosenthal, ed., *Sepher Joseph Hamekane* (Jerusalem, 1970), p. 61; cf. pp. 100–101. Anti-usury sentiment is further revealed in the condemnation of Jacob for usurious practice in buying so cheaply Esau's valuable birthright (ibid., pp. 40–41).

[49] Ibid., p. 61. A more extensive defense of the Jewish rights to usury can be found in the writings of the southern French leader, R. Meir b. Simeon. These writings include a purported epistle addressed to the king of France, a series of seemingly actual discussions with the archbishops of Narbonne, and a number of literary debates between Jews and churchmen. On this material, see Siegfried Stein, "A Disputation on Moneylending between Jews and Gentiles in Me'ir b. Simeon's *Milḥemeth Miṣwah*," *Journal of Jewish Studies* 10 (1959): 45–61; and idem, *Jewish-Christian Disputations in Thirteenth-Century Narbonne* (London, 1969).

[50] Delisle, "Recueil des jugements de l'Echiquier de Normandie," doc. no. 662.

many complaints are unfortunately couched in vague and ambiguous terms, also detracting from their usefulness. Such problems notwithstanding, enough clear evidence remains to show us the continuation of many prohibited procedures.[51]

A few complaints indicate that the abuses in enforcing Jewish loans which Philip Augustus had attempted to eradicate in 1219 were still in vogue. In one case the plaintiff refers to forced sale of his mill in 1230 in order to pay a debt for which he had supposedly served as surety.[52] In two cases the plaintiffs mention imprisonment as a result of debts supposedly owed the Jews.[53] Both of these practices had been outlawed in 1219. It is curious that not one of the three claimants based his case on the legislation of 1219; there is no overt recollection of the prohibition of these practices.

More evidence is available for the continued enforcement of Jewish usury, despite the ordinance of 1223. A number of incidents from 1227 through 1237 reveal governmental support for usury and are the occasion for complaints against the governmental officials involved.[54] One of these claims details explicitly the forced return of 64 shillings of usury to a Jew after the king had ordered that usury not be enforced.[55] In the cases dating from 1227 and 1229, it is possible that the loans may have been contracted prior to 1223 and that the claims were thus invalid; the cases dating from the 1230's seem to be blatant instances of failure to observe the statute of 1223.

There is but one overt reference to the 1230 prohibition of governmental enforcement of Jewish loans altogether, and that reference is incorrect. A Christian claimant, William Petit, charged that, in 1227, a former royal provost had enforced a debt of 11 pounds owed to a certain Jew, although the king had prohibited forced repayment of obligations owed to Jews.[56] There are a number of post-1230 claims that cite official enforcement of debts owed Jews; in no instance, however, is the claim based on breach of the 1230 legislation.[57] It is possi-

---

[51] The complaints were edited by Léopold Delisle in volume 24 of *RHF* and in "Fragments d'un registre des enquêteurs de Saint Louis," *Journal des Savants* 7 (1909): 38-41. On these complaints, see Charles-Victor Langlois, "Doléances recueillies par les Enquêteurs de Saint Louis," *Revue historique* 92 (1906): 1-41. On the claims pertaining to the Jews, see Nahon, "Le credit et les Juifs dans la France du XIIIe siècle."

[52] *RHF*, vol. 24, p. 201, doc. no. 1262.

[53] Ibid., p. 222, doc. no. 1512; p. 286, doc. no. 88.

[54] Ibid., p. 161, doc. no. 727; p. 199, doc. no. 1217; p. 200, doc. no. 1218; p. 201, doc. no. 1260; p. 216, doc. no. 1460.

[55] Ibid., p. 216, doc. no. 1460.

[56] Ibid., p. 164, doc. no. 745.

[57] Ibid., p. 188, doc. no. 1086; p. 188, doc. no. 1093; p. 223, doc. no. 1530.

ble that the debts predated this edict and that hence no complaint could be filed on that basis. One complaint mentions official extortion of additional sums on grounds that the claimant "had not been deleted from the roll of the king."[58] This seems to refer to the rolls drawn up in the wake of the 1230 legislation, examples of which have survived. This particular obligation thus predated 1230, and the same may be true for others.

The practice most widely attested as ignoring the legislation of the 1220's and 1230's was Jewish usury itself. We have already suggested that the prohibition of usury promulgated in 1235 would have been the most difficult of the edicts to execute; the complaints of 1247-1248 support this contention. Indications of Jewish usury abound.[59] In some instances mention of Jewish usury is made in passing; in other instances it is directly referred to as the basis for a certain kind of claim against the government.[60] The earlier legislation, while relatively effective in curbing governmental involvement in Jewish business, had been less successful in forcing the Jews into more "wholesome" economic outlets.

Realization of this failure, coupled with the heightened royal religiosity that characterized the years immediately prior to Louis's first crusading venture, triggered the second wave of royal action against Jewish usury. In this campaign the major concern was no longer governmental involvement; it was the continued practice of usury by the Jews themselves.

The second campaign began prior to Louis's departure for Outremer with a general confiscation of Jewish funds and of obligations owed the Jews. While the first evidence for this seizure comes in two documents addressed to the royal seneschal of Carcassonne, it is clear that this was a wide-ranging despoliation of the Jews.[61] The rationale for this seizure was, in all likelihood, the desire to order the affairs of the realm by restoring Jewish usury. Louis himself, in his order of 1257 appointing a special commission to return Jewish usury, specifies that prior to embarking on his Crusade he had received certain goods from the Jews,

---

[58] Ibid., p. 188, doc. no. 1093.

[59] Note, for example, ibid., p. 89, doc. no. 199; p. 90, doc. no. 204; p. 281, doc. nos. 53, 55, 57; p. 291, doc. nos. 121, 122, 123, 126; pp. 742-44, doc. nos. 121-28.

[60] On these special claims, see below.

[61] Claude de Vic and Joseph Vaissète, *Histoire générale de Languedoc*, 15 vols. (Toulouse, 1872-92), vol. 8, pp. 1191-92. In the first document, dated July 1246, the seneschal is ordered not to collect outstanding loans. In the second, dated a month later, he is ordered to collect the principal but not the interest. Both prohibited the Jews from any further usury.

"not indeed with the intention of retaining them."[62] Precisely the same expression—"non tamen animo retendi"—is used by Louis's biographer, William of Chartres, with added elaboration:

> He caused them (the Jews) and their goods to be taken, not indeed with the intention of retaining them, but rather so that the goods might be restored to those from whom the Jews had extorted them through usurious viciousness—when legitimate proofs had been given. For this purpose, he appointed diligent and prudent inquisitors, placing in their hands the goods, so that they themselves might freely restore them. If some were left—concerning which it could not be proved or found to whom they should be returned—he disbursed them, with ecclesiastical permission, for pious purposes and for the churches.[63]

The crudest royal attempt to correct the wrongs of Jewish lending was simply to repeat the earlier legislation of 1234. In his edict of 1248, the king called for reduction by a third of all debts owed the Jews at the time of the general confiscation. Where the obligation had already been discharged, a third was to be returned; for the debts as yet unpaid, a third was to be deducted. All outstanding obligations were to be repaid within the ensuing half-year, in two equal installments. Philip Augustus's prohibition of forced sale of ancestral property and of imprisonment was, however, to be scrupulously observed.[64]

While this ordinance addressed itself effectively to the problem of Jewish usury still owed at the time of the general confiscation, the king remained deeply troubled over prior usury paid out to the Jews. In order to rectify these injustices, the king urged the bishops of France to appoint inquisitors who would investigate properly all complaints against Jewish usury and would return the usurious sums whenever sufficient proof was adduced. The ordinance governing these inquests is unusually detailed.[65] The royal bailiffs were to announce publicly in each diocese times and places where complaints against Jewish usury could be heard and restitution could be made. All cases involving sums

---

[62] *Ordonnances*, vol. 1, p. 85.

[63] *RHF*, vol. 20, p. 34.

[64] Delisle, "Recueil des jugements de l'Echiquier de Normandie," doc. no. 735. In his important register, Archbishop Eudes of Rouen notes his visit to the monastery of Saint-Pierre-des-Preaux in early 1249. He found that the monks "owe four hundred pounds without interest to a certain Jew, and they do not know whether they will be cleared of this debt or whether they will have to pay it" (Sydney Brown, trans., and J. F. O'Sullivan, ed., *The Register of Eudes of Rouen* [New York, 1964], p. 66).

[65] Bibliothèque nationale, fonds Dupuy, vol. 532, 88r–90v.

under 100 shillings were to be dealt with directly by the inquisitors. Upon receipt of acceptable testimony, they were empowered to disburse the proper sums; they were only responsible for providing adequate records as to the sums, the Jewish creditors, and the Christian debtors involved. Cases involving sums exceeding 100 shillings were to be referred to the royal court, with written evidence supplied by the inquisitors as well as with direct participation of an inquisitor deputized to attend the royal hearing. A number of provisions were made to ease the process of reclaiming usury. Where the inquisitors had difficulty in eliciting the necessary evidence, they were to be aided by the secular authorities, who would compel reluctant witnesses to testify. Many witnesses normally excluded from testifying at court proceedings were to be admitted in these cases. Finally, elaborate arrangements were specified for those instances where a full set of witnesses was not available. In sum, every possible effort was made to ease strict requirements and to ensure that, whenever possible, usury be restored.

A number of lists drawn up as a result of these special investigations are extant. These records follow precisely the guidelines set forth in the royal order: they involve sums under 100 shillings, with but one exception; they list carefully the amounts involved, the Jewish creditor by whom the usury was extorted, and the Christian claimants; and they generally add as well the names of the witnesses upon whose testimony the claim was substantiated.[66]

Once again, as during the 1230's, the royal initiative against Jewish usury triggered wide imitation. At precisely the same period, Pope Innocent IV wrote to Theobald of Champagne, describing again Jewish pleas and ordering justice for these Jews.

> On behalf of the Jews of Champagne a complaint was made to us that some of your Christian subjects, to whom the Jews had shown themselves liberal in a money transaction and who ought therefore to be kind and well-disposed toward them, have on the contrary repaid evil for good, and consider them odious and despicable. These same Christians not only make no effort to repay to the said Jews the money so liberally loaned, nor to observe the legitimate contracts entered into with regard to this, but they even wickedly rage in their midst, conducting themselves with inhumanity, showing themselves oppressive and injurious. That is why the Jews have had recourse to the protection of the Apostolic Throne.

[66]Note, for example, *RHF*, vol. 24, pp. 742-43, doc. nos. 121-44; pp. 743-44, doc. nos. 145-54; p. 744, doc. nos. 155-68; Delisle, "Fragments d'un registre des enquêteurs de Saint Louis."

Wherefore, no matter how great their perfidy may be, since He who wants none to perish, mercifully still awaits their conversion, for God will not forever forsake His people, therefore, we warn and urge Your Serenity to use the power granted you by God to compel the said Christians your subjects to give satisfaction to the Jews for the money due them, and to try to observe the contracts above-named, and to desist from oppressing and injuring them. Thus will you prove that you hate iniquity and love justice, when even the Jews may enjoy their rights under the protection of your power.[67]

The proximity of the second major confiscation of the reign of Saint Louis to a crusading venture must be noted. The scrupulous efforts at restitution of Jewish usury in the late 1240's and again in the 1250's concerned themselves with usury alone—the principal in Jewish loans also had been confiscated and these funds presumably were directed into the royal treasury. It is not difficult to envision the pious French monarch using these sums in the great Crusade upon which he embarked in June 1248.

Sometime during his sojourn in Outremer, probably in 1253, Louis sent back instructions that his earlier prohibition of Jewish usury be repeated, but this time with sanctions specified. This ordinance was included, along with the statute of Melun of 1230, in the great general reform enacted by Louis upon his return from the Crusade in 1254.

(1) The Jews must desist from usury, blasphemy, magic, and necromancy.
(2) Both the Talmud and other books in which blasphemies are to be found must be burned.
(3) Those Jews unwilling to abide by this legislation are to be expelled; transgressors are to be properly punished.
(4) Let all Jews live by the labor of their hands or by commerce without interest or usury.[68]

A number of reports indicate that the threatened expulsion of recalcitrant Jews was in fact carried out. The most compelling evidence comes from Louis himself. Appointing a commission in the late 1250's to seek further restitution of Jewish usury held by the king, Louis describes the means by which he had come into possession of these funds. Part had come from the pre-Crusade confiscation; "afterwards, when we ordered that these Jews be expelled from our domain, we accumulated further Jewish possessions."[69] The link between outlawed Jewish usury and

---

[67]Grayzel, *The Church and the Jews in the XIIIth Century*, pp. 268–69.
[68]*Ordonnances*, vol. 1, p. 75.
[69]Ibid., p. 85.

expulsion is reinforced by Louis's biographer William of Chartres. In his depiction of the monarch's antipathy to Jewish usury, William has the king warning that "the Jews must abandon usury or they must totally leave the royal domain."[70] The same connection is made by the English historian, Matthew Paris, who in addition supplies a date, the year 1253.[71] Finally, a dispute in 1271 between Louis's successor and the duke of Burgundy has the latter claiming that a certain wealthy Jew had been part of the expulsion ordered by Louis and had as a result come into Burgundy and resided there for the intervening eighteen years.[72] This corresponds perfectly to the 1253 date suggested by Matthew Paris. Given the fact that this was a partial expulsion only—banishment of those unwilling to abide by the king's absolute prohibition of Jewish usury—it is difficult to evaluate its impact. The alternatives posed, however, were stark—ruin through exile or ruin through acceptance of the royal prohibition.

The king's religious scruples about the possession and utilization of funds tainted with Jewish usury continued to plague him. In 1257, he empaneled a royal commission to check on the confiscated goods, to make certain that they were all properly accounted for, and to continue the effort to return unclaimed usury.[73] The panel, composed of the bishop of Orléans, the abbot of Bonneval, and the archdeacon of Poissy, began its activities immediately. Norman records show this commission selling a mill at Fresney-le-Puceux, part of which had belonged to the wealthy Morel of Falaise.[74] While one concern was thus the sale of Jewish holdings to raise the funds necessary for continued reimbursement, the king also stipulated that synagogues and cemeteries, if they had been confiscated, were to be returned to the Jews—a beneficial step from the Jewish point of view and a good indication that a substantial segment of the Jewish community remained.[75]

Finally, Louis also petitioned the pope and the bishops of France for permission to use unreturned funds for pious purposes. William of Char-

---

[70] *RHF*, vol. 20, p. 34.

[71] Henry Luard, ed., *Matthaei Parisiensis monachi Sancti Albani Chronica Majora*, 7 vols. (London, 1872–83), vol. 5, pp. 361–62. The expulsion is dated 1252 in two Christian chronicles: *RHF*, vol. 23, pp. 215, 402, and after Louis's return to France in 1254 in *Shevet Yehudah*, pp. 69, 149.

[72] *Olim*, vol. 1, p. 364, case no. 6.

[73] *Ordonnances*, vol. 1, p. 85.

[74] Lucien Musset, "Morel de Falaise," *Bulletin de la Société des Antiquaires de Normandie* 57 (1963–64): 559. Interestingly, two of the three commissioners specified by the king were involved in this transaction—the abbot of Bonneval and the archdeacon of Poissy. Instead of the bishop of Orléans, the third figure active here was a canon of Paris.

[75] *Ordonnances*, vol. 1, p. 85.

tres's testimony on the royal request is substantiated by a long series of letters received by the monarch, granting the permission which he had sought.[76]

There remains a very precious insight into Jewish reaction to this extended attack on Jewish economic life. R. Meir b. Simeon of Narbonne, whose fellow Jews were now suffering along with their northern brethren, formulated a Hebrew missive which was supposed to be addressed to the king himself. The charges leveled against the royal authority correspond precisely to the series of blows just described. After citing a number of scriptural passages—binding on Christians as well as on Jews—for the obligation to hear the cry of the oppressed, the author begins to count off the unjust steps taken by the king against all the Jews of his many domains:

> First, he enacted a decree upon our people that a Jew not be permitted to leave the authority of one ruler and pass under the authority of another. Behold how difficult this decree is! By this decree, he consigned us to daily destruction and decimation at the hands of the barons. . . .

> Secondly, he stole the debts owed us and our moneys. As a result we are unable to sustain ourselves and our children. How much more are we unable to provide for our poor—many of them are dying of hunger.

> Thirdly, [despite the above] he has kept in force the payment of taxes and has not annulled them. He should have ordered throughout all his kingdom that no tax be taken from any Jew, since he has confiscated their money.

> Fourthly, he has commanded the barons—even though it does not meet with their favor—that neither they nor their officials may enforce debts owed Jews by Christians, neither the principal nor the interest.

> Fifthly, he has commanded that, if a Jew be indebted to a Christian, they force the Jew to pay his debt to the Christian.

> Sixthly, that we not lend money usuriously at all, even in those situations permitted to us in Scripture according to the view of our ancestors. Thus he robs us of provision for our poor and indigent, who find for themselves no sustenance.[77]

---

[76] *RHF*, vol. 20, p. 34; *Layettes*, vol. 3, doc. nos. 4502, 4508, 4510–36, 4541–48.

[77] Moshe Blau, ed., *Sefer ha-Meorot ve-Sefer ha-Hashlamah, Berakhot and Pesaḥim* (New York, 1964), pp. 16–18.

These complaints were not figments of the author's imagination. Each of the actions cited has been authenticated in our description of the royal campaign. It is interesting, however, to note the Jewish perception of these blows. For the author, the limitation of Jewish mobility was extremely serious, since it deprived the Jews of the possibility of flight and emboldened the barony to treat their Jews with greater cruelty. Also very damaging were the tangible losses emanating from the confiscation of funds and debts. While the removal of governmental support for Jewish business is not featured prominently in the list of royal decrees, it is the complaint that recurs most prominently throughout the rest of the letter. This innovation obviously hurt the Jews very badly. The tone of the Jewish complaint is bitter, and the description of Jewish suffering extreme. If this reflects accurately the southern reality, then in the north, where the anti-usury campaign had begun earlier and had been pursued more zealously, the Jewish economy must have been well-nigh shattered.

The same reign that produced an extended and ultimately successful campaign against the economic foundations of Jewish life in northern France saw a parallel assault on the pillars of Jewish religion as well. The attack on the Talmud and related literature began in 1239, during a period of lull in the government's anti-usury efforts, and continued unabated through the rest of the years of Louis's rule, renewed vigorously on the eve of his second crusading venture and his death. By 1270 the spiritual well-being of northern French Jewry had been as effectively undermined as its financial health.[78]

In this instance the initial spark to the royal assault was externally introduced. In 1236, Pope Gregory IX sponsored the conversion of a Jew named Nicholas Donin.[79] As was often the case with such converts, Donin immediately embarked on a vigorous attack against his former coreligionists. The new convert remained close to the papal court,

---

[78] On Jewish intellectual life during this period, see Urbach, *Ba'aley ha-Tosafot*, pp. 371–404. The first stage of Louis's assault on the Talmud has been extensively studied. See *inter alia* Isidore Loeb, "La controverse de 1240 sur le Talmud," *REJ* 1 (1880): 247–61, 2 (1881): 248–70, 3 (1881): 39–57; Yitzhak Baer, "The Disputation of R. Yehiel of Paris and of Nachmanides" (Hebrew), *Tarbiz* 2 (1930–31): 172–87; Judah Rosenthal, "The Talmud on Trial," *JQR* 47 (1956–57): 58–76, 145–69; Ch. Merchavia, *Ha-Talmud be-Rei ha-Naẓrut* (Jerusalem, 1970), pp. 227–360. The essential sources are the papal letters published by Grayzel, the Latin materials published in part by Loeb, and the Hebrew *Vikuah R. Yehiel mi-Pariz* (Thorn, 1873).

[79] The little material available on Nicholas Donin has been collected by Grayzel, *The Church and the Jews in the XIIIth Century*, pp. 339–40. It seems probable that Donin was originally from northern France. Both R. Yehiel of Paris and R. Jacob b. Eli mention excommunication of Donin by R. Yehiel prior to his conversion.

gathering material designed to illuminate the horrors of Talmudic literature. His attempts to convince Gregory of the "vicious malice" of the
rabbinic writings were eventually successful and, in mid 1239, Donin
was sent forth, armed with papal letters, to counteract this evil.[80]

It is highly significant that the area through which the campaign was
chaneled was northern France. Donin, with his papal letters and his
collected materials, made his way to Paris. There the materials were to
be examined, and from there they were to be transmitted "to our
venerable brethren the archbishops and to our dear sons the Kings of
France, England, Aragon, Navarre, Castile, Leon, and Portugal."[81]

The choice of the bishop of Paris as a central figure was dictated by a
number of considerations. Paris was, of course, a great center of both
canonical and theological studies, where expert opinion, were it ever
needed, would be readily available. Yet more important was the position of Paris as the capital of the French kingdom and the abode of the
most pious of the kings of western Christendom. Gregory IX recognized
from the outset the necessity of secular support in carrying out his
designs. The French king, whose authority was based in Paris, was
clearly the most likely candidate among all of European royalty to
support such a program. He had already proven widely his deep concern
for matters of faith and had shown diligence and zeal in those areas that
specifically related to the Jews. Subsequent events show that the papal
choice of Paris as a starting point was a wise one—it was only Louis who
supported the effort and it was only in France that success was
achieved.

The charges on the basis of which the Talmud was to be seized are
indicated in cursory fashion in the letters addressed by the pope to the
archbishops of France, the kings of western Europe, and the heads of
the Franciscans and Dominicans of Paris:

> If what is said about the Jews of France and of the other lands is
> true, no punishment would be sufficiently great or sufficiently
> worthy of their crime. For they, so we have heard, are not content
> with the Old Law which God gave to Moses in writing: they even
> ignore it completely, and affirm that God gave another Law which is
> called "Talmud," that is "Teaching," handed down to Moses orally.
> Falsely they allege that it was implanted within their minds and,
> unwritten, was there preserved until certain men came, whom they
> call "Sages" and "Scribes," who, fearing that this Law may be lost

[80]Grayzel, *The Church and the Jews in the XIIIth Century*, pp. 238-43.
[81]Ibid., pp. 238-41.

from the minds of men through forgetfulness, reduced it to writing, and the volume of this by far exceeds the text of the Bible. In this is contained matter so abusive and so unspeakable that it arouses shame in those who mention it and horror in those who hear it.

Wherefore, since this is said to be the chief cause that holds the Jews obstinate in their perfidy, we thought that Your Fraternity should be warned and urged, and we herewith order you by Apostolic Letters, that on the first Saturday of the Lent to come, in the morning, while the Jews are gathered in the synagogues, you shall, by our order, seize all the books of the Jews who live in your districts, and have these books carefully guarded in the possession of the Dominican and Franciscan Friars.[82]

The vagueness of these charges is dispelled by the series of thirty-five accusations drawn up seemingly by Nicholas Donin. These charges fall under five major headings: (1) Jewish emphasis on the sanctity of Oral Law, which is in itself a blasphemy of sorts against the holiness of Scriptures recognized by Jew and Christian alike; (2) Talmudic material that overtly fosters anti-Christian attitudes and actions; (3) Talmudic materials that, in their puerile descriptions of the deity, constitute sacrilege against God; (4) Talmudic materials that blaspheme Jesus and the leaders of the Christian faith; and (5) Talmudic materials that are in a general way morally and intellectually offensive.[83] The first of these categories corresponds accurately to the opening remarks of the papal letters; the remaining four specify the "matter so abusive and so unspeakable that it arouses shame in those who mention it and horror in those who hear it."

The program was presented in only the most general terms to the archbishops and the kings addressed. Both groups were enjoined to have the books of the Jews seized on the first Saturday of the coming Lent, which was March 3, 1240. The archbishops were told that they might utilize the support of the secular authorities whenever necessary. The kings were bidden to make the effort royal in scope; it was to extend beyond their personal domains to the kingdoms at large. The instructions merely ordered that the confiscated volumes be turned over to the Dominicans and the Franciscans.[84]

---

[82] Ibid., pp. 240-43.

[83] See Loeb, "La controverse de 1240 sur le Talmud," *REJ* 2 (1881): 253-54; Rosenthal, "The Talmud on Trial," pp. 74-75, 145-66; and Merchavia, *Ha-Talmud be-Rei ha-Naẓrut*, pp. 249-83. On the significance of the first charge, see Amos Funkenstein, "Changes in the Patterns of Christian Anti-Jewish Polemics in the 12th Century" (Hebrew), *Zion* 33 (1968): 137.

[84] Grayzel, *The Church and the Jews in the XIIIth Century*, pp. 240-43.

Just as the letters ordering seizure of Jewish books were channeled through Paris, so too the books themselves were to be channeled into the capital city. The responsibility for the sequestered tomes seems to have devolved upon the Dominicans and Franciscans of Paris. The letter addressed to them is specific as to the action commanded.

> We, through Apostolic Letters, order Your Discretion to have the Jews who live in the Kingdoms of France, England, Aragon, Navarre, Castile, Leon and Portugal, forced by secular arm to give up their books. Those books, in which you will find errors of this sort, you shall cause to be burned at the stake. By Apostolic Power, and through use of ecclesiastical censure, you will silence all opponents. You will also report to us faithfully what you have done in the matter. But, should all of you be unable to be present at the fulfillment of these instructions, someone of you, none the less, shall carry out its execution.[85]

While the papal order seems to imply carte blanche for direct action against the Jewish books, the next step was some kind of inquisitorial proceeding to ascertain the validity of the charges.[86] The basis for these proceedings seems to have been the aforementioned thirty-five accusations drawn up by Donin. A number of important rabbis, chief among them R. Yehiel of Paris (Vivant of Meaux) and R. Judah of Melun, were called upon to testify on behalf of the accused Talmudic tradition. Their testimony is briefly recapitulated in an unofficial set of two Latin *confessiones* and in an embellished Hebrew account that transforms the Jewish defense into a vigorous disputation between the chief accuser, Donin, and the most important of the Jewish leaders, R. Yehiel. There is sufficient similarity between the thirty-five accusations drawn up by Donin, the Latin *confessiones*, and the Hebrew *Vikuah* to indicate substantial factual information underlying both of the latter two sources.[87]

The papal directive had ordered burning of those books in which abusive errors were found. The investigation at Paris had revealed such errors. The next step was thus a major conflagration of condemned Jewish books, which took place during the summer of 1242.[88] This was an incident which deeply shook northern European Jewry, occasioning

---

[85] Ibid., pp. 242–43.

[86] Emphasized by Baer, "The Disputation of R. Yehiel of Paris and of Nachmanides."

[87] Loeb, "La controverse de 1240 sur le Talmud," *REJ* 2 (1881): 253–54.

[88] On the dating, see S. H. Kuk, "The Date of the Burning of the Talmud in France," and David Tamar, "More on the Date of the Burning of the Talmud in France," both in *Kiryat Sefer* 29 (1953–54), pp. 281 and 430–31, respectively.

inter alia a pathetic lament by the young Meir of Rothenburg, at that time a student in France and destined to become a major figure in German Jewry:

O thou consumed by fire—seek out
    the welfare of those who mourn thee,
Who desire desperately to dwell
    in your courtyards;
Those who yearn for the soil of the one
    true land,
Who suffer in astonishment over the
    scorching of your parchment pages;
Those who walk in dark despair
    without illumination,
Who hope daily for a light that will
    burst forth upon them and upon you.[89]

The next information comes from a papal letter, dated May 9, 1244, sent by Innocent IV to Louis IX. This letter begins with a repetition of the charges against the Talmud, again corresponding accurately to the thirty-five accusations leveled by Donin.

The wicked perfidy of the Jews, from whose hearts our Redeemer has not removed the veil of blindness because of the enormity of their crime, but has so far permitted to remain in blindness such as in a measure covers Israel, does not heed, as it should, the fact that Christian piety received them and patiently allows them to live among them through pity only. Instead, it (the perfidy) commits such enormities as are stupifying to those who hear of them, and horrible to those who tell them. For, ungrateful to the Lord Jesus Christ, who, in the abundance of His kindliness, patiently expects their conversion, they, displaying no shame for their guilt nor reverence for the honor of the Christian Faith, throw away and despise the Law of Moses and the prophets, and follow some tradition of their elders. On account of these same traditions the Lord reproves them in the Gospel saying: "Wherefore do you transgress the law of God, and render it void because of your traditions, teaching doctrines and commands of men?"

In traditions of this sort they rear and nurture their children, which traditions are called "Talmud" in Hebrew. It is a big book among them, exceeding in size the text of the Bible. In it are found blasphemies against God and His Christ, and obviously entangled

[89] Conveniently available in Abraham Habermann, ed., *Sefer Gezerot Ashkenaz ve-Ẓarfat* (Jerusalem, 1945), p. 183.

fables about the Blessed Virgin, and abusive errors, and unheard of follies. But of the laws and doctrines of the prophets they make their sons altogether ignorant. They fear that if the forbidden truth, which is found in the Law and the Prophets, be understood, and the testimony concerning the only-begotten Son of God that He appeared in the flesh, be furnished, these (children) would be converted to the Faith and humbly return to their Redeemer.[90]

The pope then describes the action taken in Paris, culminating in the burning of the Talmud. He commends the French king for his zealous support and urges him to pursue the matter with further vigor, extending the eradication of condemned Jewish books throughout the kingdom.

Indeed our beloved son the Chancellor of Paris, and the doctors, the Regents of Paris, after having at the command of our predecessor, Pope Gregory of happy memory, as expressed in a sacred decree, read the above-named book of abuse, as well as others which, along with their glosses, they had in their possession, and after having examined them, they consigned them to the flames, in the presence of clergy and laity, to the confusion of the perfidy of the Jews, as we have seen in their letters. You, also, Catholic King and most Christian Prince, have given fitting help in these matters and extended your favor, and on account of this we commend the Royal Excellency with fitting praise to God, and bestow our gratitude upon you. Nevertheless, because the blasphemous abuse of these Jews has not yet ceased, nor their troubles as yet given them understanding, we ask your Royal Highness and we beseech you in the name of the Lord Jesus Christ, to strike down with merited severity all the detestable and heinous excesses of this sort which they have committed in insult of the Creator and to the injury of the Christian name, and which you have with laudable piety begun to prosecute. Also the above-mentioned abusive books, condemned by these doctors, as well as all the commentaries which have been examined and condemned by them, should, at your order, be burned in fire wherever they can be found throughout your kingdom.[91]

The results of Innocent IV's exhortations are unknown. Whatever their impact may have been, by 1247 a curious papal reversal had taken place. From late 1244 through early 1251, the pope resided at Lyons. There he seems to have been particularly accessible to Jewish petitions. The Jews advanced the claim that prohibition of the Talmud was tanta-

---

[90]Grayzel, *The Church and the Jews in the XIIIth Century*, pp. 250–53.
[91]Ibid., pp. 252–53.

mount to the outlawing of the Jewish faith. In a sense, this had been perceived by Innocent and his predecessor. Gregory IX had described the Talmud as "the chief cause that holds the Jews obstinate in their perfidy," and Innocent himself had charged that the Talmud was used to prevent direct study of the Bible lest the Jews perceive the true message of the Scriptures and abandon their obdurate faith.[92] Now, however, the Jews emphasized for their purposes the contention that without the Talmud practice of Jewish religion was impossible, asserting that the effective prohibition of Jewish life blatantly contravened established Church doctrine.[93] The pressures brought to bear upon the pope alongside this legal argument are unknown. In any case, the letter of 1247 addressed to Louis indicates that the matter of the Talmud had been reopened and that a new investigation had been ordered under the aegis of the papal legate in Paris. The purpose of this new investigation was to restore to the Jews as much of their rabbinic literature as possible—without injury to the Christian faith.[94]

While it had been papal instructions that sparked the campaign against the Talmud, in northern France this assault had become self-sustaining. Innocent's recommendation received little hearing in northern French circles. Just as in the case of usury, the stand of the French clergy—and along with them the king—was far more radical than the position of the central ecclesiastical authorities.

While the royal response to the pope's new directive has been lost, the vigorous reply of the papal legate delegated to undertake the reexamination remains. The legate Odo began his rejoinder with a precise narration of earlier developments—the charges assembled by Donin, the series of papal letters, substantiation of the accusations through a careful study of the Jewish books and through personal questioning of a number of Jewish teachers, and finally the public burning of the condemned volumes. From all this Odo concludes that it would be a grievous error to restore the Talmud to the Jews.

> It would therefore be most disgraceful, and a cause of shame for the Apostolic Throne, if books that had been so solemnly and so justly burned in the presence of all the scholars, and of the clergy, and of the populace of Paris, were to be given back to the masters of the Jews at the order of the pope,—for such tolerance would seem to mean approval. Saint Jerome, speaking of the lepers whom the Lord

---

[92] Ibid., pp. 240-43, 250-53.
[93] Ibid., pp. 274-81.
[94] Ibid.

cured, says that there is no perverse doctrine that does not contain some truth, and so likewise no heretics are to be found who do not think well of some one article of the Faith. These are books that contained errors, and hence no matter how much good they contain, they were, nevertheless, condemned by the authority of the councils, in the same way that heretics are condemned although they do not err in everything. Thus, although these books contain some good things, though not many, nevertheless, they deserve condemnation. This is the very teaching of which Saint Jerome made mention in the Gospel of Matthew, that it makes errors into commands of God, as the Lord Himself bore witness.[95]

Whatever the papal response may have been, Odo and his colleagues proceeded to a second public condemnation of the Talmud in 1248.

Certain books by the name of Talmud having been presented by the Jewish masters to us armed with Apostolic Authority, we have examined these books and caused them to be carefully examined by men of discretion, expert in these matters, God-fearing, and zealous for the Christian Faith. Whereas we found that these books were full of innumerable errors, abuses, blasphemies and wickedness such as arouse shame in those who speak of them and horrify the hearer, to such an extent that these books cannot be tolerated in the name of God without injury to the Christian Faith, therefore, with the advice of those pious men whom we caused to be gathered especially for that purpose, we pronounced that the said books are unworthy of tolerance, and they are not to be restored to the Jewish masters, and we decisively condemn them. We are also possessed of full knowledge as to the place and time of other books not shown to us by the Jewish masters nor by us examined, although we have often made demands for them; and we shall do what there is to be done with regard to them.[96]

The edict of 1248 framed by the papal legate remained in force for some time. The important royal ordinance of 1253, which outlawed Jewish usury and enacted sanctions for noncompliance, included also a prohibition of the Talmud.[97] While those sources which do describe the resultant expulsion in any detail link it with the anti-usury clause of the ordinance, it is possible that some Jews may have left France as a

---

[95] Ibid., pp. 275–78. It is interesting to note that Odo had been sent to Paris primarily in order to preach the new Crusade. Again the nexus between crusading and anti-Jewish activity is striking.

[96] Ibid., pp. 278–79.

[97] *Ordonnances*, vol. 1, p. 75.

result of the overt royal prohibition of Talmudic study. Such may have been the case, for example, with the distinguished defender of the Talmud at the 1240 Paris trial, R. Yehiel.[98]

In 1257 Pope Alexander IV addressed almost identical letters to three of the most important political figures in northern France—the duke of Burgundy, the count of Anjou, and the king.[99] In these letters the pope exhorted the three leaders to exhibit zeal in their enforcement of ecclesiastical legislation concerning the Jews. It seems highly significant that the letter to Louis omits entirely the matter of offensive Jewish books highlighted in the other two messages. This omission reflects papal awareness of the energetic and protracted efforts of the French king in this regard.

Thus the campaign initiated by the papacy in 1239 did not flag, in the late 1240's, with a papal change of heart. It was steadily pursued by the French authorities all through the remaining years of the reign of Louis IX. For the Jews this meant a devastating blow to the impressive achievements of northern French Jewish scholarship. While we have noted the immediate and agonized reaction to the burning of Jewish books, it is more difficult to trace the long-range effects of the ongoing attack against rabbinic literature. R. Samuel b. Solomon, a major Jewish figure in the mid-century French Jewish community, opened a letter to the same R. Meir of Rothenburg who had eulogized the charred Jewish books, with the following remarks:

> My spirit has left me, my strength has departed, the light of my eyes has dissipated, because of the oppressor. His hand has fallen heavily upon us; he has taken from us the delight of our eyes—we no longer have books for study and for understanding. May the Lord be zealous on behalf of his people and say to our oppressor—"Enough!"[100]

Whatever the measures one chooses, the mid thirteenth century represents a major turning point in the intellectual life of northern French Jewry. The great academies whose fame had spread throughout European Jewry declined. There were no longer major leaders on a par with the distinguished galaxy of twelfth- and early-thirteenth-century giants such as R. Jacob Tam, R. Samuel b. Meir, R. Isaac of Dampierre, R. Samson of Sens, his brother R. Isaac b. Abraham, R. Judah Sire Leon,

---

[98] S. H. Kuk, "R. Yehiel of Paris and Erez Yisrael," *Zion—Measef* 5 (1933): 97-107; Urbach, *Ba'aley ha-Tosafot*, pp. 378-79.

[99] Isidore Loeb, "Bulles inédites des papes," *REJ* 1 (1880): 116-17.

[100] Recorded by R. Meir of Rothenberg and cited by Urbach, *Ba'aley ha-Tosafot*, pp. 377-78.

and R. Yehiel. The steady stream of German students making their way to the leading academies of France dried up. In the view of Ephraim Urbach, the outstanding student of the Jewish intellectual life of this period, the anti-Talmud legislation "brought in its wake a lessening of studies and, with the passage of time, a complete decline in the intellectual life of the Jews of France."[101]

Capetian policy on Jewish settlement underwent total change during the period from 1223 to 1270. In the first year of his reign, Louis VIII went beyond the efforts of his father to stabilize Jewish residence patterns by leading a number of important barons in the signing of a nonretention clause, which was to bind signers and nonsigners alike.[102] This direction was pursued by Blanche and Louis as well. The Melun ordinance of 1230 included a similar nonretention clause, augmented by specification of the responsibilities of the signers for enforcement.[103]

As royal interest in revenue from the Jews declined and royal concern with Jewish offenses increased, the government's efforts to limit Jewish population movement waned. By 1253 the king was perfectly willing to see substantial segments of the Jewish community—possibly the wealthiest elements at that—leave his domain.[104] While there was some profit from this expulsion, the motivation was quite different from that of Philip Augustus in expelling his Jews in 1182. How large a percentage of the Jewish community was affected by this expulsion is unclear. Many of the barons of northern France did not share the royal disdain for Jewish settlement. A series of parliamentary cases in the wake of the confiscation of 1268 shows key seigneurs adamant in emphasizing their proprietary rights over certain Jews.[105] Lists drawn up in a number of Champenois towns during the 1240's reflect the same concerns.[106]

While significant emigration may have resulted from the edict of 1253, there was during this period at least one important instance of

[101] Ibid.

[102] *Layettes*, vol. 2, doc. no. 1610; see Langmuir, " 'Judei Nostri' and the Beginning of Capetian Legislation," pp. 217-21, and Chazan, "Jewish Settlement in Northern France, 1096-1306," p. 52.

[103] *Layettes*, vol. 2, doc. no. 2083; Langmuir, " 'Judei Nostri' and the Beginning of Capetian Legislation," pp. 225-30.

[104] See above.

[105] *Olim*, vol. 1, p. 791, case no. 4; p. 793, case no. 7; p. 811, case no. 32; p. 821, case no. 16.

[106] Arbois de Jubainville, *Histoire des ducs et des comtes de Champagne*, vol. 5, doc. nos. 2792-95.

mass immigration. In 1239, as a result of pressures exerted by both ecclesiastical and secular authorities, John I, count of Brittany, expelled the Jews from that western French territory. It seems reasonable to suppose that most of the fugitives made their way eastward into the settled centers of northern French Jewish life.[107]

Shifts in Jewish population notwithstanding, the increasing availability of documentary materials brings to light new Jewish enclaves and reinforces the impression already established of widespread Jewish settlement.[108] In this regard, the Champenois tax record of 1252 offers some very valuable insight. This record, available only in extracts, shows Jewish revenue bailliage by bailliage and town by town.[109] It reveals Jews in a total of forty-two Champenois towns—a rather large number. It is quite possible, in fact, that the list preserves only the major Jewish settlements and that Jews living in smaller locales may well have paid their taxes through the central Jewish communities listed. It is significant to compare the pattern of Jewish settlement with that of the other "foreign" element in Champagne at the time, namely, the Lombards. Against the forty-two Jewish communities attested we find only twenty-two Lombard groups, almost exclusively centered in the major towns of the county.

While economic necessity forced the Jews into smaller settlements spread widely over northern France, such a trend could only develop against a background of considerable physical security. It is curious, however, that the reign of the king heralded for his emphasis on justice should have seen major incidents of popular attack on the Jews. Earlier, only the attack on the Jewish community of Rouen during the First Crusade disturbed the pattern of adequate protection of Jews from popular hostility.[110] The Crusades of the twelfth and early thirteenth centuries passed without serious incident in northern France. The violence suffered by northern French Jewry was, in every instance, the result of governmental initiative, rather than an outpouring of popular sentiment.[111] Now, during the reign of that king famed for his commitment to the eradication of violence, the Jews began to feel the sting of popular fury. Both significant outbreaks were associated, not unexpectedly, with the Crusades of the middle years of the century.

[107] Grayzel, *The Church and the Jews in the XIIIth Century*, pp. 344–45.

[108] Chazan, "Jewish Settlement in Northern France, 1096–1306," pp. 42–45.

[109] Auguste Longnon, ed., *Documents relatifs au comté de Champagne et de Brie, 1172–1361*, 3 vols. (Paris, 1901–4), vol. 3, pp. 8–16.

[110] See above, chapter 1.

[111] See above, chapters 2 and 3.

In February 1229, Frederick II had come to a negotiated settlement with the Moslems that provided *inter alia* a ten-year period of truce. This arrangement was never terribly popular with either side, and long before its expiration Pope Gregory IX had begun to lay plans for yet another crusading expedition. The focus of papal exhortation was northern France and England, and it was from there that the expedition eventually set forth under the leadership of Theobald of Champagne. Prior to the actual organization of this Crusade in 1239, unruly bands in western France had begun to do serious damage, especially in attacks upon the Jews.[112]

The beleaguered Jews quickly turned to the instigator of the Crusade, the pope himself, imploring his protection against the vicious attacks. Gregory responded with a series of strong letters denouncing the atrocities, the first addressed to the bishops of Western France.

We have received a tearful and pitiful complaint from the Jews who live in the Kingdom of France. It shows that although the crusaders of your districts and dioceses should have prepared heart and body to fight the battles of the Lord, and to liberate the heritage of Christ from the hands of pagans who, because of the enormous sins of the Christian people, hold and defile the Temple of God, and although to the extent that such a battle is especially Christ's, so much the more humbly should they be filled with fear and love of His name, lest, God forbid, they steep themselves in their evil desires and arouse against themselves Divine displeasure; yet (despite all this) these very ones, along with others who have taken the Cross, plot impious designs against the Jews, and pay no heed to the fact that the proof for the Christian faith comes, as it were, from their archives, and that, as the prophets testified, although they should be as the sands of the sea, yet in the end of days a remnant of them shall be saved, because the Lord will not forever spurn His people. But (the crusaders) try to wipe them almost completely off the face of the earth. In an unheard of and unprecedented outburst of cruelty, they have slaughtered in this mad hostility, two thousand and five hundred of them; old and young, as well as pregnant women. Some were mortally wounded and others trampled like mud under the feet of horses. They burned their books and, for greater shame and disgrace, they exposed the bodies of those thus killed, for food to the birds of heaven, and their flesh to the beasts of the earth.

[112] Runciman, *A History of the Crusades*, vol. 3, pp. 195–217. The key contemporary sources for the attacks on the Jews are the papal letters found in Grayzel, *The Church and the Jews in the XIIIth Century*, pp. 226–31. It is impossible to identify the source for the brief description in *Shevet Yehudah*, p. 148, which specifies slaughter of over 3,000 Jews and forced conversion of over 500.

After foully and shamefully treating those who remained alive after this massacre, they carried off their goods and consumed them. And in order that they may be able to hide such an inhuman crime under the cover of virtue, and in some way justify their unholy cause, they represent themselves as having done the above, and they threaten to do worse, on the ground that they (the Jews) refuse to be baptized.

Wherefore, placed as under a new Egyptian enslavement, and fearing their extermination, the Jews turned to, and humbly besought mercy from the Apostolic Throne.

Therefore, lest such temerity if unpunished, continue to injure still others, we command that each one of you force the inhabitants of your dioceses who commit such excesses, to bring proper satisfaction for the crimes perpetrated against the Jews and for the property stolen from them. After giving due warning you may use ecclesiastical punishment without appeal.[113]

In his letter to the bishops of western France the pope enjoined that each "force the inhabitants of your dioceses who commit such excesses, to bring proper satisfaction for the crimes perpetrated against the Jews and for the property stolen from them."[114] While the attackers were in most instances Crusaders and hence technically under the jurisdiction of ecclesiastical courts, the pope realized that, in actuality, the most powerful force in northern France was the monarchy and that Louis IX was already celebrated for his dedication to the Christian faith and to justice. For this reason the pope addressed an important epistle to Louis, describing and condemning again the outrages and eloquently enjoining the king to prosecute the criminals.

Since, however it is for kings to render judgment, and do justice, for in the words of the Prophet—"The honor of a king loves judgment, and justice and judgment are the foundations of his throne," and, "to free the oppressed from the hand of those who pursue them with force," therefore, we ask Your Royal Excellency and we warn you and urge you in the name of the Lord, to use the power with which God entrusted you, to correct and to punish those who in their rashness dare commit these crimes so unspeakably and terribly offensive to God in whose image the victims were created, and so injurious to the Apostolic Throne whose privileges they have been granted. Force the crusaders to restore to the Jews all that has been

---

[113]Grayzel, *The Church and the Jews in the XIIIth Century*, pp. 226-29.
[114]Ibid., pp. 228-29.

stolen: that you may prove yourself by an exhibition of good works, to be one who hates iniquity and loves justice. Thus may we be able to commend to God the meritorious zeal of your sincerity.[115]

The papal exhortation to Louis may have had its effects. A number of the complaints before the royal inquisitors in 1247 and 1248 relate to punishments imposed for murder of Jews or assaults upon them; some of these probably stem from the incidents of 1236.[116] The complaints, while denying the charges upon which imprisonment or fines had been based, do reveal royal officialdom in northwestern France assessing stiff penalties on Christians accused of assault upon Jews.

The second major eruption of violence was also associated with the Crusades. This incident took place while Louis himself was abroad in 1251. In northern France, a popular crusading movement developed, led by the so-called Master of Hungary. Growing rapidly and attracting outcast elements in society, this bizarre aggregation made its way southward and found itself even dignified by an interview with the regent herself. Unchecked by encounters with the central authorities, this band split in a number of directions, moving westward through the Seine and Loire valleys and southward towards Bourges. The paths of these marauders were marked by pillage and devastation, with the primary targets seemingly the clergy and the well-to-do. It was almost inevitable that such an anarchic movement should turn its fury against the Jews. This happened finally in Bourges, where the Jews were attacked and despoiled in their synagogue. By this time, reaction had begun to set in against the attackers, and before long the groups had been curbed and dispersed.[117]

On the one hand, these incidents reveal a France still dedicated to preservation of internal peace and still able to suppress and punish popular excesses; it remains true nevertheless that the religious zeal evoked by the mid-century Crusades, by royal enthusiasm for those expeditions, and by royal despoiling of the Jews encouraged the growth of anti-Jewish sentiment and perhaps fostered the feeling that violence could be committed with relative impunity.

---

[115] Ibid., pp. 228–31.

[116] *RHF*, vol. 24, p. 114, doc. no. 171; p. 211, doc. no. 1410; p. 213, doc. no. 1429; p. 227, doc. no. 1575; p. 229, doc. no. 1588; p. 234, doc. no. 1637.

[117] On the Master of Hungary, see Berger, *Histoire de Blanche de Castille*, pp. 393–401, and Norman Cohn, *The Pursuit of the Millennium*, rev. ed. (New York, 1970), pp. 82–87. For evidence of attacks on Jews, see Adolphe Cheruel, ed., *Normanniae nova chronica* (Caen, 1850), pp. 23–24.

The discussion of royal attempts to stifle Jewish moneylending has already suggested a precipitous decline in Jewish economic fortunes in northern France. Such a decline is extremely difficult to document. We have noted already the general disappearance of loan documents as one index of the effectiveness of the governmental campaign. Particularly in the wake of 1253, there seems to be little doubt of the seriousness and success of the royal attempts to root out Jewish usury. The economic alternatives for those Jews who chose to remain in France must have been extremely limited. Moneylending had always drawn the Jews into related commercial activities, but how rewarding these pursuits were is questionable. The inference must necessarily be a period of substantial impoverishment.

There is one brief insight available on declining Jewish economic fortunes contained in the tax records for Champagne for the year 1252.[118] The record, already cited, is remarkably thorough in its accounting, showing normal revenues listed bailliage by bailliage and then adding a variety of special incomes as well. The impression is one of an almost complete overview of the financial resources of the county. The most striking items for our purposes are the net income of approximately 50,000 pounds, the 20,000 pounds paid by the Lombards of the county, and the 521 pounds paid by the Jews. The sum listed for the Jews is significant in a number of senses. In the first place, back in the early 1220's the Jewish community of Champagne had been assessed a fine of 70,000 pounds over a five-year period—almost 15,000 pounds per annum.[119] The decline is obvious. In the second place, the contrast between income from Lombards and from Jews is sharp. The Lombards are clearly the wealthy moneylending element in Champenois society. Finally, within the total revenues of the county, a sum of almost 50,000 pounds, the Jewish contribution represents a meager one percent, an accurate gauge of the economic catastrophe that had struck the community.

The period from 1223 to 1270 saw not only economic decline; it saw a slip in political status as well. This deterioration was, in one sense, merely an intensification of the tendencies initiated during the reign of Philip Augustus. Designs for the exploitation of Jewish wealth had already led Philip to limit Jewish population movement—a development that was correctly perceived by the Jewish leadership as a serious loss of political dignity. The general nonretention clauses of 1223 and 1230

---

[118] Longnon, *Documents relatifs au comté de Champagne et de Brie*, vol. 3, pp. 8-16.
[119] See above.

represented a far more effective method of controlling Jewish movement than the bilateral treaties struck by Philip; they were ipso facto a
step further in the political degradation of the Jews. The articulation of
the right to seize runaway Jews and of the responsibility to force recalcitrant barons to hand over such Jews only added to the realities of
political deterioration. A classic expression of the economically-based
limitation of Jewish status can be found in the *Coutume d'Anjou et de
Touraine*.[120] There the question of legal jurisdiction over the Jews was
raised. The cases adduced involved a conflict of jurisdictions—a royal
Jew bringing suit against a baron's man or a baron's Jew bringing suit
against a vassal's man. The position taken was that the case must be
brought before the possessor of the Jew, because the Jew's goods essentially belong to the king or the barons. The economic rights over the
property of the Jew thrust him even more deeply into the political
grasp of the governmental authority who "held" him.

The terminological culmination of this tendency came in the Melun
ordinance of 1230. There it was stipulated that a Jew who left his land
for another domain might be seized by his original holder "tanquam
proprium servum," as his serf, no matter what custom the Jews might
enjoy under the rule of another overlord or in another kingdom.[121] The
equation of Jewish status to that of serfs had been implied ever since
the first nonretention treaties. The earlier adoption in English circles of
overt expressions of Jewish serfdom may have had its impact as well.[122]
William of Chartres, it will be recalled, has Louis basing his anti-usury
legislation on the contention that the Jews were directly subject to
royal authority.[123]

While Louis himself began to develop his view of Jewish serfdom in a
new direction, many of the barons of northern France continued to
claim their possessory rights over the Jews, with concern for economic
gain still uppermost in their minds. Thus, for example, the great confiscations of 1268 gave rise to a series of complaints before Parliament,

---

[120] Paul Viollet, ed., *Les établissements de Saint Louis*, 4 vols. (Paris 1881–86), vol. 3, p.
82.

[121] *Layettes*, vol. 2, doc. no. 2083. For an overview of "Jewish serfdom" during this period,
see Baron, *A Social and Religious History of the Jews*, vol. 11, pp. 4–13, and the copious
literature cited in the notes. The reference to the customs enjoyed by Jews elsewhere may
reflect the type of Jewish complaints recorded in the name of R. Isaac of Dampierre (see above,
chapter 3, n. 48).

[122] Salo Baron, "Medieval Nationalism and Jewish Serfdom," *Studies and Essays in Honor
of Abraham A. Neuman*, ed. Meir Ben-Horin et al. (Leiden, 1962), pp. 31–37.

[123] *RHF*, vol. 20, p. 34. Christian emphasis on Jewish subjugation is reflected also in Jewish
literature of the period. See Rosenthal, *Sepher Joseph Hamekane*, pp. 62, 67.

charging that royal officials had arrested nonroyal Jews or had confiscated their goods. Investigation was made and, when the baronial allegations were substantiated, redress was made.[124] Slightly before these events, the count of Champagne accused the count of Grandpré of usurping rights over a number of his Jews.[125] It was in order to obviate such conflicts that, on occasion, lists would be drawn up of Jews belonging to a specific lord. Records of Jews belonging to the count of Champagne have survived for the towns of Troyes, Bray, Montereau, and Villemaur; these lists were intended to solidify the legal claim of the Champenois authorities.[126]

During this period, there emerged a new challenge to the rights exercised by the barony over the Jews. The municipalities of northern France, ever striving to expand their powers, represented a more serious threat than heretofore. Thus, the counts of Champagne, dispensers of many town charters during the years between 1230 and 1270, emphasized in these grants their own retention of certain prerogatives, including jurisdiction over the Jews.[127] The barons seem to have been relatively successful in holding the line against the municipalities in this respect. The parliamentary decision of 1260 to give the town authorities rights over converted Jews reveals the ongoing efforts of the municipalities and implies that Jews who retained their faith must have continued to fall under baronial jurisdiction.[128] The one meager reflection of any municipal success in securing rights over Jews is an agreement on the taxes which the burghers of Troyes might impose; these included a sales tax to be levied on the Jews of the town.[129]

In view of this fundamentally economic concern with the Jews, it is striking that little evidence on Jewish taxation remains. We have already noted the record of Champenois revenues for 1252 and the indication of relatively insignificant income from the Jews. It seems highly likely that the most important sums were realized from the Jews as a result of the major confiscations of 1234, 1247–1248, and 1268, with addi-

---

[124]*Olim*, vol. 1, p. 791, case no. 4; p. 793, case no. 7; p. 811, case no. 32; p. 821, case no. 16.

[125]Félix Bourquelot, *Études sur les foires de Champagne*, 2 vols. (Paris, 1865), vol. 2, p. 163.

[126]Arbois de Jubainville, *Histoire des ducs et des comtes de Champagne*, vol. 5, doc. nos. 2792–95.

[127]See, for example, *Layettes*, vol. 2, doc. nos. 2075 (Provins), 2134 (Saint-Mange), 2153 (Châtillon-sur-Marne), 2170 (Saint-Florentin); and Longnon, *Documents relatifs au comté de Champagne et de Brie*, vol. 2, pp. 40 (Villemaur), 56 (Bar-sur-Aube).

[128]*Olim*, vol. 1, p. 482, case no. 17.

[129]*Layettes*, vol. 2, doc. no. 2910.

tional revenues deriving from the goods of those Jews expelled in 1253. Despite the serious efforts of some barons—primarily the king himself— to free themselves from the stigma of utilization of Jewish usury, substantial riches were amassed for the royal and baronial treasuries.

Along with the enhanced control of Jewish affairs, which was merely a continuation of the policies of Philip Augustus, the second major element in the decline of Jewish political status was the introduction, largely by Louis himself, of ecclesiastical notions of governmental culpability for Jewish misdeeds. In a certain sense, this new emphasis flowed from the deepening alliance between the Jews and the barony. According to William of Chartres, Louis saw himself as responsible for the presence of the Jews on French soil and hence felt personally accountable for rigorous control of their behavior. Crimes on their part would mean that the Christian commonwealth had been polluted through him, an abhorrent thought for a monarch so deeply devoted to both the spotlessness of his own soul and the purity of his realm.[130] These notions represent another serious blow to Jewish political standing in northern France; the actions which they unleashed were crucial in the precipitous decline in Jewish affairs during this period.

It is significant that the three major confiscations noted above all correspond to the beginnings of important crusading efforts. While attempts had been made to rationalize Philip Augustus's seizure of Jewish property on religious grounds, it seems highly probable that the confiscations ordered by his grandson were in fact motivated by pious purposes. Twelfth-century ecclesiastical leaders had already suggested that ill-gotten Jewish gains should be used to finance holy expeditions.[131] Unless the proximity of these three confiscations to the onset of the Crusades be merely an unusual coincidence, it seems likely that Louis himself, and on occasion others with him, picked up such notions and translated them into practice.

Given the concerted attack on Jewish life, it might well be anticipated that the agencies of Jewish self-government found themselves unusually pressed during the decades of the mid century. Unfortunately the decline in Jewish source materials stemming from the campaign against the Talmud precludes the possibility of tracing Jewish communal endeavor in any detail.

There is no reason to suppose any basic diminution in the role of the institutions of Jewish self-government, in terms of their liaison function

---

[130]*RHF*, vol. 20, p. 34.
[131]See above, chapter 2.

with the non-Jewish rulers or in terms of their control of Jewish affairs from within. The condemnation of the Talmud certainly brought in its wake a decline in the caliber of communal leadership—at least of that segment of leadership whose authority derived from Jewish learning. In some instances a major leader, for example, R. Yehiel of Paris, felt the necessity for withdrawing;[132] ultimately, the learned leadership of the community was unable to reproduce itself. By the later years of Louis's reign, there was, for the first time since the eleventh century, no individual of commanding rabbinic stature functioning simultaneously in a leadership capacity in Jewish affairs. In view of this decline in scholarly elite, it is not surprising that no centralizing figure, like that of R. Jacob Tam, emerged. While the Jewish community was no longer able to generate unification from within, the non-Jewish rulers, whose interest in economic profit from the Jews was declining, exhibited no serious external interest in centralization of Jewish communal authority.

The leadership of the Jewish community was preoccupied during this period with responding to the serious assaults leveled against Jewish life. Since the basis for those attacks lay fundamentally in ecclesiastical programs, it is not surprising that much of the focus of Jewish energies was directed towards the Church. Particularly striking are the incidents of Jewish entreaty at the papal courts. Jewish leaders appeared in order to protest the excesses stemming from both the anti-usury campaign and the direct assault on the Talmud. Generally, these leaders received a sympathetic hearing and in some instances elicited significant papal pronouncements.[133]

In some cases Jewish leadership, particularly scholarly leadership, was forced to present itself in direct confrontations associated with the attacks on Jewish religious life. Thus, for example, when the charges were leveled against the Talmud, Jewish authorities were called upon to appear as witnesses for the defense. It was in such unhappy circumstances that key figures, such as R. Yehiel of Paris, stepped forward as representatives for northern French Jewry.[134] By the end of the reign of Saint Louis, the focus had shifted from the extirpation of blasphemy in Jewish literature to an engagement of the two faiths in direct debate. Once again men of stature were called upon to shoulder heavy responsi-

---

[132] See above.

[133] See, for example, Grayzel, *The Church and the Jews in the XIIIth Century*, pp. 200-203, 226-31, 268-69, 274-81.

[134] See above.

bilities. Joinville's reminiscences include mention of such an incident at Cluny.[135] By far the most serious of these debates took place in Paris under the inspiration of the convert Paul Christian.[136]

When we look into the spiritual life of northern French Jewry at this juncture, we sense an atmosphere of deep disarray. Part of the dejection flowed from the unremitting physical and material attacks mounted against the Jews; part, however, resulted from the intellectual and religious crisis of the period.

During the early years of the reign of Louis IX, the northern French intellectual elite continued to be looked upon with great respect and reverence by neighboring Jewish communities. When the issue of philosophic heterodoxy arose for a second time in the early 1230's, the leading anti-Maimunist figures turned once more to the intellectual leaders of northern French Jewry, acknowledged for their supremacy in mastery of the Talmud. R. Solomon b. Abraham, the leader of the anti-Maimunist forces, claimed that he had not approached the rabbis of northern France for a ban of excommunication; he had, however, solicited their support against the Maimunist forces opposing him. His admiration for the scholarship and the religious purity of his brethren in northern France ran deep.[137]

Those figures who were not wholeheartedly anti-Maimunist or who were even pro-Maimunist expressed admiration for some facets of northern French intellectual prowess. Thus Nachmanides, who had doubts as to the ban imposed by the northern French rabbis, addressed them nonetheless in tones of utmost respect. A major portion of his letter is given over to effusive praise of the addressees and repeated protestations that he was not rejecting the supposed ban but was only seeking to understand it fully.[138] On the other hand, the Jewish community of Narbonne, which openly opposed the alleged northern French ban on the study of Maimonides and which vigorously attacked northern French Jewry and its leadership in order to counter the effects of this ban, nonetheless recognized northern mastery of Talmudic lore: "Although they are masterful and brilliant in the wisdom of the Talmud, their very brilliance leads them to error."[139]

---

[135] John of Joinville, *The Life of St. Louis*, pp. 35–36.

[136] See below.

[137] Joseph Shatzmiller, "Towards a Picture of the First Maimonidean Controversy" (Hebrew), *Zion* 34 (1969): 127–30.

[138] *Kovez Teshuvot ha-Rambam*, 3 vols. (Leipzig, 1859), vol. 3, pp. 8–10.

[139] Shatzmiller, "Towards a Picture of the First Maimonidean Controversy," p. 144. On the letter in general, see ibid., pp. 135–37.

With the conquest of the south by the monarchy, the links between the Jewries of Languedoc and Languedoiel increased. At the outset of the new Maimonidean conflict, some of the intellectual leaders of northern France seem to have remained relatively unaware of the philosophic writings of R. Moses b. Maimon, around which the controversy swirled; they seem to have known only the *halachic* works of the North African genius. If the account of R. Solomon is to be believed, the first reaction of the northern French leadership was "letters of rebuke" phrased in generalities. These were followed by more serious examination of the books and practices in question and then by a specific ban on the study of such literature. Segments of northern French Jewry were thus forced into direct contact with the new philosophic thinking permeating southern France and Spain.[140]

While the response to southern philosophy was negative, a key northern leader of the 1230's, R. Moses of Coucy, shows extensive admiration for Maimonides the legalist, quoting him copiously and to some extent shaping his own magnum opus in accord with Maimonidean organizational principles.[141] The same R. Moses of Coucy is also the first major northern French figure to exhibit familiarity with the new teaching of the *Hasidim* of Germany.[142] The overall impression is a Jewish community much less segregated than heretofore from intellectual developments elsewhere in the Jewish world, forced to familiarize itself with new doctrines, and in some instances responding positively to these new patterns of thought.

Under other circumstances these new currents would have invigorated Jewish intellectual life. While there might have been temporary dislocation, before long these new views would probably have been usefully integrated into the religious outlook of the community. In this case, however, the new teachings intruded at a most inauspicious point in the development of northern French Jewry, the point at which the Church was expending great effort to suppress important elements in the Jewish religious tradition and to lure weakened Jews into the Christian fold. While the attack leveled in Paris by Nicholas Donin was aimed at revealing the offensive materials in classic Jewish sources, the assault led by his fellow apostate, Paul Christian, some thirty years later was a direct attempt to utilize Jewish learning in order to convince belea-

---

[140] Ibid., pp. 127-30.

[141] R. Moses of Coucy, *Sefer Miẓvot Gadol* (Jerusalem, 1961 [reprint]). On R. Moses in general, see Urbach, *Ba'aley ha-Tosafot*, pp. 384-95.

[142] Ibid., pp. 386-88; Jacob Katz, *Exclusiveness and Tolerance: Studies in Jewish-Gentile Relations in Medieval and Modern Times* (London, 1961), pp. 102-5.

guered Jews of the truth of the majority faith which they had so long resisted.[143]

The Jewish writings of the period reflect the heightened intensity of this Christian assault. The major polemic work, *Sepher Joseph Hamekane*, is devoted primarily to refuting claims of Christological references in the Hebrew Scriptures. New allegations are also rebutted, for example the contention that usury from Christians is forbidden to the Jews or the slander that Jews utilize Christian blood.[144] It is particularly noteworthy that the author introduces occasional anti-Christian materials into his discussion. In fact, the concluding section of the book is devoted to a careful and critical anaylsis of the Gospels.[145] While rebuttals of Christian claims were perhaps intended to serve as guidelines for self-defense in interfaith argumentation, anti-Christian statements could not be openly aired in Jewish-Christian debate. Surely such materials were intended primarily to buttress the faith of Jews who were being subjected to a totally new kind of frontal attack.

A serious concern with Jewish despair and wavering is reflected in the author's introductory observations to *Sepher Joseph Hamekane*.

> Behold I have named this book *Joseph ha-Mekane*. In the heavens is my witness that I have not been moved to arrange this material for self-aggrandizement. I have done this rather for two reasons. The first is because I have become exceedingly zealous for the God of Israel, while I have seen the rebellious among my people leaving the well-spring of living waters to seek after chimera, attempting to utilize the prophets of truth in order to establish the reputation of the corpse, to turn in the direction of deceitful lies. May the All-Knowing smite them mightily. . . . For the word of the Lord will be established forever; it may suffer neither addition nor detraction. Rather one must inform all men of understanding, in a manner clear and explicit, that—since the misfortune which the prophets foretold has come upon us (investigate carefully—not one has been lacking)—it must be known and believed, without wavering left or right, that the consolation will bloom forth.[146]

There follows then a detailed review of the Biblical promises of consolation, designed to assure readers of the inevitability of divine intervention on behalf of the Jews.[147]

---

[143] See below.
[144] Rosenthal, *Sepher Joseph Hamekane*, pp. 53-54, 61-62.
[145] Ibid., pp. 125-38.
[146] Ibid., pp. 15-16.
[147] Ibid., pp. 16-25.

There are a number of indications that the suppression of Jewish classics, the open debates, and the resultant waverings of Jewish faith took their toll during the middle portion of the century. The number of references, in both ecclesiastical communications and royal records, to converted Jews seems to increase sharply. Louis, who was, expectably, concerned with such accretions to the faith, was particularly generous with these new Christians.[148]

The fate of these converts is generally obscure. The bulk of them lived out their days in the shadows, slowly finding their way fully into the Christian community. A few, however, became prominent. Some of these converts achieved renown for their participation in the intensified assault on Jewish belief. These did more than simply abandon their ancestral faith; they used their familiarity with Jewish learning and practice to contribute to the attack being mounted against it. While Paul Christian is almost certainly not of northern French extraction, northern French converts such as Nicholas Donin and Theobald of Sens added significantly to the developing fund of information on Jewish life and ultimately sharpened the severity of the campaign against Judaism.[149]

In some instances, converts achieved renown in the opposite direction, that is, by reversion to the faith of their forebearers. These cases of relapse, along with the anticipated punishment, seem to have made a profound impression in Christian circles. One such incident is preserved in an anonymous journal depicting Parisian life in the late 1260's.

In that year [1268], a certain accursed Jew was seized; he had been a Christian for twenty years or more, had taken a wife according to Christian law, and through her had sired Christian children, of whom he subsequently caused two to be circumcised and to Judaize with him. On the Sunday prior to the Feast of St. Vincent, at St. Anthony near Paris, with a multitude of good men in attendance—for those who attended received major indulgences from the bishop—the accused was stripped of orders by the bishop, was degraded, and was turned over to the secular court. On the following Thursday—after he had chosen for himself fire rather than to return to the Christian faith, asserting that if all the kindling of Paris were gathered and ignited and he thrown into the midst he would not be burned by that fire—he was led into the square where hogs were sold in Paris and

---

[148] Note the material in Le Nain de Tillemont, *Vie de Saint Louis, roi de France*, 6 vols. (Paris, 1847-51), vol. 5, pp. 296-98, and in Alexandre Bruel, "Notes de Vyon d'Herouval sur les baptisés et les convers au temps de saint Louis," *BEC* 28 (1867): 609-21.

[149] Rosenthal, "The Talmud on Trial," p. 69.

there, bound fast, he was totally consumed by the fire, so that nothing remained unburned either of his body or of his limbs. Then his ashes were strewn throughout the adjacent fields.[150]

A second case of relapse is described by Eudes Rigaud, archbishop of Rouen, in his register.

> April 18 (1266). With God's grace we preached near the Mare-du-Parc, where the clergy and people of Rouen had collected after marching thither in a procession. Here we adjudged and condemned as an apostate and heretic one who had been converted from Judaism to the Catholic faith. He had again reverted from the Catholic faith to Judaic depravity, and, once again baptized, had once more reverted to Judaism, being unwilling afterwards to be restored to the Catholic faith, although several times admonished to do so. He was then burned by the bailiff.[151]

Obviously the path into the Christian faith was not always a smooth one.

In general, this was a period during which material decline and aggressive Christian religious attack combined to produce occasional confusion and despair within the Jewish community of northern France. Recognition of the problem and pride in the ability of the majority of northern French Jews to hold fast to their faith is reflected in an exchange between Christian and Jew created in a Hebrew polemic work:

> The Unbeliever: There is a major proof for our faith in that there is no people lowlier than the Jews.

> The Believer: Just the opposite! It is a major proof for *our* faith, for nonetheless we remain steadfast in it.[152]

The crusading years of the mid thirteenth century were trying for the Jews of northern France. There was more than simply fear of physical assault by exhilarated Crusaders—although that did happen both in 1236 and in 1251; there was also the more pervasive danger of heightened religiosity and the issues that might be raised in its wake. The Crusade of the late 1230's had seen not only the onslaughts in western France; the same years had also witnessed a major expulsion, a general

---

[150] Léopold Delisle, "Notes sur quelques mss. du Musée britannique," *Mémoires de la Société de l'Histoire de Paris* 4 (1877): 189.

[151] Brown and O'Sullivan, *The Register of Eudes of Rouen*, p. 618.

[152] Bibliotèca nazionale, Rome, Hebrew manuscript no. 53, 24b.

confiscation of Jewish goods probably related to the Crusade, a total prohibition of Jewish usury, and the disastrous attack on Talmudic literature. The period between 1248 and 1252, the time of Louis's first crusading misfortune, also saw physical attack, confiscation, and the sharply worded prohibition of usury, stipulating expulsion for those who refused to accept the new orders and severe punishment for transgressors. It was undoubtedly with deep trepidation that the Jews heard of renewed royal crusading plans in the late 1260's. Unfortunately for these Jews, many of their worst fears were confirmed.

On September 15, 1268, a general confiscation took place in the royal domain, in the county of Champagne, and in the domain of Alphonse of Poitiers. While the edict itself has not survived, we can confidently suggest a direct link between the seizure and the impending Crusade. Seven days after the confiscation, an order was issued by the clergy of Champagne decreeing excommunication for all those hiding Jewish goods.[153] Such ecclesiastical concern with a baronial confiscation of Jewish property surely reflects a relation to some major Church program—a Crusade, for example. The royal officials were zealous in their conduct of this seizure. Jews were taken far and wide, in many instances Jews not belonging to the confiscating authorities. Parliament, in 1270, had to deal with a number of complaints leveled by barons whose Jews had been indiscriminately seized in 1268.[154] Louis and Theobald of Champagne each had found a number of their Jews residing in the domain of the other. Since they had both been party to the confiscation, they agreed to avoid expensive litigation and to allow each to hold the Jews of the other seized during the general capture.[155] Finally, the confiscation, like the earlier one of 1247, involved more than private property of the Jews; Jewish public facilities were sequestered as well. Thus, in February 1269, Theobald of Champagne allowed the Jews of Provins to purchase new land to replace the cemetery which recently had been taken over by the comital authorities.[156]

The material losses of 1268 were only the beginning of the misfortunes of Louis's final years. The next set of problems stemmed from

[153]Arbois de Jubainville, *Histoire des ducs et des comtes de Champagne*, vol. 5, doc. no. 3526. Documents concerning this confiscation and the Jews of Alphonse of Poitiers can be found in de Vic and Vaissète, *Histoire générale de Languedoc*, vol. 8, pp. 1656–61.

[154]*Olim*, vol. 1, p. 791, case no. 4; p. 793, case no. 7; p. 811, case no. 32; p. 821, case no. 16.

[155]*Layettes*, vol. 4, doc. no. 5488.

[156]Arbois de Jubainville, *Histoire des ducs et des comtes de Champagne*, vol. 5, doc. no. 3526.

the arrival in northern France of the second of the important converted Jews of the reign of Louis IX, Paul Christian.

Paul Christian had been baptized, had joined the Dominican order, and, like Nicholas Donin, had begun to use his knowledge of Jewish sources to attack his former coreligionists. His first area of activity was Spain. There he continued Donin's effort to expurgate Jewish classics of suspected blasphemy. Paul, however, moved far beyond a negative assault on rabbinic literature to a more positive attempt to debate the issues of Jewish faith and to gain thereby new converts to Christianity. His most impressive achievement was the public disputation into which he forced the eminent R. Moses b. Nahman. From Spain he moved on to southern France and from there northward to the capital of the Capetian kingdom.[157]

In the late 1260's, Paul made his way to Paris, arriving as Louis IX prepared for his second Crusade. He found the monarch in a mood of utmost receptivity and brilliantly exploited the situation. The king was profoundly impressed by his new Dominican advisor and, under his spell, introduced a number of radical innovations concerning the Jews.

The Church's drive to segregate the Jews, ostensibly out of fear of their religious influence, was an old feature of ecclesiastical policy. Louis had been faithful in implementing many of the specifics of this policy. Thus, for example, the edict of 1235, besides outlawing usury, had prohibited Christians from functioning as nurses for Jewish children and as servants in Jewish homes, both of longstanding concern to the Church.[158] The most significant new step taken by the Church in its segregation program had been the enactment by the IV Lateran Council of special garb by means of which the Jews might be readily distinguished from their Christian neighbors.[159] This decree was only sporadically executed in northern France, never with the full backing of the monarchy.[160] Now under the influence of Paul Christian and of the impending Crusade, Louis ordered royal enforcement of the Jewish badge.

---

[157]On Paul Christian, see Ernest Renan, *Les rabbins français du commencement du quatorzième siècle* (Paris, 1877), pp. 563–71. On his activities in Spain, see Yitzhak Baer, *A History of the Jews in Christian Spain*, 2 vols. (Philadelphia, 1961–66), vol. 1, pp. 152–59.

[158]Delisle, "Recueil des jugements de l'Echiquier de Normandie," doc. no. 581.

[159]Grayzel, *The Church and the Jews in the XIIIth Century*, pp. 308–9.

[160]There is an interesting testimony by R. Isaac b. Moses of Vienna on the wearing of the badge in France right after the Lateran Council (*Or Zaru'a*, vol. 2, 20a). Grayzel discusses this testimony at length (*The Church and the Jews in the XIIIth Century*, p. 65, n. 112) and concludes that it refers only to a local ordinance. Urbach (*Ba'aley ha-Tosafot*, p. 361, n. 22) rejects Grayzel's suggestion because of the general statement of R. Isaac that "thus it was

Since we wish that the Jews be distinguishable from Christians and be recognizable, we order you that, at the order of our dear brother in Christ, Paul Christian, of the Order of Preaching Brethren, you impose signs upon each and every Jew of both sexes, viz. a circle of felt or yellow cloth, stitched upon the outer garment in front and in back. The diameter of the circle must be four fingers wide; its area must be the size of a palm. If a Jew be found henceforth without the sign, his outer garment shall be ceded to the one who noticed him, and the same Jew found without the sign shall be fined as much as ten pounds.[161]

The anonymous Parisian chronicle quoted earlier indicates that, for the capital at least, the new royal order did not remain a dead letter.

In the same year [1269], on the Thursday after the Translation of St. Martin, on the subsequent Thursday, by royal order and in the presence of the provost, the Jews at Paris were ensigned with a circle of felt, in front and in back on all the clothes which they wore.[162]

Institution of the Jewish badge was only the first of Paul Christian's successes. Already in the early 1260's he had proceeded beyond the attack of Nicholas Donin. While still concerned over the issue of blasphemy in Talmudic literature, he was even more committed to an overt assault on Jewish faith, to be effected by drawing Jews into direct religious argumentation. Rabbinic texts were now utilized in a totally new way, namely, as support for the truth of Christianity. The most famous of these confrontations was that staged in Barcelona in 1263, with the Jewish protagonist the esteemed R. Moses b. Nahman.[163]

In July 1269, Louis issued a royal order to all his officials, enjoining support for the conversionist efforts of Paul Christian.

---

decreed concerning all the Jews at that time." However, the general decree alluded to need not have been a royal decree; R. Isaac may have been referring to the IV Lateran enactment itself. We would thus agree with Grayzel that the early bearing of the badge was a local matter and that only in 1269 was it legislated for all of royal France. Between 1257 and 1263, a number of provincial councils presided over by Archbishop Eudes of Rouen had included a Jewish badge among their decrees (Brown and O'Sullivan, *The Register of Eudes of Rouen*, pp. 325, 441, and 550).

[161] *Ordonnances*, vol. 1, p. 294.

[162] Delisle, "Notes sur quelques mss. du Musée britannique," p. 189. The execution of this edict is further reflected in the southern French polemical treatise of R. Mordechai b. Joseph; see Renan, *Les rabbins français*, p. 567. It is also mentioned in *Shevet Yehudah*, p. 148.

[163] The Barcelona disputation, like the earlier confrontation in Paris, has been widely studied. For an overview, see Baer, *A History of the Jews in Christian Spain*, vol. 1, pp. 152–59.

Since our beloved brother in Christ, Paul Christian of the Order of Preaching Brethren, the bearer of the present letter, wishes and intends, for the glory of the divine name, to preach to the Jews the word of light, in order, we understand, to evangelise for the exaltation of the Christian faith, we order you to force those Jews residing in your jurisdiction to present themselves to hear from him and without objection the word of the Lord and present their books as the aforesaid brother shall require. You shall compel the Jews to respond fully, without calumny and subterfuge, on those matters which relate to their law, concerning which the aforesaid brother might interrogate them, whether in sermons in their synagogues or elsewhere.[164]

Once again, the very useful Parisian chronicle indicates that there was little pause between the edict and its execution.

In the same year (1269), close to Pentecost, a certain brother of the order of Preaching Brethren . . . , came from Lombardy. He had been a Jew and was the highest authority in Mosaic law and in our law. Publicly, in the royal court at Paris and in the court of the Preaching Brethren, he preached to the Jews—who came there by royal order—, showing them that their law was null and worthless, that they had in fact not observed it for a long time, that indeed they daily diverted from all its precepts.[165]

Precisely the kind of confrontation envisioned in the royal order did take place, in Paris at least.

The Jews themselves were not taken totally by surprise. A curious Hebrew document shows northern French Jewry fully aware of the earlier activities of Paul Christian. The document, a manual for anticipating the expected onslaught, began as follows:

Just now in the year 5029 (=1269) an apostate from Montpellier has arrived, revealing secrets of the Torah and questioning the traditions of our Talmud. He has already held a disputation with R. Moses b. Nahman before the Aragonese King in Barcelona.[166]

This is followed by a detailed summary of the arguments raised in the famous Barcelona disputation. The résumé is perfectly accurate and

---

[164] Bibliothèque nationale, fonds Dupuy, vol. 532, 79r.

[165] Delisle, "Notes sur quelques mss. du Musée britannique," p. 189.

[166] Adolf Neubauer, "Literary Gleanings V," *JQR* (old series) 4 (1891–92): 699; cited also by Ephraim Urbach, "Études sur la littérature polémique au moyen-âge," *REJ* 100 (1935): 56. Urbach's description is somewhat misleading. Only p. 21 refers to Paul Christian.

probably served the Jews usefully in the preaching to which they were subjected at Paris.

One further source seems to reflect this new blow. A Hebrew polemic work, described many decades ago and subsequently lost, reveals much information on the confrontation as seen through Jewish eyes.

> These are the responses to the unbeliever who rose up against us in the year 5032. He came from Spain to destroy totally the remnant of Israel, and his name was Paul the Dominican . . . This is the beginning of the words of Paul the heretic, who came from Spain to destroy the remnant of the holy people throughout all the territories of the King of France. He sought to wipe out and obliterate even children and women. . . .

> In the year 5033, the unbeliever Paul came and gathered all the rabbis. Thus he said to them before the bishop of Paris and the heads of the monks who were there: "Listen to me, O house of Jacob and all the clans of the house of Israel. You shall be convinced to repent and to abandon your faith in the face of the compelling claims that I shall reveal to you. I shall not rest till I am avenged of you, and I shall demand your blood. Indeed I wish to prove that you are faithless, a people of 'Bougres,' fit to be burned. I shall inform you of the charges; on each you should be judged guilty of a capital crime. Now send for your greatest sages and answer me without delay. For thus have I been commanded by the king, to bring you to your deserved end. . . . "

> Know that each day we were over a thousand souls in the royal court or in the Dominican court, pelted with stones. Praise to our Creator, not one of us turned to the religion of vanity and lies. . . .[167]

Despite the discrepancies in date, the Hebrew description corresponds accurately to the royal ordinance and to the Latin account. The king's order is cited in both chronicles; the scene is the royal court and Dominican headquarters; the same Paul appears. According to both accounts, the Latin and the Hebrew, Paul's assault seems to have taken a serious new turn. He set out to prove that the Jews were far from observing their own Talmudic law and that they deserved to be prose-

---

[167] Adolph Neubauer, "Literary Gleanings VIII," *JQR* (old series) 5 (1892-93): 714. Neubauer rejects the identification with Paul Christian because of the designation חובל, which he takes to mean "cordelier" or Franciscan. The parallels to other data make it obvious, however, that the reference is to the Dominican Paul Christian. What is called for is reinvestigation of the term חובל.

cuted as a totally faithless people, the alternative being of course conversion to Christianity. This is a departure from both Donin's condemnation of Talmudic blasphemy and Paul's earlier attempt to use Talmudic sources to prove the veracity of Christian faith. How thoroughly this new approach was developed cannot be ascertained in the absence of the remainder of the Hebrew account.

The final years of King Louis represent unquestionably the nadir of Jewish fortunes in northern France. The community's economic activities had been sharply curtailed, it had just suffered a major confiscation, the most radical ecclesiastical policy of segregation had been legislated into effect by the king, and now the very right of the Jews to live as Jews had once more been questioned in the conversionist efforts of Paul Christian.

On the afternoon of August 25, 1270, off the coast of North Africa, the most pious of French kings expired. As the news reached northern France, the Jews could scarcely have participated deeply in the mourning over the soon-to-be-sainted monarch. The more than four decades of his rule had been an unmitigated disaster. These Jews might well have wondered apprehensively what the reign of Louis's son held in store.

V

PHILIP IV—REVIVAL AND RUIN

I T WAS THE UNFORTUNATE FATE of Philip III to be obscured by the long and dynamic reigns of both his father and his son. The fifteen years between 1270 and 1285 represent a shadowy transition between the piety of Saint Louis and the *raison d'état* of Philip the Fair.[1]

At the outset of Philip's reign, the monarchy was strengthened territorially by the death of Alphonse of Poitiers without heir and the subsequent reversion of his lands to the crown. Philip himself engineered the addition of vast and wealthy eastern domains through the marriage of his son to the heiress to the county of Champagne.

This territorial growth, however, does not seem to have been matched by aggressive and purposeful administration. Louis's advisors played a major role in controlling court affairs, and the members of the royal family exerted an influence on governmental policy that was unusual in the annals of the Capetian monarchy. Philip himself does not appear as a commanding figure at the center of a powerful administration.

---

[1] The best treatment of Philip III is that of Charles-Victor Langlois, *Le règne de Philippe III le Hardi* (Paris, 1887). Langlois also wrote the brief section on Philip in Ernest Lavisse, *Histoire de France*, 9 vols. in 18 (Paris, 1900–1911), vol. 3, pt. 2.

At the same time, the administrative machinery which Louis had begun to fashion for his expanding holdings must have been cultivated, so that a full-blown bureaucracy could emerge under Philip IV. Also the shift in values away from the ecclesiastical orientation of Saint Louis towards the secular statecraft of his grandson must have been underway, despite the acknowledged religiosity of Philip III himself. A transitional reign necessarily implies such development, as difficult as it may be to trace the process in detail.

The period between 1270 and 1285 surely represents a transition for the Jews of northern France. As is the case for the broader changes in French society, details are sparse. French Jewry, however, as it emerges into clearer light in the late 1280's, will have changed substantially from the shattered community of the last years of Saint Louis.[2]

For the Jews of northern France, the reign of Philip III must have been a welcome respite. While there was concerted royal effort to preserve Louis's anti-Jewish innovations, some of these programs were allowed to lapse. The decade and a half of Philip's rule are marred by no major demographic upheavals and no discernible physical assault. Jewish moneylending, successfully prohibited by Louis, began to revive, renewing the economic viability of Jewish life. For the Jews, this was a period of rebuilding and revival.

Philip III, though not cutting the same saintly figure as his illustrious father, was nonetheless seriously committed to the execution of ecclesiastical policy, particularly to the continuation of his father's efforts in that direction. Thus, on September 23, 1271, shortly after his return to Paris and his assumption of the reins of government, Philip renewed Louis's enactment of the Jewish badge, strictly enjoining his royal officials that the edict be enforced.[3] Sometime thereafter, still early in his reign, Philip again renewed the badge, along with his father's prohibition of Jewish moneylending.[4] Royal concern with segregation of the Jews was not limited to instituting special insignia. In 1280 Parliament reenacted into law the traditional Church demand that Christians not function in Jewish houses as servants or nurses.[5]

---

[2] For the fate of the Jews during this period, see Georg Caro, *Sozial- und Wirtschaftsgeschichte der Juden im Mittelalter und der Neuzeit*, 2 vols. (Frankfort, 1908–20), vol. 2, and Salo Baron, *A Social and Religious History of the Jews*, 2nd ed., 14 vols. (New York, 1952–69), vol. 10.

[3] *Ordonnances*, vol. 1, p. 312, where the act is undated. Another copy, however, in the Bibliothèque nationale, fonds Dupuy, vol. 532, 111r, gives the date as September 23, 1271.

[4] *Ordonnances*, vol. 3, p. 323.

[5] *Olim*, vol. 2, p. 158, case no. 13.

In one respect, Philip went beyond the segregation legislation of his predecessor. In April 1276, the Exchequer of Normandy registered a decree expelling the Jews from the villages of France.[6] The concern was over the impact of the Jews on the villagers, who were apt to be unlettered and unsophisticated and also likely to have far more contact with local Jews than would urban burghers.

Philip's major pronouncement on the issue of the Jews came on April 19, 1283. This ordinance, like the edicts of Louis IX, bears the unmistakable imprint of ecclesiastical policy, which the king proudly avows in his preamble.

(1) Since nothing reflects more glory on a prince than zeal for the faith, unceasingly devoted to the promotion and exaltation of the Christian faith, we order and require—in accordance with the statute already enacted—that Jews, so that they may be distinguishable from Christians, bear a badge of felt on their chest and add a second between their shoulders.

(2) Also in accordance with a prohibition already enacted by me, they may not have in their homes Christian nurses, maidservants, or male servants.

(3) Also, they may not institute nor construct new cemeteries or new synagogues, nor may they repair old ones, nor may they chant loudly. When the contrary be found, it must be corrected.

(4) Also, in our kingdom, they may not dwell or reside in small towns, among the rustics; rather they must reside in large towns and in well-known locales, in which they have been accustomed to dwell of yore.

(5) Also, these Jews must not have the Talmud and other books condemned in Paris; rather they must be publicly burned in your territories and in the jurisdictions committed to you.[7]

The concern for the faith proclaimed in the preamble is certainly borne out by the provisions of the ordinance. Most of the items are not new but merely reiterations of earlier legislation. The general thrust of the enactments is defensive. Christians must be protected from the pernicious influence of the Jews; hence the removal of the Jews from villages where contact was likely, the prohibition of Christians serving

---

[6] Ernest Perrot, ed., *Arresta communia Scaccarii* (Caen, 1910), doc. no. 1.

[7] Gustave Saige, *Les Juifs du Languedoc antérieurement au XIVe siècle* (Paris, 1881), pp. 212-13.

in Jewish homes where religious impact might result, and the require-
ment of the Jewish badge so that each Jew could be readily identified
as such. Christian dignity and honor were also to be safeguarded by
outlawing the erection of new religious facilities and by calling once
more for the burning of offensive Jewish literature. The inquisitors had
already played a key role in Jewish affairs, beginning back in the early
1240's. Their role is specifically recognized in this ordinance; they are
empowered to pass judgment on the literary materials brought to their
attention.

Given the substantial backlog of Capetian legislation already in existence, it is important to note not only items that were included in this
major general pronouncement but those items omitted as well. Philip
seems to have retreated to the more defensive stance of the middle
years of his father's reign; he stopped short of the all-out offensive
against the Jewish faith embodied in Louis's 1269 support for the
conversionist preaching of Paul Christian. More significant yet is the
deletion of a key item in Louis's long campaign against the Jews, his
attack on Jewish moneylending. The failure to persevere in Louis's
anti-lending assault must have been a matter of utmost importance for
the Jews. It is the contributing factor to the revitalization of Jewish
economic life, reflected, for example, in the heavy taxation of the latter
decades of the thirteenth century.

In fact, a year prior to the ordinance of 1283, a royal order was
promulgated which reveals the resumption of Jewish moneylending
and, by dealing with some of the technicalities of such lending, im-
plicitly condones this resumption.[8] The two clauses dealing with Jewish
lending provide regulations for the return of pledges held by the Jews
and minimal limitations on the kinds of pledges which Jews might
accept. The measures afford important protection for the Jewish creditor, thus not only recognizing Jewish lending but strengthening it as
well. It is not surprising that the first post-Louis IX legislation on
Jewish lending should deal with pawnbroking transactions. These were
the last financial operations to be outlawed, and they were the first to
be legally resumed. From the point of view of the government, these
were of course the simplest kind of loans, requiring no documentation
and no official involvement.

While formal recognition of at least some kinds of Jewish lending
came in the last years of Philip's reign, it is unlikely that resumption of
usury awaited official governmental sanction. In fact, the regulation of

---

[8] Langlois, *Le règne de Philippe III le Hardi*, pp. 440–41, doc. no. 21.

1282 reflects de facto Jewish lending already in progress. All that was really necessary for renewed Jewish lending was a slackening in governmental concern with the problem. Quite clearly this had already happened long before 1282. Thus, for example, a list of court cases from 1273 to 1275 includes proceedings against the Jews of Orléans for excessive usury.[9] Such a case would have been inconceivable in the final years of the reign of Louis IX, since all usury had been outlawed. Even in the early years of Philip's rule, despite the pious repetition of his father's negation of usury, the Jews had begun to lend once more, and the government was willing to let this happen, prosecuting only instances of exorbitant interest. The slow resumption of usury during the early years of Philip III and the overt recognition of certain kinds of lending by 1282 represent the beginning of a Jewish economic revival, which was more fully realized under Philip IV.

For the government, a Jewry once more financially sound presented itself again as a most tempting source of revenues. Information on standard taxation of the Jews is almost nonexistent for the years between 1270 and 1285. There are signs, however, of special levies upon the Jews during the latter years of the reign. A parliamentary decision of 1282 exempted the wealthy Abraham of Falaise from any contribution to the tallage of 60,000 pounds imposed upon his fellow Jews.[10] While the time span over which this tallage was to be paid is not indicated, 60,000 pounds was certainly a substantial sum of money. As with the resumption of lending, so too with the return of heavy taxation there is an inescapable sense of retreat from the impractical stance of Louis IX towards the worldly policies of Philip Augustus.

In the light of revived Jewish business and the return of utilitarian governmental concern with the Jews, it is not surprising to see a renewal of interest in clearly established control over specific Jews. While such efforts had not disappeared altogether during the days of Saint Louis, they were bound to be intensified with the resurgence of fiscal benefit from the Jews.

One of the last acts of Louis IX had been a major confiscation of Jewish property, carried out in concert with Alphonse of Poitiers and Theobald of Champagne, just prior to departure for the Crusade.[11] The zealousness of royal officials occasioned a number of court cases, in 1270 and 1271, concerning the rights of neighboring barons over cer-

---

[9] Charles-Victor Langlois, ed., *Textes relatifs à l'histoire du Parlement depuis les origines jusqu'en 1314* (Paris, 1888), p. 89.

[10] *Olim*, vol. 3, p. 218, case no. 45.

[11] See above, chapter 4.

tain arrested Jews and their confiscated properties.[12] It is interesting to note that the decisions of Parliament generally favored the barons in their contention against the crown and its agents. A second spate of such litigations surfaced in 1281 and 1282.[13]

The Champenois investigation of the domain of the count from 1276 to 1278 elicited a number of lists of Jews belonging to the count.[14] These lists, reminiscent of those of the mid 1240's, were in all probability not exhaustive accounts of all the Jews in any given locality; they dealt only with those Jews whose status might have been in doubt. They represent, then, another kind of affirmation of baronial prerogatives over specific Jews.

Control of the Jews was claimed not only by the king and the barony; there were other elements in society contesting these rights. For the municipalities, the Jews as an urban element responsible only to royal or baronial jurisdiction still represented a constant source of irritation. While the middle decades of the century had seen some minimal gains by the municipalities in their struggle towards authority over the Jews in their midst, it is significant that the extensive court records surviving from Provins show not a single instance of Jews appearing before the town magistrates. The rights of jurisdiction reserved by the count of Champagne over his Jews seems to have been scrupulously respected.[15] It is also noteworthy that, while the Jews do appear rather often in the financial records from Provins, they are generally cited as tax collectors, tax farmers, or creditors; there is no indication of direct taxation of the Jews by the municipality.[16] In one instance, the question of Jewish obligation to share in municipal burdens was brought before the Exchequer of Normandy. In April 1276, the Exchequer decreed that the Jews of Bernay could not be compelled to aid in the town watch.[17] Once again the lack of municipal rights over the Jews was reaffirmed. The only evidence that reflects any progress in town rights comes from the parliamentary decision of 1275 allowing the commune of Senlis jurisdiction in the case of a Jew charged by a Christian neighbor with attempting to violate the latter's wife.[18] As had

[12] Ibid.

[13] *Olim*, vol. 2, p. 195, case no. 23; p. 196, case no. 30; p. 212, case no. 33.

[14] Auguste Longnon, ed., *Documents relatifs au comté de Champagne et de Brie, 1172-1361*, 3 vols. (Paris, 1901-4), vol. 2, pp. 54-55, 83, 149, 182.

[15] Maurice Prou and S. d'Auriac, eds., *Actes et comptes de la commune de Provins* (Provins, 1933).

[16] Ibid.

[17] Perrot, *Arresta communia Scaccarii*, doc. no. 6.

[18] *Olim*, vol. 2, p. 61, case no. 1.

been the case throughout the century, the monarchy and the barony continued to protect assiduously their prerogatives in the face of continued municipal effort at jurisdictional expansion.

There seems to have been little strife between the barons and the ecclesiastical authorities over the Jews. Here the legacy of Saint Louis was probably still influential. Louis had strenuously attempted to regulate the status of the Jews in accordance with the dictates of the Church and had shown perfect willingness to entrust certain aspects of Jewish affairs, such as the return of usury and the investigation of Jewish books, to ecclesiastical commissions. There is no noticeable rekindling of Church-state friction over the Jews, despite the revival of Jewish lending and the return of more utilitarian governmental policies. The resumption of Jewish lending occasioned no major clerical outcry. On the other hand, Philip was content to support Church influence in those areas where it was appropriate, noting specifically in his clause concerning continued prosecution of the Talmud and other baneful literature that such books were to be brought to the attention of the inquisitors.[19]

The most general and emphatic statement on jurisdiction over the Jews came in the royal decree of 1282, which adopts a positive and protective stance towards the Jews; it has the flavor of a set of guarantees that the Jews themselves may have lobbied for. While the focus in this decree is revived Jewish pawnbroking, there is also an important statement on the sensitive issue of jurisdiction: "It is granted that no Jews be constrained to respond legally except before their bailiffs or their viscounts or to those designated by the bailiffs."[20] This arrangement seems to reflect Jewish desires, as well as royal interest. Unfortunately, the agencies whose jurisdictions are negated are not specified. The most likely possibilities are of course the municipal and ecclesiastical courts; the Jews seem to have felt far safer in the hands of the royal courts than at the mercy of either town or Church.

Turning to the internal affairs of northern French Jewry, we find very little evidence on Jewish community activities and intellectual achievement during this transitional period. The Jewish community and its institutions certainly continued to function during these years—without them Jewish life would have been unthinkable. At the same time, the quality of Jewish communal leadership and the level of Jewish religious creativity do not measure up to the heights achieved by

---

[19] Saige, *Les Juifs du Languedoc*, p. 213.

[20] Langlois, *Le règne de Philippe III le Hardi*, pp. 440-41, doc. no. 21.

northern French Jewry prior to the determined assault by Louis IX. Philip's major legislation on the Jews, the edict of 1283, features prominently the continued ban on the Talmud and on related materials considered offensive to the ruling faith. Not only is the prohibition strongly worded but provisions for its enforcement, including involvement of the inquisitorial agents in France, are included.[21] The impression is that the beginnings of a more utilitarian attitude towards Jewish business affairs, accompanied by an end to the outright attack on Jewish faith initiated by Paul Christian, did not extend to a lessening of anxiety over the injurious results of Talmudic study. In other words, while Jewish economic life was slowly allowed to revive, Jewish intellectual activities remained restricted.

In sum, the general transitional qualities of the reign of Philip III are revealed in the fate of the Jews as well. Loyal in many regards to the legacy of his great father, Philip relaxed the stifling royal pressures in key areas. The Jews can only have greeted these developments with relief. They must have sensed a new lease on life. While some may have lamented the lack of concomitant intellectual renaissance, optimists may well have hoped that the ensuing decades would bring that also. Few could have sensed the ominous overtones in the heavy levies of the early 1280's. Little could they have imagined that the realpolitik of Philip III was but a prelude to that of Philip IV and that a mere two decades of this new and seemingly more permissive policy would bring to a sudden close the rich saga of medieval northern French Jewish history.

Philip IV was the third of the great French monarchs of the thirteenth century. No such close descendant of Saint Louis could fail to pursue ostensibly a program of intimate cooperation with the Church, which his grandfather had so zealously supported. The real direction of Philip's reign, however, lay elsewhere. The primary emphasis of his governance shifted to the worldly sphere, as had been the case with Philip Augustus at the beginning of the century.[22]

The France over which Philip the Fair ruled had grown enormously from the restricted royal domain which Philip Augustus had inherited in 1180. Not only was royal France far larger, the Europe of which it

---

[21] Saige, *Les Juifs du Languedoc*, p. 213.

[22] There has been no detailed treatment of this highly significant reign. The most valuable résumé is that by Langlois in Lavisse, *Histoire de France*, vol. 3, pt. 2. Useful for the purposes of this study is Joseph Strayer, "Consent to Taxation under Philip the Fair," in *Studies in Early French Taxation*, ed. Joseph R. Strayer and Charles H. Taylor (Cambridge, Mass., 1939).

was a part was a century more mature. The result was a set of involvements that fostered new needs and extensive exploitation of the riches of a large and prosperous land. Bureaucratic organization and personnel proliferated, with one major goal—more effective collection of a bewildering set of revenues. The preoccupation with royal income led to the injustices traditionally resulting from an ever-expanding bureaucracy and to most of the causes célèbres of a troubled reign. Serious clashes with the papacy and the destruction of the Order of Knights Templar, masked as they were by concern for refinement of the faith, were in reality reflections of the worldly thrust of the government of Philip the Fair.

For the Jews of northern France, the demise of Saint Louis and of the pious programs which he had fostered had unquestionably been a major boon. Jewish life, while not recovering fully, had begun to show signs of revival, in the economic sphere at least. The possibilities for a full renaissance under a distinctly "worldly" monarch may have seemed promising; there was probably little suspicion that worldly rule, when carried to the extreme, could prove as devastating as the religiosity of Saint Louis. Some sensitive Jews may have been aware of the slow strangulation of English Jewry by the revenue-hungry English rulers of the latter half of the thirteenth century. Even these, however, could probably not have anticipated that by 1290, five years after the accession of Philip the Fair, medieval Anglo-Jewish history would draw to an abrupt end and that a scant sixteen years later their own turn would come.[23]

As governmental concern with the Jews shifted more and more strongly towards financial exploitation, the thoroughgoing attempts of Louis IX to implement Church teachings, particularly in the area of usury, had to fall into neglect. The reign of Philip III had already seen the revival of Jewish lending and an acceptance of this renewal in the legislation of 1282. The policies of Philip IV accelerated the tendency. In April 1287, early in the reign of Philip the Fair, the Exchequer of Normandy proclaimed a curious set of stipulations. Henceforth, no Christian was to be imprisoned for debts owed the Jews, nor was any

---

[23]The most significant studies of the period are once more those of Caro and Baron. Useful are the monographs of Gérard Nahon, "Contribution à l'histoire des Juifs en France sous Philippe le Bel," *REJ* 121 (1962): 59–80, and Lucien Lazard, "Les revenus tirés des Juifs de France dans le domaine royal," *REJ* 15 (1887): 233–61, which concentrates on the reign of Philip IV. Again, Ephraim Urbach's *Ba'aley ha-Tosafot* (Jerusalem, 1955) is helpful.

Christian debtor to be forced to sell his family heritage.[24] This, of course, was not a new policy for royal France. Philip Augustus had made the same provisions in his more inclusive legislation of 1219.[25] These measures, however, had fallen into desuetude as a result of the extreme position on Jewish lending taken by Saint Louis. Once Jewish lending had been totally prohibited, there was no longer any purpose to such partial safeguards. It seems that, by the early years of Philip IV, Jewish lending had revived to the point where certain older abuses had begun to manifest themselves once more and had to be specifically addressed and outlawed. Not only does this royal order reflect the rebirth of certain usury-related practices; it indicates also the reinvolvement of governmental authorities in Jewish business affairs. Long before the outright prohibition of Jewish lending, Saint Louis had taken steps to ensure that his government not be besmirched by support for Jewish lending. Now, a decade and a half since the saintly monarch's death, Jewish lending had begun again; governmental support had been regained; and some older abuses had become sufficiently widespread to arouse the attention of the Exchequer of Normandy.

Sometime during the early 1290's, the revival of Jewish business excited the cupidity of royal officialdom, and a confiscation of Jewish debts was decreed. As soon as this move was undertaken, however, it proved counterproductive. As a result, Philip quickly backtracked. In his ordinance of January 31, 1292, he repudiated the confiscation policy on the grounds that it had interfered with realization of normal revenues from the Jews.[26] He therefore ordered his agents to provide necessary aid to the Jews in the collection of obligations owed them, so that governmental exploitation be in no way impeded. Thus in this ordinance there is overt indication of the resumption of governmental support for Jewish lending, a development which we had already inferred from the first years of Philip's reign.

The ordinance of 1292 contains a second stipulation worthy of some attention. The king provided that "all commercial dealings and contracts which the Jews in the future might lawfully draw up—if it be proven that there be in these contracts special usury—shall be totally forfeited to us."[27] There are two noteworthy aspects to this stipulation. In the first place, the offense is "special usury," reminiscent of the

---

[24] Perrot, *Arresta communia Scaccarii*, doc. no. 143.

[25] See above, chapter 3.

[26] Saige, *Les Juifs du Languedoc*, pp. 228–29.

[27] Ibid., p. 229.

"heavy and immoderate Jewish usury" outlawed by the IV Lateran Council of 1215.[28] Once again there has been a major retreat from the uncompromising stand of Saint Louis, which had totally prohibited Jewish usury. Indeed, by concerning himself with "special usury," Philip IV had in effect condoned normal cases of Jewish usury. While such usury had already resumed, overt governmental approval is significant. The penalty for misdeed—in this instance unduly heavy usury—is also striking. Breach of the law was to be punished by confiscation, which meant direct royal profit. Once again, the contrast with the policies and practices of Saint Louis is instructive. For Louis, the affront to Christian ethics resulting from usury necessitated an extensive effort to return the money extorted as usury or, all else failing, to use those funds for pious purposes.[29] The relentless search for revenues that characterized the reign of Philip IV transformed the crime of "special usury" from an injustice to be remedied into yet another source of royal income.

The period between 1296 and 1300 represented a lull in serious strife between Philip IV and the Church. The years immediately prior to 1296 had seen skirmishing between Church and state, but this battling subsided in the last years of the century. In 1297, papal desire for ingratiation with the Capetian monarchy was reflected in the elevation of its noblest son, Louis IX, to the rank of saint. These brief years of peaceful relations prior to the outbreak of new and profound animosities that would reach their climax at Anagni produced the only significant limitation of Jewish lending during Philip's reign. On June 29, 1299, in an edict rich in pious phraseology and heavily spiced with recollection of the newly beatified Saint Louis, Philip recalled the Melun ordinance of 1230, enacted by Louis in the presence of France's prelates and barons, and ordered that henceforth the government was to withdraw from involvement in the enforcement of Jewish loans.[30] As had been decreed by Saint Louis, governmental officials were no longer to write up Jewish loan documents nor to have them officially sealed. We have already noted evidence for such governmental involvement under Philip the Fair. The legislation of 1299, influenced no doubt by the temporary cordiality between the king and the Church, represents major retrogression in the developing pattern of enhanced

---

[28] Solomon Grayzel, *The Church and the Jews in the XIIIth Century* (Philadelphia, 1933), pp. 306–7.

[29] See above, chapter 4.

[30] *Ordonnances*, vol. 1, pp. 333–34.

support for Jewish lending. Jewish moneylending had revived steadily, with occasional overt governmental recognition of the de facto situation, from 1270 down through 1299. The edict of June 1299 represents a significant backward step. However, if the extensive references to Jewish loan documents in the post-1306 materials are indicative, the effort to eliminate governmental involvement in Jewish lending seems to have borne little fruit. It seems quite likely that this new anti-usury effort, spawned by the halcyon days of Church-state amity, dissipated quickly with the rekindling of Church-state tension in the early 1300's.

There is but one bit of follow-up legislation to the edict of 1299. On April 27, 1303, the king responded to certain complaints leveled by his Jews. While the ordinance of 1299 had specified that debts contracted prior to that date were to be enforced by royal officials, it was claimed by the Jews that in some instances such support was being withheld. As had been suggested on an earlier occasion, declining Jewish business was resulting in a decrease in revenue from the Jews—for Philip IV an intolerable situation. The king therefore instructed his officials to apply themselves assiduously to the enforcement of pre-1299 obligations.[31]

This same royal order addresses itself once more to the issue of Jewish usury in general. It takes a far harsher stand than the ordinance of 1292. Where usury could be proved, the interest was to be forgiven, with the debtor responsible only for payment of the principal. There are two significant shifts in this clause, as compared with the royal position of 1292. In the first place, usury in general is at issue, with no indication of "special usury." In the second place, in ordering simply remittance of the usury rather than a forfeiture to the royal coffers, the penalty shows more of the spirit of Saint Louis. Again the impression is one of governmental concern with the ecclesiastical stand on Jewish usury. However, once more, the widespread indication of Jewish lending in the post-1306 documentation raises serious doubts as to the effective withdrawal of governmental support and the annulment of usury.

Review of royal legislation on Jewish usury reveals deep concern over revenues to be realized from the Jews. Twice decrees were enacted as a direct result of diminishing income. The importance attached to taxation of the Jews is further reflected in an edict of June 1292, which in a sense defines a royal Jew as one who pays taxes to the king.[32] In this order it is stipulated that only those Jews who contribute to the royal

---

[31] Ibid., p. 545.

[32] Saige, *Les Juifs du Languedoc*, pp. 229-30.

treasury can enjoy the privileges extended to the king's Jews. This definition of a royal Jew in terms of taxation is yet another index of the new emphasis on revenue. The fiscal documentation from the reign of Philip the Fair indicates the seriousness with which Jewish taxation was taken and the concerted efforts to maximize royal profit from the Jews.

Taxation of the Jews took a number of forms. There was little royal desire to streamline the forms of revenue; since the primary concern was for the fullest income, every possible avenue was explored. A rather lengthy entry in the *Journaux du Trésor* for June 21, 1298, affords some indication of the varieties of Jewish taxation. The entry includes the following items:

> From the tallage of the Jews of Champagne—960 l.t.
> From Fantin, a Jew of Champagne, for his tallage—24 l., 10 s.t.
> From Haquin of Fère, of the bailliage of Vermandois, for the same—20 l.t.
> From Samuel of Roye, a Jew, and his offspring, formerly belonging to the dowry of the deceased Queen Marguerite, for the same—140 l.t.
> From Thyerma of Corbeil, a Jewess, belonging to the same dowry, for the same—41 l., 5 s.t.
> From Amand of Avalon, a Jew, for the same—4 l.t.—he has fled.
> From a certain Jew of Bayeux—17 l., 5 s.t.
> From the tallage of the Jews of the bailliage of Bourges—30 l.t.
> From the remnant of the *quatorzième* of the Jews of the bailliage of Troyes, for the needs of the army and arms—21 l.t.
> From Vivans, a Jew, for the same subvention—25 l.t.
> From the bailliage of Auverne, for the aforesaid remnant—13 l.t.
> From the bailliage of Rouen, for the same residue—32 l., 7 s.t.
> From the bailliage of Gisors, for the same—12 l.t.
> From the badges of the Jews of Paris, for the period of All Saints 1297—50 l.t.
> From the badges of the Jews of the bailliage of Bourges . . . 35 l.t.
> From the badges of the Jews of Champagne . . . 100 l.t.
> From the fine of Vitul, a Jew, who caused Renaud Monach to be harmed and imprisoned—50 l.t.
> From the fine of Sonin, a Jew of Château-Thierry, for falsely, in the name of the marshall of Champagne, causing false documents to be written and to be sealed . . . 50 l.t.
> From the fine of Manasses of Épernay, a Jew, for a certain instance of insubordination to John Clersens—6 l., 5 s.t.[33]

---

[33] *Journaux*, item no. 707.

The major source of royal revenue from the Jews was the tallage. While the precise fluctuations in the tallage of the Jews cannot be traced, certain developments are clear. On March 18, 1288, Philip, still early in his reign, showed extreme displeasure with the revenue collected from his Jews. He ordered his bailiffs and seneschals to inquire carefully into the deficiencies in tallage of the Jews over the previous seven years, stretching back into the reign of his father. All such deficiencies were to be remedied.[34] It seems likely that the king continued to be dissatisfied with royal revenue from the Jewish tallage. In the early 1290's, he shifted procedures and turned the Jewish tallage over to the Italian bankers Biche and Mouche. Mignon, in his description of tax rolls, indicates "an account of receipts and expenses encountered in regard to the 100,000 l.t., for the tallage of the Jews from Candlemas 1291 to All Saints' Day 1292."[35] He notes also "four other accounts of Biche and Mouche concerning the new tallage of the Jews and the arrears of the old tallage, from the Feast of John the Baptist 1293 to Ascension Day 1296."[36] We find here a series of tallages levied upon the Jews between 1291 and 1296, with seemingly substantial income. A 1297 account of war revenues shows the tallage of the Jews as producing 215,000 pounds, a significant sum, exceeded only by the 530,000 pounds raised from wealthy burghers and the 315,000 pounds raised from the *centième*.[37] This may well refer to the sums raised by Biche and Mouche between 1293 and 1296. For unknown reasons, Philip abandoned his reliance on the Italian bankers for the Jewish tallage after 1296. The receipts at the Treasury from Tours, dated November 1, 1296, show approximately 15,000 pounds from the tallage of the Jews, reported by regular officials.[38] In the extensive *Journaux* records of 1298 through 1301, royal bailiffs and their officials are cited time and again as responsible for raising and reporting the Jewish tallage. While the revenues reflected in the *Journaux* are not nearly so impressive as the moneys raised by Biche and Mouche, it is unlikely that the *Journaux* records are an accurate reflection of the sum total of Jewish tallage over this period. There is simply no accurate way to

---

[34] Saige, *Les Juifs du Languedoc*, p. 220.

[35] Mignon, item no. 2113; also see Strayer, "Consent to Taxation under Philip the Fair," p. 18, n. 54.

[36] Mignon, item no. 2114. On these Italian bankers and their activities, see Joseph Strayer, "Italian Bankers and Philip the Fair," *Explorations in Economic History* 7 (1969): 113–21.

[37] Edgard Boutaric, "Documents inédits relatifs à l'histoire de France sous Philippe le Bel," *Notices et extraits des manuscrits de la Bibliothèque nationale* 20, 2 (1862): 128.

[38] *Comptes du Trésor*, item nos. 288–91.

evaluate the change in revenues that accompanied the shift in tax responsibilities.

A second major source of revenue from the Jews was the income raised from the Jewish badges, which had been instituted by Saint Louis in 1269 at the urging of Paul Christian.[39] Louis had been moved by traditional ecclesiastical desires for segregation of the Jews as a separate and easily identifiable element in society. Early in his reign, Philip IV had transformed the badge into a source of additional revenue. His tax ordinance of March 18, 1288, included the following reference to earlier legislation on the Jewish badge:

> You shall compell the Jews subordinate to us to bear badges, in accordance with the ordinance enacted by our court concerning these badges. In instances where the badge is not worn, you must levy the required fine along with the amount required annually for the aforementioned badge according to the aforesaid ordinance.[40]

While the earlier ordinance has not survived, it clearly stipulated some annual levy on the Jewish badges. The receipts from this tax are regularly mentioned, both in the accounts of royal officials and in the records of the Treasury. It has often been noted that the sums actually realized from this tax are in most instances insignificant. They certainly come nowhere near the revenue accruing from the tallages.

During the period between 1295 and 1300, the government attempted to establish a broadly based war subsidy. Eschewing the old notion of war tax as a commutation of direct service, there was an effort to force all to contribute towards the mounting cost of military campaigning.[41] This expansion of the war subsidy extended to the Jews as well. During 1298 and 1299, there are a number of references to the collection of the revenues of a *quatorzième* levied on the Jews. The lengthy *Journaux* entry of June 21, 1298, included five references to this revenue, labeling it "the remnant of the *quatorzième* of the Jews for the needs of the army and of arms."[42]

A recurring item in governmental receipts from the Jews is the *emenda*, or fine. Such fines often produced substantial income, for example, the 500 pound fine paid by a Jew of the bailliage of Tours in 1285 and the 300 pound fine levied on the Jewish community of Paris

---

[39] See above, chapter 4.
[40] Saige, *Les Juifs du Languedoc*, p. 220.
[41] Strayer, "Consent to Taxation under Philip the Fair," pp. 8-11.
[42] *Journaux*, item no. 707.

in 1288.[43] The offenses for which such fines were assessed varied widely. The 1288 fine on Parisian Jewry was for "chanting too loudly," an offense prohibited earlier by Philip III and later included in Philip IV's catalogue of serious Jewish misdeeds.[44] Such singing was viewed as an affront to the ruling faith. Other offenses specifically noted in the royal records are far more prosaic, usually involving business malpractice. Again the *Journaux* entry of June 6, 1298, is useful. It specified, for example, a fine levied on Sonin of Château-Thierry for forging governmental documents and a fine on Manasses of Épernay for insubordination towards an important royal official.[45]

While the tallage, the assessment on Jewish badges, the *quatorzième*, and the fine were the most regular forms of Jewish taxation, there are a number of special levies that may be noted as well. The most significant of these was the "gift" bestowed by Champenois Jewry on Philip in 1285, the year in which he became both count of Champagne through marriage and king of France through inheritance. This gift amounted to 25,000 pounds. The first installment, 5,000 pounds, was paid in 1285. After that, subsequent installments were spread out over a number of years, with the final payment of approximately 7,000 pounds recorded in 1292 or 1293.[46]

There is also some evidence of an inheritance tax, or perhaps an inheritance agreement, established for the estates of unusually wealthy Jews. The one figure for whom such a tax is revealed is the important Calot of Rouen. Calot, whose governmental activities were varied, died shortly after Easter in 1300. After his death, an inventory of his possessions was made by four royal officials, including the bailiff of Rouen.[47] The *Journaux* entry of May 9, 1301, mentions a *finatio* of 4,000 pounds owed by the widow of Calot.[48] While this may be a simple instance of tallage of a wealthy individual Jew, it seems more likely that it involves some kind of special assessment on the estate left by Calot. The entry of May 9 indicates payment of 300 pounds towards the 4,000, and a later entry, dated November 5, 1301, records payment of

---

[43] *RHF*, vol. 22, p. 663; Nicolas Brussel, *Nouvel examen de l'usage des fiefs en France*, 2 vols. (Paris, 1750), vol. 1, p. 603.

[44] Saige, *Les Juifs du Languedoc*, pp. 212–13, 235–36.

[45] *Journaux*, item no. 707.

[46] Longnon, *Documents relatifs au comté de Champagne et de Brie*, vol. 3, p. 27; *Comptes royaux*, vol. 2, item no. 15263.

[47] Mignon, item no. 2142.

[48] *Journaux*, item no. 4644.

an additional 700.[49] By the end of 1301, then, at least a quarter of the obligation had been met.

While the Jews were generally absolved of obligations towards the municipalities, Parisian Jews did contribute towards the local sales tax in the years between 1292 and 1300. The tax lists for 1292, 1296, and 1297 show a series of Jewish payments.[50] The basis for imposition of these obligations and the conclusions which may legitimately be drawn from this material are shrouded in obscurity. Puzzling, for example, is the fact that the records for the last years of the century fail to mention the Jews. While it has been suggested that the deletion of the Jews may reflect an expulsion, other tax records reveal a Jewish community in Paris down through 1306.[51] The reasons for the removal of the Jews, like the extent of their involvement, must remain an unresolved question.

Closely related to taxation of the Jews was confiscation of Jewish property and wealth. While the major confiscation of the period came in the wake of the expulsion of 1306, earlier seizures of Jewish goods by Philip IV are documented. Mention has already been made of confiscation of Jewish debts prior to early 1292 and revocation of that seizure on the grounds that taxation revenues were being impeded.[52] The terrible tragedy of April 1288, in which thirteen distinguished Champenois Jews were executed on what seems to be a murder charge, resulted in confiscation of the substantial possessions of these well-to-do Jews. Some of this income is listed in the tax records from Champagne of December 31, 1288.[53] Royal profits from these Jews were still being recorded six years later. In 1294, Philip sold five houses of those earlier confiscated to the Jewish community of Troyes.[54] Early in 1304 two Jewish houses were expropriated at Lormaye, and a Jewish home in Marcilly-sur-Eure was similarly taken in early 1305.[55] While the basis

---

[49] Ibid., item no. 5377.

[50] Hercule Géraud, *Paris sous Philippe-le-Bel* (Paris, 1837), pp. 178–79; Karl Michaëlsson, ed., *Le Livre de la taille de Paris l'an 1297* (Göteborg, 1958), pp. 264–67. The latter lists were also published by Isidore Loeb, "Le rôle des Juifs de Paris en 1296 et 1297," *REJ* 1 (1880): 60–71.

[51] The suggestion of expulsion is made by Loeb, "Le rôle des Juifs de Paris," p. 62. For Jews in Paris between 1296 and 1306 see, *inter alia, Journaux*, item nos. 1607, 2445, 4097, 5806.

[52] See above.

[53] On the incident itself, see below. For the royal revenues, see Longnon, *Documents relatifs au comté de Champagne et de Brie*, vol. 3, p. 72.

[54] Pierre Piétresson de Saint Aubin, "Document inédit relatif aux Juifs de Troyes," *Le moyen âge* 22 (1920): 87.

[55] Siméon Luce, "Catalogue des documents du Trésor des Chartes relatifs aux Juifs sous le règne de Philippe le Bel," *REJ* 2 (1881), doc. no. 19; *Registres*, doc. no. 223.

for these confiscations is not clearly delineated, the 1304 document does claim that the two homes were held "in contradiction to the ordinance of the kingdom of France." It seems most probable that the reference is to the royal legislation of April 1, 1291, outlawing Jewish residence in the small towns of France.[56] If this supposition be correct, it then follows that failure to abide by the edict could result in the loss of the houses illegally held by the Jews.

In a curiously twisted way, the Jews of northern France made one further contribution to royal and baronial coffers. In 1288, the count of Anjou and Maine expelled his Jews in return for a grant of 3 shillings per hearth. This was a move that at one and the same time curried favor with the local populace and enriched the treasury.[57] It is the most bizarre form of Jewish assistance to the fiscal well-being of their governmental overlords.

Having analyzed the variety of taxes imposed upon the Jews, we must finally attempt to estimate the relative significance of the revenue which they produced. This is, unfortunately, a hopeless task. The data are simply too fragmentary. Even the tables of Treasury receipts drawn up by Fawtier are far from complete as reflections of income drawn from the Jews.[58] The most useful general indication that the profit derived from the Jews was substantial comes from the records of heavy tallages levied between 1291 and 1296 through Biche and Mouche and from the extensive evidence for major royal revenue from the confiscated property and business dealings of the Jews expelled in 1306. While these two periods may have represented peaks in royal profit from the Jews, the rest of the years of Philip IV in all probability saw a generally high level of income. The inflated prices paid by the king for the Jews whom he purchased reinforces this impression.[59] Philip the Fair, adroit businessman that he was, would certainly not have expended such considerable sums without the anticipation of even greater gains. The taxation raised from the Jews of northern France in the last decades of the thirteenth century must have added substantially to baronial, and particularly to royal, wealth.

An important factor in insuring maximum revenue from the Jews was effective taxation procedures and personnel. The administration of Jewish affairs underwent a number of major changes through the course

---

[56] Saige, *Les Juifs du Languedoc*, p. 223.

[57] Pierre Rangeard, *Histoire de l'Université d'Angers*, 2 vols. (Angers, 1877), vol. 2, pp. 183–87. On the expulsion itself, see below.

[58] *Comptes du Trésor*, pp. 46–58.

[59] See below.

of Philip's reign. The ordinance of March 18, 1288, represents his first significant attempt to organize Jewish affairs. The decree was addressed to all the king's seneschals and bailiffs, who had hitherto been responsible for Jewish taxation and were to continue to bear this responsibility. The first two clauses of the edict are concerned with delinquencies in the collection and reporting of the Jewish tallage and with a stern reminder related to the tax on Jewish badges. The third clause reflects both current procedures and an attempt to centralize these practices:

> You must come or send a delegate to make reckoning concerning these matters [i.e., Jewish taxation] with our men, at the day set aside for your seneschally and bailliage during the coming Parliament of Pentecost. You must turn over our letter patent, bearing the tenor of the present matters, to the carrier of the present document, our clerk Gaufrid Gornic, and to John Point Lanne, a burgher of Paris, whom we have assigned to Jewish affairs. You must carefully heed and obey documents sealed with the seal of the aforesaid Gaufrid and John—even without our own letters—when they order you or require something of you as regards the affairs of the aforesaid Jews.[60]

While the bailiffs and seneschals were to remain responsible for Jewish taxation, there is an effort here to centralize control of Jewish affairs. There would henceforth be two key Treasury officials to whom the local personnel would report. This new arrangement afforded the king far closer supervision of Jewish revenues.

A drastic revision in procedure seems to have been set in motion in 1291. At this point, responsibility for the tallage, which was after all the major item in Jewish revenue, was removed from the hands of the bailiffs and seneschals and turned over to the wealthy and influential Italian banking firm of Biche and Mouche. Mignon's record of five accounts relating to the tallages from 1291 through early 1296 indicates substantial royal profit accruing from this period.[61]

For unknown reasons, in 1296 Philip lifted the responsibility for Jewish taxation from the Italians and returned it to his own officials. The first major items recorded under the new system are a series of returns from the Jewish tallage received by the Treasury on November

---

[60]Saige, *Les Juifs du Languedoc*, p. 223.

[61]Mignon, item nos. 2113–14. On Biche and Mouche, see again Strayer, "Italian Bankers and Philip the Fair."

1, 1296. These revenues are listed by bailliage, with many well-known royal officials responsible for them.[62]

In the subsequent records, particularly the extensive *Journaux* entries, a number of interesting developments can be traced. The first is the emergence alongside the regular officials of certain figures particularly prominent in the collection of Jewish revenues. The most important of these is Daniel Cleric, who bore responsibility for the Jews who had formerly belonged to Queen Marguerite and for the Jews of the *prévôté* of Paris. Daniel is mentioned widely as reporting Jewish income and often received sums from the Treasury for expenses incurred in relation to Jewish affairs.[63]

In addition to these governmental officials deeply involved in Jewish taxation, there appears also a set of Jews who play a role in collection of Jewish obligations. Such Jews include, for example, Vivans Godemar of Troyes and Hagi of Provins, responsible for the taxes of the Jews of the bailliage of Troyes; Fantin of Bar, responsible for the taxes of the Jews of the bailliage of Chaumont; and Perrequin of Milli, responsible for the Jews of the bailliage of Bourges.[64] Probably the most important of these Jewish tax collectors were Joce of Pontoise and Calot of Rouen.[65] The latter bears the official designation *procurator communitatis Judeorum regni nostri*; however the precise implications of this title are not clear.[66]

Little is known of these important figures. It seems highly likely, however, that they rose to prominence as a result of substantial wealth. Mention has already been made of the inquest into the possessions amassed by Calot and the signs of an inheritance tax paid by his widow.[67] A number of Jewish tax collectors were among those Jews individually taxed—again indicative of private riches. Such is the case, for example, with Vivans of Troyes and Fantin of Bar, cited above. It is of course likely that involvement in governmental affairs presented an opportunity for wealthy Jews to enrich themselves still further. These Jews seem to have enjoyed a number of useful privileges. A safe-

---

[62] *Comptes du Trésor*, item nos. 288–91.

[63] See the index to the *Journaux*, s.v. "Danyel Brito" and "Danyel seu Daniel, clericus."

[64] For Vivans and Hagi, see *Journaux*, item nos. 3910, 3919; for Fantin, see ibid., item no. 4403; for Perrequin, ibid., item no. 707.

[65] Joce is indicated as a tax collector in *Comptes du Trésor*, item no. 288, and in *Journaux*, item no. 4599. For transactions involving Joce, see below. Calot is recorded as a tax collector in *Comptes du Trésor*, item no. 289, and in *Journaux*, item no. 3127. Calot is reimbursed for his activities in ibid., item nos. 3066, 4323.

[66] Luce, "Catalogue des documents," doc. no. 5.

[67] See above.

conduct issued in May 1293 for Manassier of Touri, described as a collector of royal taxes on the Jews, indicates some of these privileges, the most striking being removal of the normal obligation to wear the Jewish badge.[68]

The development of personnel devoted specifically to the collection of Jewish taxes is paralleled by indications of separate accounting within the Treasury. There are frequent references to disbursements for expenses incurred in Jewish affairs. These disbursements are usually recorded "super Judeos," "super expensas Judeorum," or "super compotum Judeorum." Perhaps the most interesting of these expenses are the pensions paid out to royal officials formerly involved with Jewish affairs. The *Journaux* show a pension of 200 pounds to William de Hangesto "quam capet super Judeos"; a pension of 40 pounds to Magister Johannes de Ribemont; and a payment of 100 pounds to Magister Johannes de Auxeyo "pro pensione sua de tempore quo fuit in officio Judeorum."[69]

One result of the new governmental concern with Jewish revenues was increased possessiveness on the part of the king and his barons towards their Jews. Jurisdictional strife over the Jews is prominent, as is enhanced commerce in Jews.

While sale of Jews or bestowal of Jews as gifts is known throughout the thirteenth century, the most significant of these commercial operations came during the reign of Philip IV. A number of sales of Jews are recorded, with the most spectacular taking place between the king and his brother Charles. In April 1296, the king bestowed upon Charles the Jew Joce of Pontoise and his six children.[70] This was a gift of no mean proportions. Joce had already emerged as an important Jew, involved in the collection of royal revenues. His stature is reflected in the fact that, when a quarrel over Jews broke out early the following year, the newcomer Joce was chosen to represent Count Charles's interest, while the king was served by the well-known Calot of Rouens.[71] Philip's gift and the subsequent contention over Jews were soon obliterated by the largest single sale of Jews known in this period. On June 2, 1299, Philip and his brother agreed to a sale of all the count's Jews for the price of

---

[68] Charles-Victor Langlois, "Formulaires de lettres du XIIe, du XIIIe et du XIVe siècle," *Notices et extraits des manuscrits de la Bibliothèque nationale* 34, 2 (1891): 17–18.

[69] *Journaux*, item nos. 1854, 3950, 5659.

[70] Lucien Broche, "Documents pontoisiens inédits," *Mémoires de la Société historique et archéologique de Pontoise et du Vexin* 23 (1901): 3–4.

[71] Luce, "Catalogue des documents," doc. no. 5.

20,000 pounds.[72] The sale was consummated very rapidly. Within two weeks, on June 17, the first installment, 2,000 pounds, had been paid.[73] The remaining installments are recorded in the *Journaux* over the ensuing six months, with the final 5,000 pounds disbursed on November 19.[74] It is worth noting that the *Journaux* entry for December 17, 1299, already shows substantial income from a Jew who was part of this massive purchase.[75] Philip did not tarry in realizing the income for which the expenditure of 20,000 pounds had been made.

While sales of Jews are one feature of the reign of Philip, contention is another. The extensive dispute between Philip and Charles of Valois prior to the large-scale sale of 1299 has already been mentioned—it was by no means an isolated phenomenon. Numerous quarrels between the king and the feudal authorities of northern France are recorded. Those contending with the king, occasionally successfully, include the archbishops of Bourges and Reims, the abbey of Fécamp, the countess of Brittany, and the seigneurs of Harcourt and Montmorency.[76] There were also disputes between nonroyal powers themselves, for example, between the count and the archbishop of Soissons.[77]

In an attempt to safeguard rights over his Jews, the king made two major pronouncements during the early 1290's. In June 1292, he addressed his attention to the Jews themselves, warning that any Jew not paying royal taxes would not be allowed to enjoy royal privileges.[78] This was one way of warding off undue baronial pressures on the Jews. The second tack was an announcement to the barons themselves. On May 2, 1293, Philip forbade directly the barons of his realm from taxing royal Jews.[79]

A minor set of conflicts all through the century had been aroused by the municipalities, out of their desire to expand their authority. The reign of Philip was not a period of extensive activity and progress for

---

[72] Ibid., doc. no. 6.

[73] *Journaux*, item no. 2819.

[74] Ibid., item no. 3750.

[75] Ibid., item no. 3963.

[76] *Olim*, vol. 2, p. 322, case no. 1 (archbishop of Bourges); Pierre Varin, ed., *Archives administratives de la ville de Reims*, 3 vols. (Paris, 1838–48), vol. 2, p. 20 (archbishop of Reims); *Olim*, vol. 2, p. 437, case no. 19 (abbey of Fécamp); *Journaux*, item no. 5343 (countess of Brittany); ibid., item, no. 1745 (seigneur of Harcourt); *Olim*, vol. 2, p. 73, case no. 15 (seigneur of Montmorency).

[77] Georges Bourgin, *La commune de Soissons et le groupe communal soissonnois* (Paris, 1908), pp. 410–11.

[78] Saige, *Les Juifs du Languedoc*, pp. 229–30.

[79] Ibid., p. 234.

the municipalities. The only indication of conflict comes in a decision of Parliament, dated February 17, 1300, ordering that if the mayor of Chaumont had been accustomed to judging the Jews of his town, he must be allowed to continue to do so.[80] While this represents a most unusual privilege when viewed against the history of royal and baronial limitation of municipal rights over the Jews, it probably reflects nothing more than a local custom widely divergent from standard procedure. There is certainly no sign of a general expansion of municipal rights at this juncture.

The sharpest internal conflict of the reign of Philip the Fair was the break between Philip and the Church. One of the foundations of Capetian policy had been a strong and consistent alliance with the ecclesiastical authorities. This policy of cooperation had reached its apogee during the reign of Louis IX, who was to be canonized as a saint during the reign of his grandson. Many of the basic programs of Philip and his advisors brought on an almost inevitable clash with Church leadership, most notably with the papacy.

As regards the Jews, the rule of Saint Louis represented a high-water mark in ecclesiastical influence. The mendicant orders, so close to the pious monarch, swayed him strongly on issues related to the Jews and were widely used by the king in administering his programs. One of the irritants in Church-state relations under Philip IV was the royal desire to reverse his grandfather's policies on the Jews. The reign of Philip is studded with admonitions to churchmen, particularly to inquisitors, to refrain from interfering in Jewish affairs. On May 16, 1288, Parliament issued two important orders, the first prohibiting clerics from levying financial penalties on Jews and the second outlawing imprisonment by clerics of Jews.[81] It has been suggested that the sanguinary events of April 1288, seemingly carried out with the involvement of the inquisitors, may have stimulated this strong royal stand.[82]

On March 18, 1293, the issue of the power of the inquisitors over the Jews was squarely joined. The bailiffs and seneschals of France, generally responsible for Jewish affairs, were ordered to permit no Jew under their jurisdiction to be seized or imprisoned by any of the friars in the absence of prior consultation with the responsible officials and without clear and unequivocal indication of the legitimate reasons for such cap-

---

[80] *Olim*, vol. 2, p. 439, case no. 23.

[81] *Olim*, vol. 2, p. 278, case no. 13; Edgard Boutaric, ed., *Actes du Parlement de Paris*, 2 vols. (Paris, 1863–67), vol. 1, p. 414.

[82] Arsène Darmesteter, "L'Autodafé de Troyes (24 avril 1288)," *REJ* 2 (1881): 245–46.

ture.[83] The statement was an overt repudiation of inquisitorial interference with the king's Jews.

Even the singularly Church-oriented edict of June 6, 1299, concerned with a series of supposed Jewish crimes and ordering governmental cooperation with ecclesiastical officialdom in rooting out the
evils, makes clear that action was to be taken only by royal function-
aries. Only royal officials were to seize, imprison, and punish guilty
Jews. While the inquisitors were to bring the charges, action on the
allegations was restricted to the king's men alone.[84]

By 1302 the brief truce between the king and the papacy, which had
occasioned the cooperative spirit of the legislation of 1299, had run its
course, and serious discord had resumed. The tone and content of the
edict of 1302 are far removed from that of 1299. The emphasis has
shifted from cooperation to an emphatic assertion of noncompliance.
More than that, there is even a reversal of some of the particulars of the
earlier order.

> We order you and each one of you that, if the aforesaid inquisitors
> involve themselves or attempt to involve themselves against the Jews
> of our kingdom in questions of usury, blasphemy, and so forth—
> which do not pertain to these inquisitors by virtue of the office of
> inquisitor—, you must seize no Jew at the behest or request of these
> inquisitors; nor cause any Jew to be seized, nor to be molested in any
> way; nor are you to extend any aid to the same inquisitors as regards
> these Jews.[85]

Church-state tension over the Jews involved more than just the interference of ecclesiastical personnel. There were substantive issues involved as well. We have already followed the vagaries of royal policy on
Jewish usury. The monarchy under Philip IV liberalized substantially
the uncompromising stand of Louis IX against Jewish moneylending. It
was only in 1299, under the influence of the brief Church-state rapprochement of the last years of the century, that a resumption of some
of the controls imposed by Louis was enacted.[86] Philip's support of
Jewish lending was, on the one hand, a reflection of his fiscal concern
with the Jews; at the same time, it represented a policy opposed to a
very important set of Church attitudes.

---

[83] Saige, *Les Juifs du Languedoc*, pp. 233–34.

[84] Ibid., pp. 235–36.

[85] *Ordonnances*, vol. 1, p. 346.

[86] See above.

While the government was covertly and overtly condoning the revival of Jewish lending, it was remarkably quiescent in many of the areas vigorously pursued by Saint Louis. It is not surprising that the one major pronouncement of Philip IV that addressed itself to traditional ecclesiastical concerns stems from precisely the period of rapprochement noted above.

> We understand that the Jews, in diverse parts of the kingdom, solicit Christians on behalf of heresy and ensnare many with their wiles and with their promises and bribes, to the extent that they receive from many and presume to handle wretchedly the most holy body of Christ and to blaspheme the other sacraments of our faith, by seducing many simple men and by circumcising those seduced. They receive and conceal fugitive heretics. To the scandal of our faith, they complete new synagogues, singing in a loud voice as though they were officiating in a Church service. They multiply copies of the condemned Talmud, containing innumerable blasphemies about the most glorious Virgin Mary. . . . [87]

The purpose of this catalogue of Jewish atrocities was to arouse royal officialdom to heed the allegations of the inquisitors on these matters and to enact the appropriate penalties. These matters, however, were not pursued diligently and consistently throughout the reign of Philip the Fair. The interest of the monarch and of his advisors lay elsewhere, and the royal ordinance of June 6, 1299, remained a special item in the flow of royal legislation, an order only fitfully executed it would seem. The royal desire to keep ecclesiastical personnel at bay was paralleled, not surprisingly, by a marked lack of enthusiasm for ecclesiastical programs.

Thus far the focus has centered on governmental policies towards the Jews under Philip IV, with an emphasis on the development of a fiscally-oriented outlook. For the Jews themselves, however, all this must have been perceived as both a blessing and a curse. The Jews must have welcomed the increasing encouragement of Jewish lending and the economic revival that this facilitated. The emergence of a new class of wealthy Jews, deeply involved in governmental administration, is but one index of this economic renewal. The Jewish wealth confiscated and the Jewish debts taken over by the government in the wake of the expulsion of 1306 is another.

---

[87]Saige, *Les Juifs du Languedoc*, p. 235.

While welcoming the economic revival, the Jews could hardly have been oblivious to some of the negative features of Philip's new policies. In the economic sphere itself, much of the new Jewish income was being diverted into royal coffers. The rise to prominence of a new elite of wealth undoubtedly afforded the Jews a useful set of intermediaries in negotiating taxation problems. The new Jewish officials may well have been responsible for gaining annulment in 1292 of a prior seizure of Jewish debts. The essential fact remains, however, that taxation of the Jews became an increasingly heavy burden.

Along with the financial ramifications of the new policy came deleterious changes in Jewish political status. The reign of Philip the Fair marks the high point in royal and baronial possessiveness towards the Jews. While assertions of baronial rights over specific Jews are found from the reign of Philip Augustus on, at no point were the claims over Jews, the sale and exchange of Jews, and the contention over Jews as prominent as they were in the final decades of the thirteenth century. We have already noted the early–thirteenth-century attempts to bind the Jews directly. The most extreme of these measures, however, was enacted by Philip the Fair as part of his major taxation ordinance of March 18, 1288.

> Upon the advice of two important Jews per seneschally or bailliage, you should receive for each Jew two additional Jews as pledges of continued residence. You shall have lists drawn up with the name of each Jew and of those serving as pledges for him, and you shall send these lists to the aforesaid Gaufrid and John [the central officials responsible for Jewish affairs].[88]

While clearly intended as an administrative measure designed for maximizing revenues from his Jewish subjects, Philip's enactment represents the most drastic infringement on Jewish rights, and with this enactment Jewish political status reaches its nadir.

At precisely this point, a period of economic rejuvenation coupled with increased fiscal exploitation and political control, the popular animosity that had been a factor in Jewish fate all through the twelfth and thirteenth centuries came increasingly to the fore. This animosity did not result in direct attack on the Jews, as it had during the reign of Saint Louis. Once more the king was able to suppress successfully the anti-Jewish animus. Both of the major tragedies of the pre-1306 decades were the results of quasi-legal proceedings.

---

[88] Ibid., p. 220.

The first of these two incidents came in April 1288 in the important Jewish community of Troyes. The sources for this incident are a series of Jewish lamentations over the victims of the tragedy, emphasizing primarily their meritorious lives and unflinching readiness for death, and some random financial records that deal with the aftermath. While the basic progression of events can be discerned, the resulting picture is not clear in all its details.[89]

The period during which the crisis fell was—not unusually—the spring months, when the celebration of Easter regularly generated strong tensions in Jewish-Christian relations.

The wicked conspired to destroy the chosen,
While still under the spell of mourning their crucified lord.[90]

According to the Hebrew sources, against this background of tension a dangerous plot was hatched.

They [the wicked] went on with the plotting, each strapping on his sword
On behalf of the crucified imposter.
They came to the house of Isaac, a man still in his prime;
They spoke peaceably with him, while covertly preparing a snare.
Isaac trembled mightily
When he heard the sound of the mob.
Rejoicing and good cheer turned into mourning;
The sun and the moon stood in their tracks.[91]

The texts not only deal cursorily with the incident itself; when they do describe it, they use the most ambiguous terms. The basic situation seems to be the deposition of a cadaver in the home of the wealthy Jew Isaac Châtelain. Despite the Passover-Easter dating, there is no reference to the Blood Libel. The indication of deposition of a corpse and subsequent "discovery" would put the crime into the category of the simpler malicious-murder allegations of the late twelfth century. It is quite likely that the juxtaposition of this incident with the Easter period—the crime was supposed to have occurred on Good Friday itself—reflects

---

[89]The sources are collected in Darmesteter, "L'Autodafé de Troyes," pp. 199–236, and are followed by a historical reconstruction of the events. To the materials gathered by Darmesteter must be added the document published by Piétresson de Saint Aubin, "Document inédit relatif aux Juifs de Troyes."

[90]Darmesteter, "L'Autodafé de Troyes," p. 222; reprinted in Abraham Habermann, ed., Sefer Gezerot Ashkenaz ve-Zarfat (Jerusalem, 1945), p. 209.

[91]Darmesteter, "L'Autodafé de Troyes," p. 222; Habermann, Sefer Gezerot, p. 210.

the inclusion of the religious motif of murder as a compulsive reenactment of the crucifixion.[92]

Only the assumption that the imputed crime had such religious overtones explains the role of the inquisitors in the trial proceedings. The evidence for this is again not overwhelming. The term חובלים, while a general designation for destructive enemies, usually refers to the Dominicans or Franciscans in Hebrew texts of this period. This term abounds in the Hebrew poems and probably reflects inquisitorial involvement based on the imputed religious elements in the alleged offense.[93] It has been suggested that the parliamentary orders of May 16, 1288, prohibiting clerics from imposing financial penalties or imprisoning Jews may have resulted from the proceedings in Troyes. While the evidence is slim, the suggestion seems plausible.[94]

What emerges then is substantial religious animosity against the Jews, leading to the fastening of responsibility for a supposed religious crime. While the situation was tense, it did not explode into popular attack but was handled in semi-legal fashion by the inquisitorial authorities. The result was the trial and execution of thirteen Jews prominent for their wealth, learning, and piety. The incident must be counted among the major catastrophes of medieval northern French Jewish history.

A scant two years later, another incident threatened northern French Jewry, revealing once more the depth of anti-Jewish feelings in the late thirteenth century. Again the time was the Easter period; the locale shifted from the chief city of Champagne to the great capital of the entire realm, Paris. The charge was a new one, yet not unrelated to the allegations of 1288. The notion that the Jews were pathologically compelled to reenact their historic sin of the crucifixion was still central. The shift, however, lay in transferring this supposed compulsion from a human victim to the *sacrosanctum Christi corpus*, the host wafer.[95]

The story, as presented in a number of Latin and French accounts, depicts a Jewish moneylender who exploited the leverage inhering in financial obligations to seduce a young Christian girl into bringing him the wafer. He then attempted to torture the wafer, but through divine intervention his vicious efforts were thwarted and his malevolence re-

---

[92] On the twelfth-century development of these motifs, see Robert Chazan, "The Bray Incident of 1192: *Realpolitik* and Folk Slander," *PAAJR* 37 (1969): 9–14, and above, chapter 2.

[93] Suggested by Darmesteter, "L'Autodafé de Troyes," pp. 243–44. On the problems associated with the term חובלים, see above, chapter 4, n. 166.

[94] Darmesteter, "L'Autodafé de Troyes," pp. 245–46.

[95] Sources include Jules Viard, ed., *Les grandes chroniques de France*, 10 vols. (Paris, 1920–53), vol. 8, p. 144; *RHF*, vol. 21, pp. 127, 133; vol. 22, p. 32; vol. 23, p. 145.

vealed. The result was imprisonment by the authorities, seemingly the bishop of Paris, and eventually public execution. According to a number of the sources, the death of the malefactor was accompanied by the conversion of his wife and children.

There are both parallels and contrasts to be drawn between the results of the incidents of 1288 and 1290. In terms of immediate results, the incident of 1290 was accompanied by no imputation of corporate guilt, as had been the case in 1288 and in most earlier incidents. For unknown reasons, there was no transfer of responsibility from an individual to a community at large. In long-range terms, however, the impact of the incident of 1290 was profound. While the crucifixion allegation reflected in the Troyes affair of 1288 received no significant new recognition, the host slander was indirectly acknowledged by the highest possible authorities and became a firm feature of subsequent anti-Jewish animosity. On July 17, 1295, Pope Boniface VIII authorized the erection of a chapel on the site of the supposed miracle of the host. Papal recognition of the site of the alleged miracle, and ostensibly of the Jewish crime as well, was a significant development.[96] The king of France lent the prestige of his high office to the allegation as well. Royal legislation of June 6, 1299, cataloguing serious Jewish offenses against the Christian faith, included mention of the accusation of host profanation.[97] The dignity conferred upon this charge by papal and royal recognition cannot be exaggerated. The well-known assertion of the fifteenth-century Alfonso de Espina, in his *Fortalitium fidei*, that the expulsion of 1306 was in reaction to the sacrilege of 1290 may be readily dismissed; Alfonso's indication, however, that this story was celebrated in the paintings and decorations of many French churches may be as readily accepted.[98] The incident of 1290 was thus, on the one hand, a result of the deepening antipathy felt towards the Jews; at the same time, it added a powerful new motif to the storehouse of anti-Jewish mythology and thus enhanced the climate of popular opinion which made the expulsion of 1306 possible.

While the growing animosity towards the Jews is most dramatically illustrated by the events of 1288 and 1290, there are additional indices of these feelings available which reflect the breadth and scope of the anti-Jewish sentiment. The most significant of these indices is the growing tendency towards exclusion of the Jews from localities or, in some

[96] Georges Digard et al., eds., *Les registres de Boniface VIII*, 4 vols. (Paris, 1904– 39), vol. 1, doc. no. 441.

[97] Saige, *Les Juifs du Languedoc*, p. 235.

[98] Alfonso de Espina, *Fortalitium Fidei* (Lyons, 1511), bk. 3, chap. 9.

cases, from important principalities. In most instances, popular desire for the removal of the Jews contributed heavily to such exclusion.

A number of local expulsions are recorded for the last decade of the thirteenth century. On May 21, 1290, the Jews were expelled from Saint-Pierre-sur-Dives.[99] The following year, on September 14, 1291, the bailiff of Cotentin decided that the Jews might not settle in the town of Saint-Pair.[100] At the very outset of the new century, on January 24, 1300, Philip the Fair banished the Jews from the town of Angy.[101] All of these actions seem to represent royal acceding to local sentiments. Such popular feeling was to play an important role in the fateful year 1306.

A broader expulsion was decreed by Philip on April 1, 1291.[102] This ordinance was actually only a repetition of his father's order expelling the Jews from the villages and small towns of France. The major motivation seems to have been insistent ecclesiastical pressures for the alleviation of potentially dangerous Jewish influence on the unsophisticated and easily seduced rural elements in the Christian population. Again, this is a climate of opinion conducive to a more general edict of expulsion.

On February 16, 1291, Philip ordered the expulsion of those Jews newly arrived from England.[103] Quite naturally many English Jews had made their way to France, from which they had originated and with which they had always maintained significant contact. This edict seems to reflect merely royal desire to keep the realm free of unprofitable Jews who had already been stripped of most of their wealth prior to departure from England. While the edict does not imply popular feeling, it is consistent with the negative mood towards Jewish presence—"superfluous" Jews were to be eschewed.

In this regard, it must be noted that some English Jews were allowed to stay. There are a number of indications of the continued presence of certain English Jews subsequent to 1291.[104] It is clear that in most instances these Jews were highly profitable to Philip and were kept on that basis. The most prominent example was Bon Ami of York. In 1292, after the expulsion ordered by Philip in 1291, Bon Ami was still

---

[99] *Olim*, vol. 2, p. 299, case no. 3.

[100] *RHF*, vol. 24, p. 152*.

[101] Ibid., p. 64*.

[102] Saige, *Les Juifs du Languedoc*, p. 223.

[103] *Olim*, vol. 2, p. 311, case no. 1.

[104] Note, for example, the English Jews listed in the Paris tax rolls of 1292, 1296, and 1297 (see above).

in Paris, doing business as a matter of fact with the archbishop of York in regard to heavy obligations still owed him in England.[105] Sometime after the edict of 1291, Bon Ami and his family were issued a special royal charter granting them the right to settle in any of those locales in which French Jews were accustomed to dwell. The price for this royal privilege was 100 pounds to be paid annually, one half on All Saints' Day and one half on Pentecost.[106] The tax records for Ascension 1298 do show Bon Ami paying the required sum.[107] The privileges granted this well-to-do Jew went beyond mere settlement; for example, he and his family were given the right to dispense with the badge normally mandatory for French Jews. While the climate of anti-Jewish feeling made the settlement of impoverished English Jews objectionable, wealth could still persuade the king to overcome his sense of antipathy.

The edict of Philip IV concerning destitute English Jews was only an aftermath to the expulsion of 1290 ordered by Edward I of England. The expulsion of 1290 itself, however, was but the most serious of a rash of expulsions that struck northwestern European Jewry during the late 1280's and the early 1290's. The first of these came in 1288, ordered by the same Edward of England for the Jews in his continental possession of Gascony. The motivation for Edward's edicts of 1288 and 1290 seems clearly to have been royal profit, the income accruing from confiscation of Jewish lands and goods.[108]

It remained, however, for Charles II, king of Sicily and count of Anjou and Maine, to add a new twist to the expulsion theme, enabling himself both to satisfy the growing popular clamor for expulsion of the Jews and to profit handsomely at the same time. Charles, whose life was so deeply complicated by the intrigues and complexities of European politics, had spent the years between mid 1284 and late 1288 in captivity. Only in October 1288, with substantial aid from Edward of England, was Charles freed. He immediately visited France and then proceeded on to Italy. In late 1289, he returned once more to France and ordered an expulsion of the Jews from the counties of Maine and Anjou. While this banishment reflected basically the same desperate need for funds that had animated the related expulsion from Gascony, the stance and technique were somewhat different. Charles issued his edict in consultation with major ecclesiastical and lay figures in the

---

[105] Cecil Roth, *A History of the Jews in England*, 3rd ed. (Oxford, 1964), p. 88.

[106] Langlois, "Formulaires de lettres," p. 18.

[107] *Comptes royaux*, vol. 1, item no. 243.

[108] On this expulsion, see H. G. Richardson, *The English Jewry under Angevin Kings* (London, 1960), pp. 225–27.

affected counties, levying a tax on the residents of the affected areas for the privilege of having the Jews expelled.

Charles II, by the grace of God king of Jerusalem, prince of Sicily and of Apulia and of Capua, count of Achea and Anjou and Forcalquier, we give notice to all by the contents of the present letter, that we, weighing carefully the fine words of sacred authority, in which it is warned that a mouse or a viper or a serpent in the bosom tend to confer unjust retribution on their hosts, and perceiving through diligent inspection the conditions and mores of the counties of Anjou and Maine—which by the will of God are subject to our rule—, discovered the state of the aforesaid land and have found that it is subject to many enormities and crimes odious to God and abhorrent to the Christian faith. In many places in those lands, a multitude of Jews, enemies of the life-giving Cross and of all of Christianity, subvert perfidiously Christians, with whom they live at random and publicly, many of either sex, who are counted among professors of Christianity, from the way of truth. They seem to subvert as many as they can. They despoil them of their goods both movable and immovable by their devious deceits and by the endless abyss of usury; they force them to beg; and—most unthinkable!— they cohabit evilly with many Christian maidens. Therefore, we, to whom the duty falls to purge the provinces entrusted to us of evil men, disheartened by pangs of compassion, with the reverend fathers the bishops and many clerics and also with the faithful counts and princes and with others worthy of faith, both through us and through our faithful deputies, held conference on these matters, so that we be able to overcome powerful maladies and to extirpate acknowledged frauds from those lands. Indeed it is pleasing to our Majesty—with divine approval, we believe—that we should provide for our aforesaid counties and for their inhabitants through an expulsion of the aforesaid Jews.

Therefore, for the honor of God and the tranquillity of the aforesaid locales, exhibiting zeal for the life-giving Cross—although we enjoy extensive temporal benefit from the aforesaid Jews—, preferring to provide for the peace of our subjects rather than to fill our coffers with the mammon of iniquity, especially when for the loss of temporal goods spiritual gains are achieved, we expell and order expelled from our aforesaid counties of Anjou and Maine and from each and every locality in those counties all Jews, male and female, adults through infants, of whatsoever sex and condition they may have been born or raised, not only for the present but for all times. . . .

Indeed, since according to the prophetic gift of the holy spirit all, from the most insignificant to the most important, strive after avarice, fearing lest any of our successors be moved by the promise of iniquitous mammon to recall the aforesaid persons, we wish and we oblige ourselves and each of our successors in the aforesaid places not to recall any of the aforesaid persons and not to consent to the habitation, temporary visitation or contracts of the aforesaid Jews, as has been indicated concerning them above, even if we be implored to annul.

Indeed, with the assent of our fathers in Christ Nicholas bishop of Angers and Durrand bishop of Nantes and the chapters of those places, along with the chapters of Le Mans, Poitiers, and St. Martin of Tours, and along with the abbeys, Hospitaliers, Templars, barons, counts, knights, and others worthy of faith, all holding land or living within the bounds of the aforesaid counties, it has been conceded to us freely and without force that we ought to receive from each hearth three shillings once only and from each wage earner six pence once only, as some recompense for the profit which we lose through the expulsion of the aforesaid. . . . [109]

While justification of expulsion of the Jews on moral and religious grounds is not new or unparalleled, the utilization of anti-Jewish sentiment for profit through an "expulsion tax" is certainly a striking innovation. The lesson was not lost on the wily Philip the Fair. By the early 1290's Philip had made the same arrangements with the inhabitants of Saintonge and Poitou, at an increased rate in fact. In the case of Saintonge and Poitou, evidence for substantial profit from this taxation is available.[110]

Yet one more major expulsion must be added. On March 20, 1294, the count of Nevers obtained from Philip IV permission to expel the Jews from those areas of the county in which they still remained, thereby completing the total exclusion of the Jews from this important principality.[111]

The late 1280's and early 1290's thus saw a spate of expulsions. While the essential motivation for these orders was the urgent need for ready cash generated by the intrigues of contemporary European politics, the rationale for such expulsions was usually drawn from the fund of ecclesiastical charges leveled against the Jews, and the acceptability of such decrees was rooted in the general anti-Jewish animus of the period. In a number of cases, in fact, this antipathy was overtly ex-

---

[109] Rangeard, *Histoire de l'Université d'Angers*, vol. 2, pp. 183–87.

[110] Strayer, "Consent to Taxation under Philip the Fair," p. 19.

[111] René de Lespinasse, *Le Nivernais et les comtes de Nevers*, 3 vols. (Paris, 1909–14), vol. 2, p. 373.

ploited, with the inhabitants of a particular area taxed directly for the privilege of having their Jewish neighbors driven out.

The decline in Jewish source materials makes it difficult to discern developments in Jewish community organization. The rise to power of a new class of wealthy Jews and their direct involvement in governmental affairs probably affected substantially Jewish self-government at the close of the thirteenth century. On the one hand, such men of wealth and power undoubtedly afforded the Jews a useful voice in governmental circles. In fact, at one point, a major Jewish financier and governmental official, Calot of Rouen, borrowed 500 pounds, ostensibly on behalf of the Jewish community of France.[112] The association of such men with an ever more centralized governmental bureaucracy moved the Jewish community itself increasingly towards centralization. The breakdown of particularism and the ability to cooperate meaningfully on a broad scale must also have enhanced the political power of French Jewry. At the same time, the involvement of prominent Jews in governmental circles and the centralization of Jewish affairs reflected above all else the thrust towards exploitation that characterized the reign of Philip the Fair. It is thus impossible to judge whether ultimately these developments proved beneficial or detrimental. Finally, it is difficult to assess the quality of Jewish leadership. There is a sense that men like Calot of Rouen and Joce of Pontoise do not represent the same combination of wealth and political power with religious training and moral standing that had been personified in leaders like R. Jacob Tam. If this were so, it would simply reflect in the Jewish community a specialization and secularization parallel to that which was developing in Christian society. It should be noted, however, that the panegyrics composed over the fallen martyrs of Troyes emphasize strongly that the wealthy and influential victims of the tragedy were also men of erudition and deep piety.[113] Allowing for the extravagances often associated with such lamentations, it is still possible that the tradition of R. Tam had not totally dissipated.

While economic resurgence was the chief quality of Jewish life under Philip the Fair, signs of a religious and intellectual renaissance are also in evidence. There is no sense of return to the glorious days of the twelfth and early thirteenth centuries, but there is indication of a relaxation of the intense pressures mounted by Louis IX against the study of the Talmud and related materials. In the legislation issued by Philip the

---

[112] *Journaux*, item nos. 1107, 1387, 1662.
[113] Darmesteter, "L'Autodafé de Troyes," pp. 199-233.

Fair, there is but one reference to the Talmud. The legislation of 1299, which enumerates a series of Jewish religious abuses, mentions among them that the Jews "spread the condemned books called the Talmud, which contain innumerable blasphemies concerning the glorious Virgin Mary."[114] The provisions of this legislation, however, make no specific reference to the Talmud; they consist merely of a call for cooperation with the inquisitors responsible for ferreting out offensive behavior. This is a far cry from the legislation of 1283 enacted by Philip's father, which called directly for renewed burnings of the condemned volumes.

With removal of the tight constraints of the last decades of Louis IX, Jewish studies in northern France seem to have resumed. Once again a number of important figures emerge.[115] Chief among these were R. Isaac of Corbeil, R. Eliezer of Touques, and R. Peretz. It is, however, curious to note the extent to which the old centers of Jewish learning, particularly Paris and Troyes, were no longer part of this revival. The major scholars of this period are associated with towns that are relatively new to intensive Jewish learning and also minor centers of French civilization in general. The growing prominence of Paris as the hub of the realm, in which governmental affairs were being increasingly concentrated and within which the splendor associated with a great capital was rapidly developing, makes the absence of a significant Jewish academy all the more striking. It seems quite likely that this shift in locus of Jewish scholarship is far from accidental. Although governmental pressures had abated, it was probably still unwise to relocate in cities where Church activity was extensive and where a renewal of Jewish learning might fan old sparks of opposition.

While the keynote of this revived northern French scholarship remained Talmudic studies, particularly the special variety of exegesis developed in the twelfth century under R. Jacob Tam, the great student of Ashkenazic legal studies, Ephraim Urbach, sees in these figures who close out the thirteenth century the normal signs of a creative movement coming to an end. According to Urbach, the chief concern of the final decades of the century was the collection of the fruits of the earlier, more creative thinkers. Urbach finds this tendency both in the work of the exegetes, devoted to collecting the glosses of their predecessors, and in the legal compendium of R. Isaac of Corbeil, designed to make readily available to large numbers of Jews the scholarship of earlier generations.[116]

---

[114] Saige, *Les Juifs du Languedoc*, p. 235.

[115] See Urbach, *Ba'aley ha-Tosafot*, pp. 447–58.

[116] Ibid.

The period then exhibits clear signs of resurgence, but the revival is far from complete. Perhaps the most significant index of continued religious decline is the evidence for substantial conversion. While the edict of 1299 had featured prominently untoward Jewish religious influence on unsuspecting Christians and while the danger of such influence was the motivating factor in the expulsion of the Jews from the villages of France, there is little evidence of Christian conversion to Judaism but substantial indication of movement in the opposite direction. Royal records list numerous converts supported by governmental doles, many extending over long periods of time. The grants reflect royal willingness to smooth somewhat the lot of the convert.[117]

In some instances, the new converts rose to positions of eminence. The most striking of these was the family headed by Philip le Convers.[118] Philip was one of the most trusted royal officials during the reign of Philip IV. He involved himself in a wide variety of governmental activities, eventually specializing in the area of forest revenues. There are no overt reflections of Philip's Jewish origins. Unlike Nicholas Donin or Paul Christian, Philip became simply another of the key royal advisors in this more secular age, a convert not strongly animated by a sense of conflict with his ancestral faith.

The process of conversion, however, was not always simple and untroubled. We have already noted from the late 1260's major incidents of relapse. The reign of Philip the Fair saw further instances of this phenomenon, particularly in the wake of the upheaval occasioned by the expulsion of 1306. The continuation of the chronicle of William of Nangis has preserved three incidents of relapse to Judaism on the part of converts, all stemming from the city of Paris, the first two in 1307 and the third in 1310.[119] It is plausible that such events in the capital caught the attention of the chronicler while similar occurrences in the provinces went unrecorded. In all likelihood, these three incidents were symptoms of occasional dislocation in the psyches of new converts. The allegations made concerning the *relapsi* represent the kind of behavior that might be expected from disenchanted converts; they reflect deeply-held Jewish objections to the dogmas and practices of the ruling faith.

---

[117]Note the material gathered by Nahon, "Contribution à l'histoire des Juifs en France sous Philippe le Bel," pp. 76-78.

[118]On Philip le Convers, see Franklin Pegues, *The Lawyers of the Last Capetians* (Princeton, 1962), pp. 124-40.

[119]Hercule Géraud, ed., *Chronique latine de Guillaume de Nangis de 1113 à 1300*, 2 vols. (Paris, 1843), vol. 2, pp. 363, 380.

The problems, both material and spiritual, which continued to afflict the Jews even during the less troubled years of Philip the Fair occasionally led to a renunciation of Jewish faith. These conversions were sometimes carried out relatively smoothly, with the new converts finding an acceptable place in Christian society. In rare instances, the attempts failed, bringing grief and sometimes death in their wake.

For the Jews of France, Philip IV did represent a breathing spell from onerous oppression, the acceleration of economic revival, and even the possibility of spiritual resurgence. Signs were not lacking, however, that the positive developments of his reign were occasioned primarily by the monarchy's own economical needs and by the realization that a combination of support and exploitation might prove highly profitable. One can only wonder whether astute Jewish observers recognized the inherent danger in these new arrangements. Once before a great Capetian monarch and a shrewd politican had concluded that desperate financial pressures could best be alleviated by expulsion of the Jews and confiscation of their belongings. Could the Jews of early-fourteenth-century France have suspected that Philip the Fair was about to ape the radical policies of his distinguished predecessor, Philip Augustus?

VI

EXPULSION AND ITS AFTERMATH

THE REIGN OF Philip the Fair was plagued by the problems of periodic warfare and the heavy strains which military campaigning imposed on the royal Treasury. During the last years of the thirteenth century, general taxes were widely levied, based on the new and often resisted principle that all inhabitants of the kingdom bore the obligation of aiding in the defense of the realm. This innovation elicited strenuous objections and, as a result, the government reverted to the older view of military taxation as commutation of the personal obligation to fight. This shift caused a serious drop in royal revenues. It is against this background of continued needs and limited resources that the expulsion of French Jewry in 1306 must be seen.[1]

Certainly precedents for such an expulsion were available. The banishment of 1182 at the hands of Philip Augustus had probably not been forgotten. It was, however, unnecessary to conjure up such distant recollections. The late 1280's and the early 1290's had seen a series of

---

[1] Joseph Strayer, "Consent to Taxation under Philip the Fair," in *Studies in Early French Taxation*, ed. Joseph R. Strayer and Charles H. Taylor (Cambridge, Mass., 1939). On some of the fiscal factors influencing the expulsion, see Simon Schwarzfuchs, "The Expulsion of the Jews from France (1306)," *The Seventy Fifth Anniversary Volume of the Jewish Quarterly Review*, ed. A. A. Neuman (New York, 1967), pp. 482-89.

expulsions, including one from the entire kingdom of England.[2] These precedents served a number of purposes. In the first place, they simply made wholesale expulsion a feasible act and a viable option. Philip did not have to take upon himself the burdensome onus of innovation. In the second place, the prior expulsions served as a clear indication of the potential profit in banishing the Jews. In these earlier incidents, a number of techniques had been developed. In some instances, the simple expedient of confiscation of the Jews' real estate and the debts owed them was invoked. In others, the animosities of the Christian populace and the widespread desire to see the Jews evicted were exploited, with the local residents taxed for the privilege of having their Jewish neighbors removed. Whatever the technique, the precedents of the late 1280's and early 1290's promised substantial profit to a government perpetually in need of new funds.[3]

An important factor in the royal decision was unquestionably the climate of opinion regarding the Jews. While public sentiment was never pro-Jewish in medieval Christendom, the intensity of anti-Jewish animus did vary, and the deeper the hostility the more easily executed a general expulsion. In fact, at those points at which feelings against the Jews ran high, the king or baron contemplating banishment could hope for both immediate financial gain and significant popular approbation. In this regard, the climate was propitious in the early fourteenth century. We have already noted the proliferation of new anti-Jewish motifs during the last decade of the thirteenth century.[4] The number of localities clamoring for a prohibition of Jewish settlement was on the rise.[5] Perhaps the most striking expression of strong anti-Jewish sentiment was the willingness of the inhabitants of some western French principalities to pay for the privilege of having the Jews expelled from their territories.[6] Philip the Fair and his advisors must certainly have felt that a broad expulsion of the Jews would be greeted with widespread enthusiasm throughout their kingdom. While not a motivation for the expulsion, this popular support undoubtedly made the move a much more appealing one for the royal authorities.

---

[2] See above, chapter 5.

[3] On the profit realized from these expulsions, see H. G. Richardson, *The English Jewry under Angevin Kings* (London, 1960), pp. 225–31, and Strayer, "Consent to Taxation under Philip the Fair," pp. 18–19.

[4] See above, chapter 5.

[5] Ibid.

[6] Ibid.

Related to this is the availability of charges against the Jews, which could serve as rationalization and legitimization for an act that was essentially one of despoliation. As is the case for most major expulsions of this period, the decree itself has not survived. The one significant contemporary edict of expulsion which is available is that issued by Charles of Sicily for the counties of Anjou and Maine. In that decree, it will be recalled, heavy emphasis was laid upon the misdeeds of the Jews, despite the influence of discernible economic considerations.[7] It seems quite likely that the expulsion of 1306 was similarly overlaid with a veneer of ostensible piety.

The precise details of the events of mid 1306 are difficult to unravel. There is no extensive Hebrew material on this expulsion; the Latin chronicles are sketchy in their description; and the documentary sources are concerned almost exclusively with the efforts to realize revenues in the wake of the banishment. A number of Latin accounts do indicate that there was a sequence of royal moves against the Jews, beginning with a general arrest, moving to a confiscation of goods, and culminating with expulsion.[8] This was not the gradual progression of actions initiated by Philip Augustus in the early 1180's; in 1306 the three stages followed quickly one upon the other, with the climactic act of expulsion obviously in mind throughout.

The initial arrest of the Jews seems to have been intended to prevent concealment of goods or funds; the government was interested, above all else, in maximum revenue from the expulsion and despoliation of the Jews. There are reflections of this earliest stage of the royal program in the *Journaux*. The *Journaux* records for February 10, 1308, indicate the payment of over 270 pounds to a knight named Hugo de Cella for his expenses in the seizure of the Jews of the bailliage of Bourges. The period of Hugo's efforts is specified as 151 days, stretching from early June through early November.[9] The arrest of the Jews thus seems to have been underway already in early June. The date widely assigned as the terminal point of the expulsion is the Feast of Mary Magdalene, falling on July 22.[10] The first extant order for sale of Jewish goods stems from August 18, 1306. A memorandum to the bailiff of Tours stipulates that he is to begin selling the goods of the

---

[7]Ibid.

[8]See, for example, *RHF*, vol. 21, pp. 647, 716; vol. 22, p. 19.

[9]*Journaux*, item no. 5874.

[10]See, for example, *RHF*, vol. 21, pp. 139, 716, 811.

Jews of his bailliage.[11] By this time, it is likely that almost all the Jews had made their exit from France.

The order established vaguely by the chronicles does then seem to be substantiated. The opening action was an arrest of the Jews, begun in early June 1306. This involved essentially a confiscation of Jewish goods, with an attempt to see that no valuables or useful records would be hidden. At this time a date for the exodus of the Jews was established. With the actual expulsion of the Jews completed by late July or early August, the arduous task of selling Jewish possessions and collecting Jewish debts began.

As noted already, the expulsion of 1306 was not the first banishment ordered by a Capetian monarch. It had, moreover, been foreshadowed by a series of similar edicts in neighboring territories during the last decades of the thirteenth century. Despite twelfth-and thirteenth-century precedents, however, the expulsion enacted by Philip the Fair was by far the most significant suffered by medieval Ashkenazic Jewry to date. The expulsion of 1182 had been serious enough, but between 1182 and 1306 the territory of royal France had grown enormously.[12] In addition, royal prerogatives had expanded as well. Thus, in 1306, Jews were expelled not only from the royal domain; they were simultaneously banished from a number of important adjacent seigneuries.[13] The result of the development of royal territory and royal power that vast areas were now affected by the royal decrees. In this respect, the expulsion of 1306 also overshadowed the edicts of the late 1280's and early 1290's. The banishments from Gascony, Anjou, Maine, and even England did not begin to compare in scope to that decreed by Philip the Fair.

The extensive areas included in the edict of Philip IV imposed double hardship on the Jews: large numbers of Jews were uprooted and the process of finding new homes was complicated by the long distances to be traversed before reaching territories open to Jewish settlement. The number of Jews expelled in 1306 is impossible to specify. The observation that it was double the 600,000 supposedly banished from Egypt in Biblical days can only serve as an indication of the fourteenth-century

---

[11] Siméon Luce, "Catalogue des documents du Trésor des Chartes relatifs aux Juifs sous le règne de Philippe le Bel," *REJ* 2 (1881), doc. no. 46.

[12] Auguste Longnon, *Atlas historique de la France* (Paris, 1888), maps 12, 13, and 14; idem and H.-François Delaborde, *La formation de l'unité française* (Paris, 1922).

[13] Léon Gauthier, "Les Juifs dans les deux Bourgognes," *REJ* 49 (1904): 219–24; Gustave Saige, *Les Juifs du Languedoc antérieurement au XIVe siècle* (Paris, 1881), p. 93.

sense of significant numbers and of terrible tragedy.[14] A recent study of late-thirteenth- and early-fourteenth-century Jewish population in royal France suggests a figure somewhere between 45,000 and 125,000 Jews.[15] Precisely how this would be broken down in terms of northern and southern France is not clear. In a vague and general way, we can only conclude that the number of Jews expelled was significant, certainly far larger than the number involved in earlier French and English expulsions, and that a substantial portion of those expelled must have been northern French Jews, long-time residents of the area under study.

The direction taken by the banished Jews is also not totally clear—again a result of the lack of sufficient Jewish source materials. It seems quite likely that the Jews of the north and those of the south, heirs to differing historical traditions and diverging links with neighboring Jewish communities, probably chose separate havens as they made their way out of France. The Jews of the south seem to have opted to remain in Mediterranean lands. The Jews of the north, on the other hand, seem to have held fast to their Franco-German orientation. Flight westward was of course impossible, since England had already been closed to Jewish habitation. The only real option then was movement eastward into imperial lands. A tangible indication of movement in this direction comes from the tax records for Bar-le-Duc in 1321, revealing the presence of numerous Jews of northern French provenance. Some of the localities from which these Jews originated include Arzillières, Doucey, Épense, Nangis, Rosières, Senonches, and Trainel.[16] While movement eastward allowed northern French Jewry to remain within the ambiance to which it had become accustomed and particularly to associate itself with Jewish communities whose life styles it shared, immigration into the German lands meant some very serious hardships.

As was the case for all such medieval expulsions of the Jews, those Jews unwilling to face the disheartening prospect of establishing new homes did have one significant alternative. Conversion to the Christian faith always saved the individual Jew from the rigors of banishment. Given the signs of some conversion among the Jews of late-thirteenth-

---

[14]Levi b. Gerson, *Perush al ha-Torah*, commentary on Leviticus 26:38. In *Shevet Yehudah*, the observation is ascribed to R. Levi b. Gerson but is cited mistakenly as part of his commentary on Numbers 23:10. Curiously, Samuel Usque transfers this estimate to the expulsion of 1182; see his *Consolation for the Tribulations of Israel*, trans. Martin Cohen (Philadelphia, 1965), pp. 177; 316, n. 28.

[15]Gérard Nahon, "Contributions à l'histoire des Juifs en France sous Philippe le Bel," *REJ* 121 (1962): 68-73.

[16]Émile Lévy, "Un document sur les Juifs de Barrois en 1321-23," *REJ* 19 (1889): 246-58.

century northern France, such action would not have been unthinkable. One of the Latin accounts of the expulsion does mention baptism on the part of Jews but indicates that it was not widespread.[17] This cautious description, coupled with the total silence of the remaining Christian sources and the lack of reference in the scanty Jewish materials, makes it plausible to conclude that conversion was in fact an option selected by only a few Jews.

By August 1306 French Jewry no longer existed. Those committed to remaining in France had ceased being Jewish; those committed to remaining Jewish had left French soil. For the government, however, the effort and the profit associated with the expulsion had just begun. Royal records from the first decades of the thirteenth century indicate how intensive the royal campaign to exploit Jewish wealth was.

Robert Mignon, writing in the early 1320's, devoted an entire section of his catalogue of royal accounts to those rolls dealing with the expulsion of 1306.[18] The records relating to the sale of Jewish goods and the realization of Jewish loans are grouped by bailliage and *prévôté*, beginning with the territories of the north and working southward. For our sector of France this includes the areas of Paris, Senlis, Virmandois, Amiens, Sens, Orléans, Bourges, Tours, Rouen, Caux, Caen, Coutances, Gisors, Troyes, Meaux, Vitry, and Chaumont. Mignon lists a total of twenty-two separate accounts for this area alone, with clear indication that his list is far from complete. Mignon makes it obvious also that the process of collecting and reporting the sums raised stretched over a long period of time. The earliest of the accounts dates from 1307; the latest were audited in the mid 1320's, almost two decades subsequent to the expulsion of 1306 and after a recall of the Jews and a second expulsion had intervened. In a number of instances, Mignon specifies the existence of more than one account for a particular bailliage, indicating a series of attempts to hunt down all possible income from the Jews. Mignon also reflects a very careful auditing of the original reports, showing extensive concern for full disclosure by responsible royal officials of all revenues. In view of the cases of malfeasance documented elsewhere, the careful checking described by Mignon was far from superfluous.

Unfortunately, Mignon is rarely precise about the sums realized in the various bailliages. In fact, in only one instance does he specify the total revenue recorded in a particular account.[19] Clearly, however, in

[17]*RHF*, vol. 21, p. 647.
[18]Mignon, item nos. 2125–80.
[19]Ibid., item no. 2137.

many instances the sums collected and carefully documented were sub-stantial. Indicative of this is Mignon's report that the account for Jew-ish goods in the bailliages of Troyes and Meaux showed almost 60,000 pounds still owed by the responsible royal officials. The account for Jewish goods in the bailliage of Vitry showed 22,694 pounds still owed, while that for the bailliage of Chaumont reveals 21,978 still unpaid by the royal collectors.[20] In the absence of more precise information, we can only conclude that the efforts partially reflected in the accounts described by Mignon must have involved substantial income for the royal coffers, over a period stretching from 1306 through the early 1320's.

Mignon indicates that the revenue realized from Jewish wealth fell basically into two classifications. Many of the rolls detail the revenue from Jewish possessions, that is, from sale of Jewish movable goods and of Jewish real estate; others record income from Jewish debts assidu-ously collected by royal officials. Each type of income presented its own problems.

Many of the documents dealing with the aftermath of the expulsion are deeds of sale. One of the most important bureaucratic activities subsequent to 1306 was the effort to sell Jewish holdings and to turn real estate into the always-needed ready cash. The substantial documen-tation shows sale of many Jewish communal possessions, such as synagogues, schools, and cemeteries. There is, in addition, disposition of private holdings as well, including homes, fields, and vineyards. In some instances the sums realized from these sales were high. The most valuable single parcel of Jewish land was the Jewish cemetery of Paris, valued at 1,000 pounds.[21] The high assessment of well-situated land in the rapidly growing capital is not surprising. The Jewish cemetery at Sens, along with an adjacent house, was sold for 400 pounds, and the cemetery at Mantes was appraised at 200 pounds.[22] While communal facilities usually fetched the highest prices, private dwellings also proved extremely valuable. Thus a 1313 document records the sale of a particularly well-situated and probably well-built Jewish home in Provins for 400 pounds.[23]

Sale of Jewish property was an arduous task, involving the energies of a plethora of royal agents. Equally important, however—and perhaps more difficult—was the attempt to collect the debts owed the expelled

---

[20] Ibid., item nos. 2151–53.

[21] *Registres*, doc. no. 1427.

[22] Luce, "Catalogue des documents," doc. no. 75; *Registres*, doc. no. 560.

[23] Luce, "Catalogue des documents," doc. no. 101.

Jews. The prerequisite for effective realization of these debts was, first of all, the availability of adequate records. With the early-fourteenth-century royal retreat from support of Jewish lending, governmental information on Jewish loans may have dwindled.[24] Thus the confiscation of Jewish records became extremely important and was a major goal of the seizure of the Jews and their assets which took place prior to expulsion. Royal officials were brutally indiscriminate in sequestering Jewish documents, with no distinction drawn between business and personal affairs. Thus, one of the major legal questions to arise in the wake of the expulsion concerned women whose marriage contracts had been seized along with their husbands' business deeds.[25]

While the materials impounded included in some instances governmentally drawn-up charters, in most cases they were far less formal. Examples of confiscated Jewish business books have survived from the neighboring duchy of Burgundy.[26] While the details of Jewish book-keeping at this stage are obscure, it is obvious that the Jewish note-books must have presented very serious problems to those royal agents striving to use them for the practical purpose of collecting pre-1306 debts. Given the difficulties involved in utilizing the Jewish records and the normal propensity of debtors to avoid payment, we can readily comprehend the dimensions of the dilemma that plagued royal official-dom.

Legislation of 1310 and 1311 reveals some of the issues which hounded the king's collectors. On January 11, 1310, Philip made his first major pronouncement on the collection of Jewish debts. He ordered, first of all, that debts more than twenty years old were to be held invalid. The assumption governing this clause was that such old debts were likely to have been paid at some earlier point. More significant was the series of provisions made for proving that less antiquated debts had been repaid. These stipulations provided that (1) a combination of the debtor's possession of the loan instrument along with his oath that the obligation had been discharged would constitute sufficient proof of payment; (2) a pre-1306 Jewish memorandum indicating discharge of the debt would alone suffice as proof of payment; and (3) in cases involving less than ten pounds, the oath of a debtor of good reputation plus the testimony of a trustworthy witness would void the obligation. A third major item in the legislation of 1310 was the disa-

---

[24]See above, chapter 5.

[25]Abba Mari of Lunel, *Minḥat Kenaot* (Brody, 1837), p. 179.

[26]Isidore Loeb, "Deux livres de commerce du commencement du XIVe siècle," *REJ* 8 (1884): 161-96; 9 (1884): 21-50, 187-213.

vowal of usury. The brief mention of this issue raises the suspicion that it was simply an empty gesture made in the direction of Church sensitivities. In view of the very complicated procedures and the extensive bureaucratic activities occasioned by Louis IX's serious attempt to free his government from the moral stigma of profit from usury, the curt provision of Philip rings hollow. Finally, imprisonment and violence were rejected as methods for the collection of unpaid obligations.[27] The edict of Philip reflects some very serious agitation on the part of—or at least on the behalf of—the debtors of France. Some amelioration of the lot of these debtors was provided, at least as regards easier avenues for proving repayment of a debt and exclusion of cruelty in the collection of unpaid obligations. Elimination of interest seems far less likely.

While the edict of 1310 reflects basically the complaints of the debtor class and the accommodations made by the government, legislation enacted the following year reveals some of the more extreme expedients adopted by royal authorities in gaining the information necessary for full collection of debts.[28] As a result of the grievous state of documentation and in light of the possibility of claims, just and unjust, that the obligation had already been discharged, the government decided to utilize the testimony of those witnesses best able to decipher the Jewish records and to refute unwarranted assertions of prior payment—namely, the Jews themselves. It is unclear precisely when the utilization of Jews for the purpose of clarifying obligations still owed began. The royal order of August 22, 1311, indicates that the practice was already in existence. In this edict, the inducement for Jewish return is spelled out. The Jews were offered one-third of the income collected with their aid. This is again reflective of the serious problems encountered by the government in enforcing Jewish debts. The willingness to forgo 33 percent of the profits is a significant gauge of the government's growing sense of futility. Actually, the edict of August 1311 represents ostensibly the termination of this partnership in loan collection and in fact proclaims the end to all enforcement of Jewish debts except those extremely well-established. The expulsion of the Jews recalled to aid in debt collection, the disavowal of further attempts to enforce obligations owed the Jews, and the call to all royal commissions to cease activities and to report their income looks again like a major victory for the debtor class.

[27] *Olim*, vol. 2, p. 506, case no. 6.
[28] *Ordonnances*, vol. 1, pp. 488–89.

In fact, however, the efforts to collect Jewish revenue continued. As noted already, the records described by Mignon show collection and auditing going on well past 1311, in fact down into the 1320's. Indeed a key stipulation of the charter extended to returning Jews by Louis X in 1315 provided that these Jews be permitted to claim debts owed them prior to 1306, with the Jew receiving one-third of the sum collected and the government two-thirds.[29] This is, of course, precisely the arrangement noted earlier. It seems quite plausible that the permission to return in 1315 was motivated—at least in part—by hopes of profiting from some of the funds still outstanding.

As indicated, it was extremely difficult to realize fully the anticipated riches from the legacy of pre-1306 French Jewry—whether through sale of Jewish property or through collection of Jewish debts. These difficulties were complicated by the normal problems of malfeasance on the part of those officials entrusted with important fiscal responsibility.

As early as 1308, the central authorities were concerned that the accounts for Jewish affairs be brought to Paris for careful reckoning.[30] The edict of August 22, 1311, which seemingly signaled the end of the campaign to collect Jewish debts, stipulated that all the commissioners dealing with Jewish affairs were to bring their records to Paris for auditing.[31] Mignon, in his description of the accounts of many of these commissions, indicates that the records were very meticulously examined.

By early 1312 evidence appears for misappropriation of funds, with suitable penalties levied against the guilty royal agents. On February 12, 1312, the viscount of Orbec was fined 1,000 pounds for his misdeeds with regard to the collection of revenues from the sale of Jewish goods.[32] More interesting yet are the proceedings of June 1312.[33] Perrequin of Milli, a Jew, who had served as a governmental agent prior to 1306 and who was probably one of the Jews recalled to aid in the pursuit of Jewish debts, brought charges of malfeasance against the commissioners for Jewish affairs in the bailliage of Bourges. The case was taken up by Parliament, and the royal officials in question were absolved of wrongdoing. Shortly thereafter, however, on June 29, the king established a new commission to look into irregularities in the

[29] Ibid., p. 596.
[30] Registres, doc. no. 752.
[31] Ordonnances, vol. 1, p. 489.
[32] Olim, vol. 3, p. 749, case no. 32.
[33] Ibid., p. 675, case no. 40.

collection of revenues from Jewish property and debts.[34] This new commission was to be composed of three members—two clerics and one lay advisor—and was to be aided by the testimony of a number of Jews recalled specifically for that purpose. These Jews were to remain in royal France only briefly, solely in connection with their function on the new royal commission. Provision was made, however, for the recall of a series of such Jews, should the situation warrant. The inducement for return was again the standard kind of sharing in the revenues gained. A number of cases during 1314 show the new commission hard at work, receiving the moneys accruing from sale of the property of those officials found guilty of absconding with funds from Jewish goods and loans.[35]

The expulsion of 1306 had been decreed with the objective of gaining significant royal income from the confiscated estates of the banished Jews. In large measure, the goal of the expulsion had been achieved—substantial sums had in fact been realized; at the same time, serious difficulties had been encountered along the way. Some of these problems had eventually necessitated the recall of a number of Jews whose aid had been enlisted through a promise of shared revenues. By 1315, with the bulk of the moneys from the Jews already collected, the new king, Louis X, decided to issue a general edict of recall for the Jews. While the factors in this shift of royal policy are complex, one hope was still related to the expulsion of 1306—the possiblity of squeezing out yet more of the moneys that had been owed prior to 1306. One of the conditions offered the returning Jews was the option of claiming old debts—with the monarchy receiving its ubiquitous 67 percent.[36]

The history of medieval Jewry in northern France concludes for all practical purposes during the summer of 1306. Sporadic Jewish presence down through 1394 forms only an epilogue to the vital chapters of medieval French Jewish life. Although our study ends also with 1306, the charter of 1315, inviting Jews to return and resettle in France, is worth brief examination. The charter of 1315 established a new foundation for Jewish settlement in France. French Jewry had never shared the German Jewish tradition of political charters. Even after the expulsion of 1182, the return of the Jews to royal France in 1198 occasioned

[34] *Registres*, doc. no. 2085.

[35] Ibid., doc. nos. 2085, 2222, 2225.

[36] *Ordonnances*, vol. 1, p. 596.

no broad statement of Jewish rights and limitations.[37] Subsequent to 1315, however, French Jewish life was to be weakly grounded in an explicit set of royal stipulations.[38]

In a pious preamble, the reasons for the recall are established. These include heavy pressures exerted by the Jews and supposedly by the populace. The case for readmission of the Jews was buttressed by appeals to the august figures of the popes and of Saint Louis, the most distinguished of the Capetian line, and by reference to traditional Church views of the basic necessity for toleration of the Jews. All of this coalesces into an impeccable argument for the return of the Jews, a move the motivation for which probably lies elsewhere.

Having established a compelling rationale for reentry of the Jews, Louis then proceeds to make the three basic stipulations which would govern their resettlement: (1) The Jews might return for a dozen years, residing in those places which prior to 1306 had been open to them. This qualification is a reflection of the growing tendency towards exclusion of the Jews from certain localities during the reign of Philip the Fair. (2) The Jews were to earn their livelihood from crafts or from dealing in good merchandise. This is taken almost verbatim from the 1235 and 1253 edicts of Saint Louis, whose image had loomed so large in the preamble to the charter. Significant is the elimination of Louis's overt repudiation of usury. The result is a curious evocation of the stance of Saint Louis, but without the actual moneylending prohibition. (3) The Jews were to display prominently the badge which distinguished them from their Christian neighbors.

The next set of provisions in this unusually well-organized charter deals with issues likely to arise in regard to pre-1306 Jewish wealth. The Jews might collect debts owed prior to 1306, retaining one-third of the money and remitting two-thirds to the government. We have already suggested that this arrangement may have had more than a little to do with the decision to readmit the Jews. Pre-1306 Jewish communal property was to be returned to the Jews in exchange for proper payment; where this would prove impossible, suitable alternatives would be offered for Jewish purchase. Books still held were to be repossessed by the Jews, with the exception of the condemned Talmud.

The final group of stipulations deals explicity with some of the issues raised by renewed Jewish presence. While the Jews were being readmitted for only twelve years, provision was made for a gradual exodus

[37] See above.
[38] *Ordonnances*, vol. 1, pp. 595–97.

should the right of settlement not be renewed. In case of nonrenewal, the Jews were to be given a full year to close down their affairs and to leave. Eventually, however, even the basic guarantee of twelve years residence was not observed.

The major concern in this third section of the charter is moneylending. The discussion of Jewish lending begins with a repetition of the encouragement of crafts and trade. If, however, the Jews should peradventure slip into moneylending, they were to take as interest no more than two pennies per pound per week, precisely the rate specified by Philip Augustus more than a century earlier. Likewise repeated from Philip Augustus is the provision that the Jews must not begin to compound interest within the first year of the loan and that the debtor might pay his obligation at any point, with the interest ceasing at that juncture. Another old prohibition is the exclusion of Church vessels from Jewish moneylending business—they were not to be accepted by the Jews as pawns. The next two clauses are reminiscent of the edict of Louis VIII and of the early legislation of Louis IX. They outlaw governmental involvement in Jewish lending. The authorities were not to enforce Jewish usury in any way. This is, of course, a rather mild stipulation, reflecting the stand taken by Louis VIII in 1223, a position which Louis IX went far beyond. Louis IX's ordinance of 1230 is represented in the provision that no royal letters were to be drawn up in support of Jewish loans. The explicit implication was that the Jews could assure return of their moneys only through the depositing of pawns. The attitude on Jewish lending is generally moderate; the charter includes no enactments from the harsher legislation which followed 1230.

Finally, arrangements were provided for adequate regulation of Jewish affairs through the appointment of two governmental agents charged with the responsibility for France's newly recalled Jewish inhabitants. This, like so much else, reflects the bureaucratic stance adopted by Philip the Fair, the monarch who had exiled these same Jews.

Most of the details of the ordinance of 1315 thus find their roots in pre-1306 Jewish life. What has changed dramatically is the foundation for renewed Jewish settlement in northern France. The totality of this change is a result of the slow erosion of Jewish status through the latter half of the preceding century and the finality of the *coup de grace* administered by Philip IV.

Thus, in mid 1306, the creative stage of medieval Jewish history in northern France drew to a close. The French kingdom had ultimately proven inhospitable to Jewish life. The Jewish presence in France would only reemerge significantly with a comprehensive restructuring of French society.

The expulsion of 1306 must not obscure the achievements of medieval French Jewry. Jewish communities had grown and spread across the face of northern France for a number of centuries. Severely limited in their economic outlets, these Jews had proven remarkably adaptable and enterprising in capitalizing on the minimal opportunities offered to them. Cultural and religious creativity had not been long in developing. Particularly the period between the late eleventh and the mid thirteenth century had seen an efflorescence of Jewish scholarship that was to enrich all subsequent Jewish intellectual endeavor. The northern French component of Ashkenazic Jewry had certainly carved out for itself a distinguished place in its people's long history.

And yet all these efforts failed to win the Jews a permanent place in medieval France. The French kingdom became and remained almost *Judenrein*. It seems fruitless to pinpoint any one specific element that brought about this failure. The constellation of factors that led to the events of 1306 has been delineated—growing popular hostility, crushing royal financial needs, the total political vulnerability of the Jews. When we proceed, however, to ask what gave rise to the popular animosity or what fostered complete dependence on the ruling powers, we shall always return to the underlying issue—a society so thoroughly organized around Christian life as to make Jewish presence inevitably peripheral and marginal. It was the distinct "otherness" of the medieval Jew that roused widespread antipathy, limited economic opportunities (often forcing the Jews into the kinds of enterprise that heightened hatreds), and threw the Jews headlong into the camp of the established authorities (again augmenting animosities). That Jews could settle as widely and as usefully as they did was the result largely of the immaturity of European society at this stage, making possible certain economic roles, and of the vigor and ingenuity of these Jewish pioneers. The economic maturation of European society and the more effective spread of Christian identity made Jewish life less and less viable.

As this process took place, there were essentially two options available. In the smaller and less organized states of central Europe, Jewish life continued, with a diminishing economic role and burgeoning dangers from popular resentment. In the larger and better organized states of the west, especially England and France, Jewish life officially and abruptly ended. Which of the two alternatives was ultimately the better can be debated.

In 1306, while Jewish life in France ended for a period, the Jews of France and the life style which they had so painstakingly created found new homes for themselves. These Jews moved eastward into Germany and eventually onward into areas of Christendom once more immature and hence once more hospitable. Eventually, many centuries later, France was to become the first great European state to restructure itself thoroughly and, in the process, to create a new and more dignified place for Jewish life. Lamentably, the tragedies of this second stage of Jewish life in France may be traceable in no small measure to the legacy of the first.

APPENDIX

JEWISH SETTLEMENT IN MEDIEVAL
NORTHERN FRANCE

THROUGHOUT THIS STUDY, there have been recurrent references to the patterns of Jewish settlement in medieval northern France. The essentially chronological framework of the investigation has made it impossible to gather all the relevant data in any one chapter. In view of the value of this information, it seems wise to collect all the available evidence and append a comprehensive map of Jewish settlements during the tenth through the fourteenth centuries.[1]

There is substantial source material for construction of such a map, although some of it poses problems of interpretation. Perhaps the most reliable data for the existence of a medieval Jewish community are tax records. Particularly useful, for example, is the Champenois tax list of 1251, indicating more than fifty Jewish communities in that county.[2] Equally conclusive are references to Jewish communal facilities, such as synagogues, cemeteries, and schools. Most of these references are found in documents disposing of Jewish communal property in the wake of

---

[1] For an earlier study of a more limited geographic area, see Robert Chazan, "Jewish Settlement in Northern France, 1096-1306," *REJ* 128 (1969): 41-65. For additional studies, see ibid., p. 41, n. 1.

[2] Auguste Longnon, ed., *Documents relatifs au comté de Champagne et de Brie, 1172-1361*, 3 vols. (Paris, 1901-4), vol. 3, pp. 11-12.

the expulsions of the period, particularly those of 1182 and 1306. Where documents attest a number of Jews settled in a particular town, a Jewish community can be safely posited, with the recognition that such communities were often quite small in size.[3] There are occasional problems associated with these data. The most persistent is the difficulty in identifying the designated site, resulting partially from changing orthography and partially from the popularity of certain place names. Thus, for example, a random reference to Jews in Chaumont is useless, since there were so many towns by that name. Occasionally of course the context indicates clearly which Chaumont is meant. Despite extensive efforts, there remain a small number of locales which we have been unable to identify or to identify conclusively. The procedure chosen has been to err in the direction of conservatism. Where significant doubt exists, we have omitted the reference.

In this regard, one special type of evidence should be noted. There is occasional mention in medieval texts of a "rue des Juifs."[4] Such a designation surely reflects the existence of a Jewish community. Because of the tendency to preserve such appellations, however, these "rues des Juifs" have not been considered, since they might possibly be carry-overs from an earlier age. While most of these designations probably do indicate a Jewish community during our period, we have once more preferred to remain as conservative as possible.

Proof of individual Jewish settlement is listed separately. In many cases, while no indications of a Jewish community have survived, there are references to Jews "of a particular town." The precise meaning of these surnames is generally unclear. They may mean that the Jew had been born in that town, that he had once lived in that town, or that he was currently a resident of that town. Although these issues are of prime importance for the biography of the individual Jew, they are less consequential for us. Such a surname can usually be taken as indicative of Jewish residence in the given locale.[5] While references to individual Jewish settlement are listed separately, it is highly likely that in the majority of cases the presence of one Jew reflects the existence of a community. Hopefully this listing of individual Jews may spur the search for evidence of the communities to which they once belonged.

[3] Chazan, "Jewish Settlement in Northern France," p. 45.

[4] For a list of towns with "rues des Juifs," see Robert Anchel, *Les Juifs de France* (Paris, 1946), pp. 41–57, and Bernhard Blumenkranz, "Contributions à la nouvelle *Gallia Judaica*," *Archives juives* 4 (1967–68): 27–29, 35–37.

[5] For the view of H. G. Richardson that such surnames may reflect only a "house of business or occasional residence" and for my disagreement, see Chazan, "Jewish Settlement in Northern France," p. 59, n. 1.

Again one special class of source material has been excluded. In thirteenth-century records there are extensive references to converts; most of these are connected with royal doles in support of these new additions to the reigning faith.[6] While almost all of these converts were formerly Jews, and while the surname designating them as converts "of a particular town" probably implies their residence in that town as Jews, this evidence has not been utilized. Again the level of uncertainty seems sufficient to warrant exclusion.

The most obvious feature of medieval Jewish settlement revealed by our map is its diffusion. Jewish residence in well over two hundred locales is attested. Given the fragmentary nature of the evidence and the problems associated with it, we may well surmise that fuller and clearer data would yield testimony to additional Jewish settlements.

While Jews are shown to be settled in all the major municipalities of northern France, it is striking to note how widely they resided in smaller towns. In fact, our investigation of the latter half of the thirteenth century reinforces this conclusion. At that point, it will be recalled, ecclesiastical pressures mounted for segregation of the Jews, in order to minimize their potential religious impact. This involved institution of the Jewish badge, in order that the individual Jew be readily identifiable, and expulsion of the Jews from smaller towns and villages, where contact with the peasantry might have deleterious effects.[7] Such an effort in and of itself surely reflects widespread Jewish settlement. It is interesting, moreover, to examine the precise formulations of Philip III and his son. While acknowledging the presence of Jews in small towns, Philip III attempted to depict this phenomenon as an aberration, ordering that the Jews be confined to the larger towns of the realm "in which they have been accustomed to dwell of yore."[8] Eight years later, however, Philip IV reissued the same order, with explicit admission that the Jews had, on the contrary, been accustomed to dwelling in many of the villages of France. He pointed, in this regard, to the bailliage of Caen in particular. This reality notwithstanding, they were henceforth to be restricted to towns large enough to support a market.[9]

It is not difficult to identify the major factor leading to such population dispersion. Our study has shown the extent to which the Jews

---

[6] For a list of such converts, drawn from royal records, see Gérard Nahon, "Contribution à l'histoire des Juifs en France sous Philippe le Bel," *REJ* 121 (1962): 76–78.

[7] See above, chapters 4 and 5.

[8] Gustave Saige, *Les Juifs du Languedoc antérieurement au XIVe siècle* (Paris, 1881), pp. 212–13.

[9] Ibid., p. 223.

Jewish Settlement in Medieval Northern France

became, during the twelfth and thirteenth centuries, rooted in one area of the economy. A group with such limited economic outlets was faced with a serious problem of overpopulation in any given town. A specific municipality could support, during our period, only a limited number of Jews. In the face of a high birth rate and an expanding Jewish population, there were only a few expedients available. One was withdrawal from the area altogether in search of better economic conditions. Our analysis has revealed little evidence of such emigration during the twelfth and thirteenth centuries. A second alternative was movement out of the major urban centers and into smaller towns. It is this tendency which is strongly indicated in our map.

While the economic motivation for Jewish movement into the countryside has often been noted, a key prerequisite for such dispersion has generally been overlooked. No matter how strong the economic pressure, Jews could not settle in small towns and villages in those areas where basic physical security was lacking. Again the findings of our investigation of medieval French Jewish life coincide with the evidence of widespread Jewish settlement. One of the striking aspects of the history of medieval French Jewry was the relative lack of popular violence. Even during the dangerous years of the Crusades, in which Frenchmen played a predominant role, there are few instances in which popular hostility led to physical assault upon the Jews. This record is largely a tribute to the effective governance of the barons and especially of the monarchs of northern France. While occasionally they themselves were responsible for bloody attacks, the control which they exercised made it possible for the Jews of northern France to venture forth from the relative safety of large Jewish settlements in major towns and to establish small enclaves across the length and the breadth of the land.

The accompanying lists attempt to advance minimal evidence for the presence of Jewish communities or Jewish individuals in the locales shown on the map. Where the Jewish community is well known, the appropriate passage in Gross's *Gallia Judaica* is cited, although additional data have occasionally been supplied. For settlements not mentioned by Gross, relevant sources are adduced. There has been, however, no attempt to produce all the evidence. We have gathered only enough data to establish the presence of a Jewish community or of a Jewish individual or, where possible, to show continued Jewish settlement over an extended period of time.

Jewish Communities

Alençon (Orne)—Henri Gross, *Gallia Judaica* (Paris, 1897), p. 56. See also Amédée Léchaudé d'Anisy, ed., *Grands rôles des echiquiers de Normandie*, 2 vols. (Paris, 1845–52), vol. 1, p. 71 (1195).

Amboise (Indre-et-Loire)—Lucien Lazard, "Les Juifs de Touraine," *REJ* 17 (1888): 227–30 (before 1306).

Andelot (Haute-Marne)—Auguste Longnon, ed., *Documents relatifs au comté de Champagne et de Brie, 1172–1361*, 3 vols. (Paris, 1901–4), vol. 3, pp. 11–12 (1251); Siméon Luce, "Catalogue des documents du Trésor des Chartes relatifs aux Juifs sous le règne de Philippe le Bel," *REJ* 2 (1881), doc. no. 82 (before 1306).

Angy (Oise)—*RHF*, vol. 24, p. 64* (1300).

Aumale (Seine-Maritime)—ibid., p. 277* (c. 1210).

Auxerre (Yonne)—Gross, *Gallia Judaica*, pp. 60–62.

Bar-sur-Aube (Aube)—Longnon, *Documents relatifs au comté de Champagne et de Brie*, vol. 3, pp. 11–12 (1251).

Bar-sur-Seine (Aube)—ibid. (1251); also ibid., vol. 2, pp. 54–55 (1276–78).

Barbonne-Fayel (Marne)—ibid., vol. 3, pp. 11–12 (1251).

Bayeux (Calvados)—*Layettes*, vol. 5, doc. no. 372 (c. 1233); *Journaux*, item no. 707 (1298).

Bernay (Eure)—Léchaudé d'Anisy, *Grands rôles*, vol. 1, p. 28 (1180); Ernest Perrot, ed., *Arresta communia Scaccarii* (Caen, 1910), doc. no. 1 (1276).

Béthisy-Saint-Pierre (Oise)—Nicolas Brussel, *Nouvel examen de l'usage des fiefs en France*, 2 vols. (Paris, 1750), vol. 2, p. CXCVII (1203).

Blois (Loir-et-Cher)—Gross, *Gallia Judaica*, p. 117.

Bonneval (Eure-et-Loir)—*Layettes*, vol. 4, doc. no. 5068 (1265); Brussel, *Nouvel examen*, vol. 1, p. 612 (before 1306).

Bourges (Cher)—Gross, *Gallia Judaica*, pp. 110–11.

Braine (Aisne)—Maxime Sars and Lucien Broche, *Histoire de Braine* (La Charité-sur-Loire, 1933), pp. 9–11.

Bray-sur-Seine (Seine-et-Marne)—Gross, *Gallia Judaica*, pp. 123–24.

Bréval (Seine-et-Oise)—*RHF*, vol. 24, p. 277* (c. 1210).

Bussy-le-Château (Marne)—Longnon, *Documents relatifs au comté de Champagne et de Brie*, vol. 3, pp. 11–12 (1251).

Caen (Calvados)—Gross, *Gallia Judaica*, pp. 541–45.

Carentan (Manche)—*Layettes*, vol. 5, doc. no. 372 (c. 1233).

Caudebec-en-Caux (Seine-Maritime)—Léchaudé d'Anisy, *Grands rôles*, vol. 1, pp. 41–42 (1195), 117 (1204); Léopold Delisle, ed., *Cartulaire normand* (Caen, 1852), doc. no. 1128 (1224).

Châlons-sur-Marne (Marne)—Luce, "Catalogue des documents," doc. no. 104 (before 1306).

Chantemerle (Marne)—Longnon, *Documents relatifs au comté de Champagne et de Brie*, vol. 3, pp. 11–12 (1251).

Chaource (Aube)—Gross, *Gallia Judaica*, p. 535. See also Longnon, *Documents relatifs au comté de Champagne et de Brie*, vol. 3, pp. 11–12 (1251).

Charray (Eure-et-Loir)—Brussel, *Nouvel examen*, vol. 1, p. 612 (before 1306).

Chartres (Eure-et-Loir)—Gross, *Gallia Judaica*, pp. 602–5.

Château-Landon (Seine-et-Marne)—ibid., pp. 259-61. See also Joseph Thillier and Eugène Jarry, eds., *Cartulaire de Sainte-Croix d'Orléans* (Orléans, 1906), pp. 496-97 (1296).

Château-Thierry (Aisne)—Gross, *Gallia Judaica*, pp. 257-59.

Châteaudun (Eure-et-Loir)—Brussel, *Nouvel examen*, vol. 1, p. 612 (before 1306).

Châteauneuf-sur-Loire (Loiret)—Théophile Cochard, *La juiverie d'Orléans* (Orléans, 1895), p. 47 (1223).

Châtillon-sur-Marne (Marne)—Edgard Boutaric, ed., *Actes du Parlement de Paris*, 2 vols. (Paris, 1863-67), vol. 1, p. 414 (1288).

Chaumont-en-Bassigny (Haute-Marne)—Longnon, *Documents relatifs au comté de Champagne et de Brie*, vol. 3, pp. 11-12 (1251).

Chaumont-en-Vexin (Oise)—*Olim*, vol. 2, p. 439, case no. 23 (1300).

Chauny (Aisne)—ibid., vol. 1, p. 944, case no. 46 (1273).

Chécy (Loiret)—Cochard, *La juiverie d'Orléans*, p. 47 (1223).

Chinon (Indre-et-Loire)—Gross, *Gallia Judaica*, pp. 577-87.

Condé-en-Brie (Aisne)—E. de l'Épinas, *Histoire de la ville et des sires de Coucy* (Paris, 1848), p. 347 (1228).

Corbeil-Essonnes (Essonne)—Gross, *Gallia Judaica*, pp. 559-72.

Cosne-sur-Loire (Nièvre)—René de Lespinasse, *Le Nivernais et les comtes de Nevers*, 3 vols. (Paris, 1909-14), vol. 2, pp. 225-26 (1250).

Coucy-le-Château-Auffrique (Aisne)—Gross, *Gallia Judaica*, pp. 554-59.

Coulommiers (Seine-et-Marne)—Longnon, *Documents relatifs au comté de Champagne et de Brie*, vol. 3, pp. 11-12 (1251); ibid., vol. 2, p. 83 (1276-78).

Coutances (Manche)—Gross, *Gallia Judaica*, p. 553. See also Léopold Delisle, "Recueil des jugements de l'Echiquier de Normandie," *Notices et extraits des manuscrits de la Bibliothèque nationale* 20,2 (1862), doc. no. 315 (1221).

Dampierre (Aube)—Gross, *Gallia Judaica*, pp. 160-70.

Dieppe (Seine-Maritime)—*Layettes*, vol. 1, doc. no. 1282 (1218).

Domfront (Orne)—Léchaudé d'Anisy, *Grands rôles*, vol. 1, p. 116 (1204).

Dormans (Marne)—*Layettes*, vol. 2, doc. no. 2153 (1231).

Dourdan (Essonne)—Brussel, *Nouvel examen*, vol. 1, p. 612 (before 1306).

Dreux (Eure-et-Loir)—Gross, *Gallia Judaica*, pp. 171-85.

Dun-sur-Auron (Cher)—Luce, "Catalogue des documents," doc. no. 63 (before 1306).

Épernay (Marne)—Gross, *Gallia Judaica*, p. 66. See also Auguste Nicaise, *Épernay et l'abbaye St.-Martin de cette ville*, 2 vols. (Châlons-sur-Marne, 1869), vol. 2, pp. 64-65 (1222), and Longnon, *Documents relatifs au comté de Champagne et de Brie*, vol. 3, pp. 11-12 (1251).

Étampes (Essonne)—Gross, *Gallia Judaica*, pp. 44-45. See also Brussel, *Nouvel examen*, vol. 1, p. 612 (before 1306).

Évreux (Eure)—Gross, *Gallia Judaica*, pp. 38-43. See also *Registres*, doc. no. 833 (before 1306).

Falaise (Calvados)—Gross, *Gallia Judaica*, pp. 476-83.

Fécamp (Seine-Maritime)—Léchaudé d'Anisy, *Grands rôles*, vol. 1, p. 41 (1195); *Olim*, vol. 2, p. 437, case no. 19 (1300).

Fismes (Marne)—Brussel, *Nouvel examen*, vol. 1, p. 612 (before 1306).

Gisors (Eure)—Léchaudé d'Anisy, *Grands rôles*, vol. 1, p. 34 (1184); *Journaux*, item no. 707 (1298).

Illiers (Eure-et-Loir)—Brussel, *Nouvel examen*, p. 612 (before 1306).

Isle-Aumont (Aube)—Longnon, *Documents relatifs au comté de Champagne et de Brie*, vol. 3, pp. 11-12 (1251).

Janville (Eure-et-Loir)—Gross, *Gallia Judaica*, pp. 253-54; Luce, "Catalogue des documents," doc. no. 99 (before 1306).

Joigny (Yonne)—Gross, *Gallia Judaica*, pp. 250-53.

Joyenval (Yvelines)—*Registres*, doc. no. 1947 (before 1306).

Laferté-sur-Aube (Haute-Marne)—Longnon, *Documents relatifs au comté de Champagne et de Brie*, vol. 3, pp. 11-12 (1251).

Laon (Aisne)—Bernhard Blumenkranz, "Géographie historique d'un thème de l'iconographie religieuse: les représentations de Synagoga en France," *Mélanges offerts à René Crozet* (Poitiers, 1966), p. 1142 (1230's); *RHF*, vol. 24, pp. 227, 290-91 (1248).

Le Mans (Sarthe)—Gross, *Gallia Judaica*, pp. 362-63. See also Robert Chazan, "The Persecution of 992," *REJ* 129 (1970): 217-21 (992).

Ligny-le-Ribault (Loiret)—Charles Petit-Dutaillis, *Étude sur la vie et le règne de Louis VIII (1187-1226)* (Paris, 1894), p. 523 (1226).

Lillebonne (Seine-Maritime)—Léchaudé d'Anisy, *Grands rôles*, vol. 1, pp. 41-42 (1195), 110 (1203), 117 (1204).

Lisieux (Calvados)—Gross, *Gallia Judaica*, pp. 291-92. See also Léchaudé d'Anisy, *Grands rôles*, vol. 1, p. 105 (1203).

Lizy-sur-Ourcq (Seine-et-Marne)—Luce, "Catalogue des documents," doc. no. 68 (before 1306).

Loches (Indre-et-Loire)—Gross, *Gallia Judaica*, pp. 292-93. See also Adolf Neubauer and Mortiz Stern, eds., *Hebräische Berichte über die Judenverfolgungen während der Kreuzzüge* (Berlin, 1892), p. 33, and Abraham Habermann, ed., *Sefer Gezerot Ashkenaz ve-Zarfat* (Jerusalem, 1945), p. 144 (1171); *RHF*, vol. 22, p. 118 (1285).

Longueville-sur-Scie (Seine-Maritime)—Léchaudé d'Anisy, *Grands rôles*, vol. 1, pp. 41-42 (1195); Léopold Delisle, ed., *Catalogue des actes de Philippe Auguste* (Paris, 1856), pp. 508-9 (c. 1204); *RHF*, vol. 24, p. 277* (c. 1210).

Lormaye (Eure-et-Loir)—Luce, "Catalogue des documents," doc. no. 19 (1304).

Mantes-la-Jolie (Yvelines)—ibid., doc. no. 85 (before 1306).

Mayenne (Mayenne)—Gross, *Gallia Judaica*, p. 314. See also Albert Grosse-Duperon, ed., *Documents sur la ville de Mayenne* (Mayenne, 1906), pp. 15 (c. 1200), 26 (1205), 77 (1209).

Meaux (Seine-et-Marne)—Gross, *Gallia Judaica*, pp. 340-42. See also Longnon, *Documents relatifs au comté de Champagne et de Brie*, vol. 3, pp. 11-12 (1251); *Comptes royaux*, vol. 2, item no. 16042 (1302); *Journaux*, item no. 5851 (before 1306).

Melun (Seine-et-Marne)—Gross, *Gallia Judaica*, pp. 351-55.

Méry-sur-Seine (Aube)—Longnon, *Documents relatifs au comté de Champagne et de Brie*, vol. 3, pp. 11-12 (1251).

Milly-sur-Thérain (Oise)—*Layettes*, vol. 4, doc. no. 5488 (1269).

Montereau-faut-Yonne (Seine-et-Marne)—Henri Stein, "Les Juifs de Montereau au Moyen Age," *Annales de la Société historique et archéologique du Gâtinais* 17 (1899): 58-59 (1247); Longnon, *Documents relatifs au comté de Champagne et de Brie*, vol. 3, pp. 11-12 (1251).

Montigny (Loiret)—Brussel, *Nouvel examen*, vol. 1, p. 612 (before 1306).

Montigny-le-Roi (Haute-Marne)—Longnon, *Documents relatifs au comté de Champagne et de Brie*, vol. 3, pp. 11-12 (1251).

Montigny-Lencoup (Seine-et-Marne)—ibid. (1251).

Montivilliers (Seine-Maritime)—Léchaudé d'Anisy, *Grands rôles*, vol. 1, pp. 41-42 (1195), 125 (1204).

Neuilly-Saint-Front (Aisne)—Longnon, *Documents relatifs au comté de Champagne et de Brie*, vol. 3, pp. 11-12 (1251).

Nevers (Nièvre)—Gross, *Gallia Judaica*, pp. 387-88.

Nogent-sur-Seine (Aube)—Longnon, *Documents relatifs au comté de Champagne et de Brie*, vol. 3, pp. 11-12 (1251).

Nonancourt (Eure)—*Olim*, vol. 2, p. 277, case no. 9 (1288).

Orléans (Loiret)—Gross, *Gallia Judaica*, pp. 30-37. See also Cochard, *La juiverie d'Orléans*.

Oulchy-le-Château (Aisne)—Longnon, *Documents relatifs au comté de Champagne et de Brie*, vol. 3, pp. 11-12 (1251).

Pacy-sur-Eure (Eure)—*RHF*, vol. 24, p. 277* (c. 1210).

Paris—Gross, *Gallia Judaica*, pp. 496-534. See also Michel Roblin, *Les Juifs de Paris* (Paris, 1952), pp. 9-24.

Passavant-en-Argonne (Marne)—Longnon, *Documents relatifs au comté de Champagne et de Brie*, vol. 3, pp. 11-12 (1251).

Payns (Aube)—ibid. (1251).

Poissy (Yvelines)—Brussel, *Nouvel examen*, vol. 2, p. CXCIX (1203); Luce, "Catalogue des documents," doc. no. 5 (1297).

Pont-Audemer (Eure)—Gross, *Gallia Judaica*, pp. 441-42. See also Léchaudé d'Anisy, *Grands rôles*, vol. 1, p. 114 (1204).

Pont-sur-Seine (Aube)—Longnon, *Documents relatifs au comté de Champagne et de Brie*, vol. 3, pp. 11-12 (1251).

Pontoise (Val-d'Oise)—Gross, *Gallia Judaica*, pp. 442-45.

Presles-et-Boves (Aisne)—Longnon, *Documents relatifs au comté de Champagne et de Brie*, vol. 3, pp. 11-12 (1251).

Provins (Seine-et-Marne)—Gross, *Gallia Judaica*, pp. 493-95. See also Félix Bourquelot, *Histoire de Provins*, 2 vols. (Provins, 1839-40), vol. 1, pp. 144-46, 264-66.

Ramerupt (Aube)—Gross, *Gallia Judaica*, pp. 634-38.

Reims (Marne)—ibid., pp. 633-34. See also Solomon Grayzel, *The Church and the Jews in the XIIIth Century* (Philadelphia, 1933), pp. 194-97 (1233); Pierre Varin, ed., *Archives administratives de la ville de Reims*, 3 vols. (Paris, 1838-48), vol. 2, p. 20 (1302).

Rouen (Seine-Maritime)—Gross, *Gallia Judaica*, pp. 622-24.

Saint-Christophe (Oise)—*RHF*, vol. 22, p. 649 (1285).

Saint-Denis (Seine-Saint-Denis)—Gross, *Gallia Judaica*, p. 151.

Saint-Fiacre (Seine-et-Marne)—Longnon, *Documents relatifs au comté de Champagne et de Brie*, vol. 3, pp. 11-12 (1251).

Saint-Florentin (Yonne)—*Layettes*, vol. 2, doc. no. 2170 (1231); Longnon, *Documents relatifs au comté de Champagne et de Brie*, vol. 3, pp. 11-12 (1251).

Saint-Jean-sur-Tourbe (Marne)—Longnon, *Documents relatifs au comté de Champagne et de Brie*, vol. 3, pp. 11-12 (1251).

Saint-Mard-sur-le-Mont (Marne)—ibid. (1251).

Saint-Pierre-sur-Dives (Calvados)—*Olim*, vol. 2, p. 299, case no. 3 (1290).

Saint-Quentin (Aisne)—*RHF*, vol. 24, pp. 281–83 (1248), 743–44 (1247–48).

Saint-Menehould (Marne)—Longnon, *Documents relatifs au comté de Champagne et de Brie*, vol. 3, pp. 11–12 (1251).

Saumur (Maine-et-Loire)—Gross, *Gallia Judaica*, p. 658. See also Léchaudé d'Anisy, *Grands rôles*, vol. 1, p. 106 (1203); *Layettes*, vol. 5, doc. no. 373 (c. 1233).

Scrupt (Marne)—Luce, "Catalogue des documents," doc. no. 10 (c. 1300).

Sées (Orne)—Léchaudé d'Anisy, *Grands rôles*, vol. 1, p. 71 (1195); Luce, "Catalogue des documents," doc. no. 5 (1297); *Journaux*, item no. 4447 (1300).

Senlis (Oise)—Gross, *Gallia Judaica*, pp. 660–61.

Sens (Yonne)—ibid., pp. 661–62. See also Grayzel, *The Church and the Jews in the XIIIth Century*, pp. 104–9 (1205); Maximilien Quantin, ed., *Recueil de pièces pour faire suite au Cartulaire général de l'Yonne* (Auxerre, 1873), doc. no. 112 (1212); Luce, "Catalogue des documents," doc. no. 75 (before 1306).

Sézanne (Marne)—Longnon, *Documents relatifs au comté de Champagne et de Brie*, vol. 3, pp. 11–12 (1251); Luce, "Catalogue des documents," doc. no. 81 (before 1306).

Soissons (Aisne)—Gross, *Gallia Judaica*, pp. 647–48. See also Melchior Regnault, *Abrégé de l'histoire de l'ancienne ville de Soissons* (Paris, 1638), preuves, p. 15 (1190); Georges Bourgin, *La commune de Soissons et le groupe communal Soissonois* (Paris, 1907), p. 175 (1284); Luce, "Catalogue des documents," doc. no. 45 (before 1306).

Soulaines-Dhuys (Aube)—Longnon, *Documents relatifs au comté de Champagne et de Brie*, vol. 3, pp. 11–12 (1251), 99 (1288).

Tonnerre (Yonne)—*Ordonnances*, vol. 11, pp. 217–19 (1174); Quantin, *Recueil des pièces*, doc. no. 254 (1220).

Touques (Calvados)—Gross, *Gallia Judaica*, pp. 209–10.

Tours (Indre-et-Loire)—ibid., pp. 216–18.

Tours-sur-Marne (Marne)—Longnon, *Documents relatifs au comté de Champagne et de Brie*, vol. 3, pp. 11–12 (1251).

Troyes (Aube)—Gross, *Gallia Judaica*, pp. 223–43.

Vauchassis (Aube)—Longnon, *Documents relatifs au comté de Champagne et de Brie*, vol. 3, pp. 11–12 (1251).

Vertus (Marne)—ibid. (1251).

Viévy-le-Rayé (Loir-et-Cher)—Brussel, *Nouvel examen*, vol. 1, p. 612 (before 1306).

Villemaur-sur-Vanne (Aube)—Longnon, *Documents relatifs au comté de Champagne et de Brie*, vol. 2, p. 40 (1231), and vol. 3, pp. 11–12 (1251).

Villers-en-Argonne (Marne)—ibid., vol. 3, pp. 11–12 (1251).

Vitry-le-François (Marne)—Gross, *Gallia Judaica*, pp. 195–97.

Wassy (Haute-Marne)—Longnon, *Documents relatifs au comté de Champagne et de Brie*, vol. 3, pp. 11–12 (1251).

Individual Jews

Anet (Eure-et-Loir)—Luce, "Catalogue des documents," doc. no. 5 (1297).

Angers (Maine-et-Loire)—Gross, *Gallia Judaica*, p. 63. See also *Layettes*, vol. 5, doc. no. 373 (c. 1233).

Argentan (Orne)—Léchaudé d'Anisy, *Grands rôles*, vol. 1, p. 71 (1195); Luce, "Catalogue des documents," doc. no. 5 (1297).

Arques-la-Bataille (Seine-Maritime)—Léchaudé d'Anisy, *Grands rôles*, vol. 1, p. 41 (1195).

Arzillières (Marne)—Émile Lévy, "Un document sur les Juifs du Barrois en 1321–23," *REJ* 19 (1889): 250 (before 1306).

Asnières-sur-Oise (Val-d'Oise)—*Journaux*, item no. 4599 (1301).

Auppegard (Seine-Maritime)—*Comptes du Trésor*, item no. 288 (1296).

Avessé (Sarthe)—Luce, "Catalogue des documents," doc. no. 5 (1297).

Avirey-Lingey (Aube)—Gross, *Gallia Judaica*, p. 24.

Avranches (Manche)—Léchaudé d'Anisy, *Grands rôles*, vol. 1, p. 141 (1222).

Beaugency (Loiret)—Gross, *Gallia Judaica*, pp. 115–16.

Beynes (Yvelines)—*Comptes royaux*, vol. 1, item no. 2194 (1299).

Blèves (Sarthe)—Luce, "Catalogue des documents," doc. no. 5 (1297).

Bonneville-sur-Touques (Calvados)—Delisle, *Catalogue des actes de Philippe Auguste*, pp. 508–9 (c. 1204).

Brienne (Eure)—ibid. (c. 1204).

Brienne-le-Château (Aube)—Gross, *Gallia Judaica*, p. 128.

Brienon-sur-Armançon (Yonne)—ibid., p. 129.

Brissac (Maine-et-Loire)—*Layettes*, vol. 5, doc. no. 373 (c. 1233).

Chappes (Aube)—Charles Lalore, ed., *Collection de principaux cartulaires du diocèse de Troyes*, 7 vols. (Paris, 1875–90), vol. 1, p. 256 (1221).

Châteaufort (Essonne)—*Layettes*, vol. 5, doc. no. 371 (1233).

Châteauneuf-en-Thymerais (Eure-et-Loir)—Luce, "Catalogue des documents," doc. no. 5 (1297).

Châteauvillain (Haute-Marne)—Gross, *Gallia Judaica*, p. 617.

Châtillon-sur-Indre (Indre)—Luce, "Catalogue des documents," doc. no. 47 (before 1306).

Cheminon (Marne)—ibid., doc. no. 10 (c. 1300).

Chennebrun (Eure)—ibid., doc. no. 5 (1297).

Chézy-sur-Marne (Aisne)—Henri d'Arbois de Jubainville, *Histoire des ducs et des comtes de Champagne*, 7 vols. in 8 (Paris, 1859–69), vol. 5, doc. no. 1851 (1228).

Clermont (Oise)—*Layettes*, vol. 5, doc. no. 371 (1233).

Compiègne (Oise)—Hercule Géraud, *Paris sous Philippe-le-Bel* (Paris, 1837), pp. 178–79 (1292); Karl Michaëlsson, ed., *Le Livre de la Taille de Paris l'an 1297* (Göteborg, 1958), pp. 264–67 (1296–97); Lévy, "Un document," p. 254 (before 1306).

Courtomer (Orne)—Luce, "Catalogue des documents," doc. no. 5 (1297).

Courville-sur-Eure (Eure-et-Loir)—*Journaux*, item no. 5823 (before 1306).

Crécy-en-Brie (Seine-et-Marne)—*Layettes*, vol. 3, doc. no. 4366 (1257).

Dangeau (Eure-et-Loir)—*Journaux*, item no. 5823 (before 1306).

Decize (Nièvre)—*Olim*, vol. 3, p. 185, case no. 51 (1306).

Doucey (Marne)—Lévy, "Un document," p. 252 (before 1306).

Écouché (Orne)—Luce, "Catalogue des documents," doc. no. 5 (1297).

Elbeuf (Seine-Maritime)—Delisle, *Catalogue des actes de Philippe Auguste*, pp. 508–9 (c. 1204).

Épense (Marne)—Lévy, "Un document," p. 251 (before 1306).

Essay (Orne)—Luce, "Catalogue des documents," doc. no. 5 (1297).

Eu (Seine-Maritime)—*Registres*, doc. no. 223 (1305).

Exmes (Orne)—Léchaudé d'Anisy, *Grands rôles*, vol. 1, p. 71 (1195).

Flixecourt (Somme)—*Journaux*, item no. 4538 (1300).

Gonesse (Val-d'Oise)—Delisle, *Catalogue des actes de Philippe Auguste*, p. 508 (c. 1204); *Journaux*, item no. 5851 (before 1306).

Gorron (Mayenne)—Luce, "Catalogue des documents," doc. no. 5 (1297).

Gournay-en-Bray (Seine-Maritime)—Gross, *Gallia Judaica*, pp. 136–39.

Gournay-sur-Marne (Seine-Saint-Denis)—Delisle, *Catalogue des actes de Philippe Auguste*, p. 508 (c. 1204).

Hodeng-au-Bosc (Seine-Maritime)—ibid., pp. 508–9 (c. 1204).

Issoudun (Indre)—Luce, "Catalogue des documents," doc. no. 97 (before 1306).

La Ferté-Frênel (Orne)—ibid., doc. no. 5 (1297).

L'Aigle (Orne)—Léchaudé d'Anisy, *Grands rôles*, vol. 2, p. 11 (1198); Luce, "Catalogue des documents," doc. no. 5 (1297).

La Neuve-Lyre (Eure)—Luce, "Catalogue des documents," doc. no. 5 (1297).

La Neuville-au-Pont (Marne)—Lévy, "Un document," p. 253 (before 1306).

Langres (Haute-Marne)—Brussel, *Nouvel examen*, vol. 2, p. CLXII (1202).

Liffol-le-Petit (Haute-Marne)—*Comptes royaux*, vol. 2, item no. 15348 (1292–93).

Longué (Maine-et-Loire)—Luce, "Catalogue des documents," doc. no. 5 (1297).

Longueville (Seine-et-Marne)—*Layettes*, vol. 5, doc. no. 371 (1233).

Lyons-la-Forêt (Eure)—Léchaudé d'Anisy, *Grands rôles*, vol. 1, p. 41 (1195).

Mainvilliers (Eure-et-Loir)—E. de Lepinas and Lucien Merlet, eds., *Cartulaire de Notre-Dame de Chartres*, 3 vols. (Chartres, 1862–65), vol. 2, p. 424 (1300).

Marcilly-sur-Eure (Eure)—*Registres*, doc. no. 223 (1305).

Mello (Oise)—*Olim*, vol. 3, p. 675, case no. 40 (before 1306).

Messei (Orne)—Luce, "Catalogue des documents," doc. no. 5 (1297).

Montargis (Loiret)—Delisle, *Catalogue des actes de Philippe Auguste*, p. 508 (c. 1204).

Montlhéry (Essonne)—Gross, *Gallia Judaica*, p. 335.

Montmorency (Val-d'Oise)—ibid., pp. 317–18. See also Joseph Depoin, ed., *Cartulaire de l'Hôtel-Dieu de Pontoise* (Montdidier, 1886), doc. no. 116 (1292).

Montrichard (Loir-et-Cher)—*Olim*, vol. 2, p. 508, case no. 8 (before 1306).

Nangis (Seine-et-Marne)—Lévy, "Un document," p. 253 (before 1306).

Neauphe-sous-Essai (Orne)—Luce, "Catalogue des documents," doc. no. 5 (1297).

Orbec (Calvados)—Delisle, *Catalogue des actes de Philippe Auguste*, pp. 508–9 (c. 1204).

Orville (Orne)—Luce, "Catalogue des documents," doc. no. 5 (1297).

Palaiseau (Essonne)—*Layettes*, vol. 5, doc. no. 371 (1233).

Pierrefonds (Oise)—Delisle, *Catalogue des actes de Philippe Auguste*, p. 508 (c. 1204).

Ribemont (Aisne)—*RHF*, vol. 24, pp. 281–82 (1248).

Rosières-près-Troyes (Aube)—Luce, "Catalogue des documents," doc. no. 10 (c. 1300).

Rosnay-l'Hôpital (Aube)—Lalore, *Collection de principaux cartulaires*, vol. 1, pp. 250–52 (1220).

Roye (Somme)—Gross, *Gallia Judaica*, p. 150.

Rugles (Eure)—Luce, "Catalogue des documents," doc. no. 5 (1297).

Saint-Céneri-le-Gerei (Orne)—ibid. (1297).

Saint-Dizier (Haute-Marne)—Grayzel, *The Church and the Jews in the XIIIth Century*, pp. 351–52 (1210); *Layettes*, vol. 2, doc. no. 1648 (1224).

Saint-Just-Sauvage (Marne)—Grayzel, *The Church and the Jews in the XIIIth Century*, pp. 351–52 (1210).

Saint-Vérain (Nièvre)—*Layettes*, vol. 2, doc. no. 2873 (1240).

Sainte-Scolasse-sur-Sarthe (Orne)—Léchaudé d'Anisy, *Grands rôles*, vol. 1, p. 71 (1195).

Senonches (Eure-et-Loir)—Luce, "Catalogue des documents," doc. no. 5 (1297).

Sermaize-les-Bains (Marne)—ibid., doc. no. 10 (c. 1300).

Thury-Harcourt (Calvados)—ibid., doc. no. 5 (1297).

Trainel (Aube)—Lévy, "Un document," p. 253 (before 1306).

Verneuil-sur-Avre (Eure)—Léchaudé d'Anisy, *Grands rôles*, vol. 2, p. 11 (1198); Delisle, *Catalogue des actes de Philippe Auguste*, pp. 508–9 (c. 1204); *RHF*, vol. 24, p. 32, doc. no. 251 (1247).

Vernon (Eure)—*RHF*, vol. 24, p. 277* (c. 1210); *Journaux*, item no. 2447 (1299); Luce, "Catalogue des documents," doc. no. 86 (before 1306).

Villenauxe-la-Grande (Aube)—Lalore, *Collection de principaux cartulaires*, vol. 1, pp. 248–49 (1220), 266–67 (1224).

BIBLIOGRAPHY

Primary Sources

Abba Mari of Lunel. *Minḥat Kenaot.* Brody, 1837.

Abraham b. Azriel. *Arugat ha-Bosem.* Edited by Ephraim Urbach. 4 vols. Jerusalem, 1939–63.

Abraham ibn Daud. *Sefer ha-Qabbalah.* Edited by Gerson Cohen. Philadelphia, 1967.

Actes du Parlement de Paris. Edited by Edgard Boutaric. 2 vols. Paris, 1863–67.

Actes et comptes de la commune de Provins. Edited by Maurice Prou and S. d'Auriac. Provins, 1933.

Adversus Judaeos. A. Lukyn Williams. Cambridge, 1935.

Alfonso de Espina. *Fortalitium Fidei.* Lyons, 1511.

Archives administratives de la ville de Reims. Edited by Pierre Varin. 3 vols. Paris, 1838–48.

Archives de l'Hôtel-Dieu de Paris. Edited by Léon Brièle. Paris, 1894.

Arresta communia Scaccarii. Edited by Ernest Perrot. Caen, 1910.

Les auteurs chrétiens latins du moyen age sur les juifs et le judaisme. Bernhard Blumenkranz. Paris, 1963.

Berechiah ha-Nakdan. *Mishley Shu'alim.* Edited by Abraham Habermann. Jerusalem, 1946.

Bernard of Clairvaux. *The Letters of St. Bernard of Clairvaux.* Translated by Bruno James. Chicago, 1953.

"Bulles inédites des papes." Isidore Loeb. *REJ 1* (1880): 114–18.

Cartulaire de l'Église Notre-Dame de Paris. Edited by Benjamin Guerard. 4 vols. Paris, 1850.

Cartulaire de l'Hôtel-Dieu de Pontoise. Edited by Joseph Depoin. Montdidier, 1886.

Cartulaire de Notre-Dame de Chartres. Edited by E. de Lepinas and Lucien Merlet. 3 vols. Chartres, 1862-65.

Cartulaire de Saint-Spire de Corbeil. Edited by Émile Coüard-Luys. Rambouillet, 1882.

Cartulaire de Sainte-Croix d'Orléans. Edited by Joseph Thillier and Eugène Jarry. Orléans, 1906.

Cartulaire général de l'Yonne. Edited by Maximilien Quantin. 2 vols. Auxerre, 1854.

Cartualaire normand. Edited by Léopold Delisle. Caen, 1852.

Catalogue des actes d'Henri Ier roi de France. Edited by Frédéric Soehnée. Paris, 1907.

Catalogue des actes de l'Abbaye de Saint-Denis relatifs à la province ecclésiastique de Sens de 1151 à 1356. Edited by Germaine Lebel. Paris, 1935.

Catalogue des actes de Philippe Auguste. Edited by Léopold Delisle. Paris, 1856.

Catalogue des actes de Robert II, roi de France. Edited by William Newman. Paris, 1939.

"Catalogue des actes relatifs aux Juifs pendant le moyen âge." Ulysse Robert. *REJ* 3 (1881): 211-24.

"Catalogue des documents du Trésor des Chartes relatifs aux Juifs sous le règne de Philippe le Bel." Siméon Luce. *REJ* 2 (1881): 15-72.

Chartularium Universitatis Parisiensis. Edited by Heinrich Denifle. 4 vols. Paris, 1889-97.

The Church and the Jews in the XIIIth Century. Solomon Grayzel. Philadelphia, 1933.

Collection de principaux cartulaires du diocèse de Troyes. Edited by Charles Lalore. 7 vols. Paris, 1875-90.

Collection de sceaux. Edited by Louis Claude Douet d'Arcq. 2 vols. Paris, 1863-67.

Comptes du Trésor. Edited by Robert Fawtier. Paris, 1930.

Comptes royaux (1285-1314). Edited by Robert Fawtier. 3 vols. Paris, 1953-56.

"Contribution à l'histoire des Juifs de Pontoise." Joseph Depoin. *Mémoires de la Société historique et archéologique de Pontoise et du Vexin* 36 (1921): 120-21.

Deux chroniques de Rouen. Edited by Alexandre Heron. Rouen, 1900.

"Document inédit relatif aux Juifs de Troyes." Pierre Piétresson de Saint Aubin. *Le moyen age* 22 (1920): 84-86.

"Un document sur les Juifs de Barrois en 1321-23." Émile Lévy. *REJ* 19 (1889): 246-58.

"Documents inédits—xi-xii." Adolf Neubauer. *REJ* 9 (1884): 63-64.

"Documents inédits relatifs à l'histoire de France sous Philippe le Bel." Edgard Boutaric. *Notices et extraits des manuscrits de la Bibliothèque nationale* 20, 2 (1862): 83-237.

"Documents pontoisiens inédits." Lucien Broche. *Mémoires de la Société historique et archéologique de Pontoise et du Vexin* 23 (1901).

Documents relatifs au comté de Champagne et de Brie, 1172-1361. Edited by Auguste Longnon. 3 vols. Paris, 1901-4.

Documents sur la ville de Mayenne. Edited by Albert Grosse-Duperon. Mayenne, 1906.

Documents sur les relations de la royauté avec les villes en France de 1180 à 1314. Edited by Arthur Giry. Paris, 1885.

Eliezer of Beaugency. *Perush al Yeḥezkel ve-Trei Asar.* Edited by Samuel Poznanski. 3 vols. Warsaw, 1900–1913.

"Enquêtes administratives du règne de Saint Louis." Léopold Delisle. *RHF* 24: 1–358.

Les établissements de Saint Louis. Edited by Paul Viollet. 4 vols. Paris, 1881–86.

Études sur les actes de Louis VII. Edited by Auguste Longnon. Paris, 1885.

"Formulaires de lettres du XIIe, du XIIIe et du XIVe siècle." Charles-Victor Langlois. *Notices et extraits des manuscrits de la Bibliothèque nationale.* 34, 2 (1891): 1–29.

"Fragments d'un registre des enquêteurs de Saint Louis." Léopold Delisle. *Journal des Savants* 7 (1909): 38–41.

Geoffroy of Courlon. *Chronique de l'abbaye St.-Pierre-le-Vif de Sens par Geoffroy de Courlon.* Edited by Gustave Julliot. Sens, 1876.

Geoffroy of Paris. *La Chronique métrique attribuée à Geoffroy de Paris.* Edited by Armel Diverrès. Paris, 1956.

Les grandes chroniques de France. Edited by Jules Viard. 10 vols. Paris, 1920–53.

Grands rôles des echiquiers de Normandie. Edited by Amédée Léchaudé d'Anisy. 2 vols. Paris, 1845–52.

Guibert of Nogent. *Histoire de sa vie.* Edited by Georges Bourgin. Paris, 1907.

———. *Self and Society in Medieval France.* Edited by John Benton. New York, 1970.

Guillaume le Breton. *Oeuvres de Rigord et de Guillaume le Breton.* Edited by H.-François Delaborde. 2 vols. Paris, 1882–85.

Guillaume of Nangis. *Chronique latine de Guillaume de Nangis de 1113 à 1300.* Edited by Hercule Géraud. 2 vols. Paris, 1843.

Guillaume of Saint-Pathus. *Vie de Saint Louis.* Edited by H.-François Delaborde. Paris, 1899.

Guiot of Provins. *Les oeuvres de Guiot de Provins, poète lyrique et satirique.* Edited by John Orr. Manchester, 1915.

Hebräische Berichte über die Judenverfolgungen während der Kreuzzüge. Edited and translated by Adolf Neubauer and Moritz Stern. Berlin, 1892.

Inventaire d'anciens comptes royaux dressé par Robert Mignon. Edited by Charles-Victor Langlois. Paris, 1894.

Isaac b. Moses of Vienna. *Or Zaru'a.* 4 vols. in 2. Zhitomir, 1862–90.

Isaac of Corbeil. *Sefer Miẓvot Katan.* Reprint. Jerusalem, 1959.

Jacob b. Meir. *Sefer ha-Yashar.* Berlin, 1898.

The Jew in the Medieval World: A Source Book: 315–1791. Jacob Marcus. Cincinnati, 1938.

Jewish Self-Government in the Middle Ages. Louis Finkelstein. New York, 1924.

John of Joinville. *Histoire de Saint Louis.* Edited by Natalis de Wailly. Paris, 1868.

———. *The Life of St. Louis.* Translated by René Hague. New York, 1955.

Joseph Bekhor Shor. *Perush al ha-Torah.* Edited by Chaim Gad. 3 vols. Jerusalem, 1957–59.

Joseph ha-Cohen. *Emek ha-Bakha.* Edited by M. Letteris. Cracow, 1895.

Judah Alharizi. *Taḥkemoni.* Edited by Paul de Lagarde. Gottingen, 1883.

Les Journaux du Trésor de Philippe IV le Bel. Edited by Jules Viard. Paris, 1940.

Ketab al-Rasil. Edited by Yehiel Brill. Paris, 1871.

Koveẓ Teshuvot ha-Rambam. 3 vols. Leipzig, 1859.

Layettes du Trésor des Chartes. Edited by Alexandre Teulet et al. 5 vols. Paris, 1863–1909.

223

Levi b. Gerson. *Perush al ha-Torah.* Venice, 1547.

"Literary Gleanings V." Adolf Neubauer. *JQR* (old series) 4 (1891–92): 699.

"Literary Gleanings VIII." Adolf Neubauer. *JQR* (old series) 5 (1892–93): 714.

Le livre de la taille de Paris l'an 1297. Edited by Karl Michaëlsson. Göteborg, 1958.

"Ma'aseh Nora." Abraham Berliner. *Oẓar Tov* 1878: 46–48.

"Ma'aseh Nora." Abraham Berliner. *Oẓar Tov* 1878: 49–52.

Matthew Paris. *Matthaei Parisiensis Monachi Sancti Albani Chronica Majora.* Edited by Henry Luard. 7 vols. London, 1872–83.

Maḥzor Vitry. Edited by S. Hurwitz. Nurnberg, 1923.

Meir b. Simeon of Narbonne and Meshullam b. Moses of Béziers. *Sefer ha-Meorot ve-Sefer ha-Hashlamah, Berakhot and Pesaḥim.* Edited by Moshe Blau. New York, 1964.

Miscellaneous Records of the Norman Exchequer, 1199–1204. Edited by Sidney Packard. Northampton, Mass., 1927.

Monuments historiques. Edited by Jules Tardif. Paris, 1866.

Moses of Coucy. *Sefer Miẓvot Gadol.* 2 vols. Reprint. Jerusalem, 1961.

Normanniae nova chronica. Edited by Adolphe Cheruel. Caen, 1850.

"Notes de comptabilité juive du XIIIe et du XIVe siècle." Moise Schwab. *REJ* 30 (1895): 289–94.

"Notes hébraiques de comptabilité au XIIIe siècle et au XIVe siècle." Moise Schwab. *REJ* 41 (1900): 149–53.

"Notes sur quelques mss. du Musée britannique." Léopold Delisle. *Mémoires de la Société de l'Histoire de Paris* 4 (1877): 183–238.

Les Olim ou registres des arrêts. Edited by Arthur Beugnot. 3 vols. in 4. Paris, 1839–48.

Ordonnances des roys de la troisième race. Edited by Eusèbe de Laurière et al. 22 vols. Paris, 1723–1849.

Otto of Freising. *The Deeds of Frederick Barbarossa.* Translated by Charles Mierow. New York, 1953.

Oẓar Vikuḥim. Edited by J. P. Eisenstein. New York, 1928.

Patriologiae cursus completus, series Latina. Edited by J. P. Migne. 217 vols. Paris, 1844–55.

Peter Abelard. "Dialogus inter Philosophum, Judaeum et Christianum." *PL* 178: 1611–84.

———. *The Story of Abelard's Adversities.* Translated by Joseph Muckle. Toronto, 1954.

Philip of Beaumanoir. *Les coutumes du Beauvoisis.* Edited by Arthur Beugnot. 2 vols. Paris, 1842.

Ralph of Diceto. *Opera historica.* Edited by William Stubbs. 2 vols. London, 1876.

Raoul Glaber. *Les cinq livres de ses histoires (900–1044).* Edited by Maurice Prou. Paris, 1886.

"Rapport sur les inscriptions hébraiques de la France." Moise Schwab. *Nouvelles archives des missions scientifiques et littéraires.* 12 (1904): 143–383.

Recueil de chartes et documents de St.-Martin-des-Champs. Edited by Joseph Depoin. 3 vols. Paris, 1912–21.

Recueil de pièces pour faire suite au Cartulaire général de l'Yonne. Edited by Maximilien Quantin. Auxerre, 1873.

Recueil des actes de Henri II, roi d'Angleterre et duc de Normandie. Edited by Léopold Delisle. 3 vols. Paris, 1909–27.

BIBLIOGRAPHY

Recueil des actes de Philippe I, roi de France. Edited by Maurice Prou. Paris, 1908.
Recueil des actes de Philippe Auguste, roi de France. Edited by H.-François Delaborde. 3 vols. Paris, 1916-66.
Recueil des actes des ducs de Normandie de 911 à 1066. Edited by Marie Fauroux. Caen, 1961.
Recueil des historiens des Croisades. Historiens occidentaux. 5 vols. Paris, 1844-95.
Recueil des historiens des Gaules et de la France. Edited by Martin Bouquet et al. 24 vols. Paris, 1737-1904.
"Recueil des jugements de l'Echiquier de Normandie." Léopold Delisle. *Notices et extraits des manuscrits de la Bibliothèque nationale* 20, 2 (1862): 238-434.
"Recueil des principales chartes de l'abbaye de Joyenval." Adolphe Dutilleux. *Mémoires de la Société historique et archéologique de Pontoise et du Vexin* 13 (1890): 74-114.
Regesten zur Geschichte der Juden in fränkischen und deutschen Reiche bis zum Jahre 1273. Edited by Julius Aronius et al. Berlin, 1902.
The Register of Eudes of Rouen. Translated by Sydney Brown. Edited by J. F. O'Sullivan. New York, 1964.
Les registres d'Alexandre IV. Edited by C. Bourel de la Roncière et al. 3 vols. Paris, 1902-53.
Les registres d'Honorius IV. Edited by Maurice Prou. Paris, 1888.
Les registres d'Urbain IV. Edited by Jean Guiraud. 4 vols. Paris, 1901-29.
Le registre de Benoit XI. Edited by Charles Grandjean. Paris, 1883-1905.
Les registres de Boniface VIII. Edited by Georges Digard et al. 4 vols. Paris, 1904-39.
Les registres de Clément IV. Edited by Édouard Jordan. Paris, 1893-1945.
Les registres de Grégoire X et de Jean XXI. Edited by Jean Guiraud and E. Cadier. Paris, 1892-1906.
Les registres de Martin IV. Edited by members of the École française de Rome. Paris, 1901-35.
Les registres de Nicholas III. Edited by Jules Gay. Paris, 1938.
Les registres de Nicholas IV. Edited by Ernest Langlois. Paris, 1886-93.
Registres du Trésor des Chartes. Edited by Robert Fawtier et al. Paris, 1958.
Reglemens sur les arts et métiers de Paris. Edited by G. B. Depping. Paris, 1837.
Rigord. *Oeuvres de Rigord et de Guillaume le Breton, historiens de Philippe-Auguste.* Edited by H.-François Delaborde. 2 vols. Paris, 1882-85.
Robert of Courçon. *Le Traité "De Usura" de Robert de Courçon.* Edited by Georges Lefèvre. Lille, 1902.
Robert of Torigni. *Chronique.* Edited by Léopold Delisle. 2 vols. Rouen, 1872-73.
"Le rôle des Juifs de Paris en 1296 et 1297." Isidore Loeb. *REJ* 1 (1880): 61-71.
Rotuli chartarum in Turri Londinensi asservati. Edited by Thomas Duffy Hardy. London, 1837.
Rotuli de liberate ac de misis et praestitis regnante Johanne. Edited by Thomas Duffy Hardy. London, 1837.
Rotuli de oblatis et finibus in Turri Londinensi asservati. Edited by Thomas Duffy Hardy. London, 1835.
Rotuli litterarum clausarum in Turri Londinensi asservati. Edited by Thomas Duffy Hardy. London, 1833.
Rotuli litterarum patentium in Turri Londinensi asservati. Edited by Thomas Duffy Hardy. London, 1835.

Sacrorum conciliorum nova et amplissima collectio. Edited by J. D. Mansi et al. 53 vols. in 58. Florence and Paris, 1759-1927.

Samuel b. Meir. *Perush ha-Torah.* Edited by David Rosin. Breslau, 1882.

Sefer Gezerot Ashkenaz ve-Zarfat. Edited by Abraham Habermann. Jerusalem, 1945.

Sefer ha-Neyar. Edited by Gerson Appel. New York, 1951.

Sefer Hasidim. Edited by Reuven Margaliot. Jerusalem, 1960.

Sefer Hasidim. Edited by Jehuda Wistinetzki and J. Freimann. 2nd ed. Frankfort, 1924.

Sefer Keritut. Edited by Simha Sofer. Jerusalem, 1965.

Sepher Joseph Hamekane. Edited by Judah Rosenthal. Jerusalem, 1970.

Solomon b. Isaac of Troyes. *Commentary on the Talmud.* Printed in all standard editions of the Talmud.

———. *Pentateuch with Rashi's Commentary Translated into English.* Translated by Morris Rosenbaum and Abraham Silbermann. 5 vols. London, 1929-34.

———. *Perush al ha-Torah.* Edited by Abraham Berliner. Berlin, 1866.

Solomon ibn Verga. *Shevet Yehudah.* Edited by Azriel Shohet. Jerusalem, 1947.

Suger. *Oeuvres complètes de Suger.* Edited by Álbert Lecoy de la Marche. Paris, 1867.

———. *Vie de Louis le Gros.* Edited by Auguste Molinier. Paris, 1887.

Teshuvot Ba'aley ha-Tosafot. Edited by Irving Agus. New York, 1954.

Teshuvot Ge'oney Mizrah ve-Ma'arav. Edited by Joel Mueller. Berlin, 1888.

Teshuvot Hakhmey Zarfat ve-Lotir. Edited by Joel Mueller. Vienna, 1881.

Teshuvot Rashi. Edited by Israel Elfenbein. New York, 1943.

Textes relatifs à l'histoire du Parlement depuis les origines jusqu'en 1314. Edited by Charles-Victor Langlois. Paris, 1888.

Tosafot (a northern French commentary on the Talmud). Printed in all standard editions of the Talmud.

Urban Civilization in Pre-Crusade Europe. Irving Agus. 2 vols. New York, 1965.

Samuel Usque. *Consolation for the Tribulations of Israel.* Translated by Martin Cohen. Philadelphia, 1965.

Veterum scriptorum et monumentorum historicorum, dogmaticorum, moralium, amplissima collectio. Edited by Edmond Martène and Ursin Durand. 9 vols. Paris, 1724-33.

Vikuah R. Yehiel mi-Pariz. Thorn, 1873.

SECONDARY READINGS

Agus, Irving. "Democracy in the Communities of the Early Middle Ages." *JQR* 43 (1952-53): 153-76.

———. *The Heroic Age of Franco-German Jewry.* New York, 1969.

Albeck, Shalom. "Rabbenu Tam's Attitude to the Problems of his Time" (Hebrew). *Zion* 19 (1954): 104-41.

The American Academy for Jewish Research. *Rashi Anniversary Volume.* New York, 1941.

Anchel, Robert. "The Early History of the Jewish Quarter in Paris." *JSS* 2 (1940): 45-60.

———. *Les Juifs de France.* Paris, 1946.

Aptowitzer, Avigdor. *Mavo le-Sefer Raviah.* Jerusalem, 1938.

Assier, Alexandre. *Nouvelle bibliothèque de l'amateur champenois.* 14 vols. Paris, 1896-98.

Baer, Yitzhak. "The Disputation of R. Yehiel of Paris and of Nachmanides" (Hebrew). *Tarbiz* 2 (1930-31): 172-87.

——. *A History of the Jews in Christian Spain.* Translated by Louis Schoffman et al. 2 vols. Philadelphia, 1961-66.

——. "The Origins of the Organisation of the Jewish Community of the Middle Ages" (Hebrew). *Zion* 15 (1950): 1-41.

——. "Rashi and the Historical Reality of his Time" (Hebrew). *Tarbiz* 20 (1949): 320-32.

Baldwin, John. *Masters, Princes and Merchants: The Social Views of Peter the Chanter and His Circle.* 2 vols. Princeton, 1969.

Baron, Salo. *The Jewish Community.* 3 vols. Philadelphia, 1942.

——. "Medieval Nationalism and Jewish Serfdom." *Studies and Essays in Honor of Abraham A. Neuman.* Edited by Meir Ben-Horin et al. Leiden, 1962.

——. " 'Plenitude of Apostolic Powers' and Medieval 'Jewish Serfdom' " (Hebrew). *Sefer Yovel le-Yitzhak Baer.* Jerusalem, 1960.

——. *A Social and Religious History of the Jews.* 2nd ed. 14 vols. New York, 1952-69.

Ben-Sasson, Haim Hillel. *Perakim be-Toldot ha-Yehudim bi-Yeme ha-Benayim.* Tel Aviv, 1958.

——. "The 'Northern' European Jewish Community and Its Ideals." *Cahiers d'histoire mondiale* 11 (1968): 208-19.

Berger, Élie. "Les dernières années de saint Louis." *Layettes* 4: iii-lxxv.

——. *Histoire de Blanche de Castille, reine de France.* Paris, 1895.

——. *Saint Louis et Innocent IV.* Paris, 1893.

Berman, Léon. *Histoire des Juifs de France des origines à nos jours.* Paris, 1937.

Bloch, Marc. *Feudal Society.* Translated by L. A. Manyon. Chicago, 1961.

——. *La France sous les derniers Capétiens.* 2nd ed. Paris, 1964.

——. *Mélanges historiques.* 2 vols. Paris, 1966.

Blumenkranz, Bernhard. *Bibliographie des Juifs en France.* Paris, 1961.

——. "Contributions à la nouvelle *Gallia Judaica.*" *Archives juives* 4 (1967-68): 27-29, 35-37.

——. "Géographie historique d'un thème de l'iconographie religieuse: les représentations de Synagoga en France." *Mélanges offerts à René Crozet.* Poitiers, 1966.

——, ed. *Histoire des Juifs en France.* Toulouse, 1972.

——. *Le juif médiéval au miroir de l'art chrétien.* Paris, 1966.

——. *Juifs et chrétiens dans le monde occidental, 430-1096.* Paris, 1960.

——. "Pour une nouvelle *Gallia Judaica.*" *L'Arche* 106 (December 1965): 42-47.

——. "Quartiers juifs en France (XIIe, XIIIe, et XIVe siècles)." *Mélanges de philosophie et de littérature juives* 3-5 (1958-62): 77-86.

Bourgeois, René. *Du mouvement communal dans le comté de Champagne.* Paris, 1904.

Bourgin, Georges. *La commune de Soissons et le groupe communal soissonnois.* Paris, 1908.

Bourquelot, Félix. *Études sur les foires de Champagne.* 2 vols. Paris, 1865.

——. *Histoire de Provins.* 2 vols. Provins, 1839-40.

Boutiot, Théophile. *Histoire de la ville Troyes et de la Champagne méridionale.* 5 vols. Paris, 1870–80.

Bouvier, H. *Historie de l'église et de l'ancien archidiocèse de Sens.* 3 vols. Paris, 1906–11.

Brown, Elizabeth. "Taxation and Morality in the Thirteenth and Fourteenth Centuries: Conscience and Political Power and the Kings of France." *French Historical Studies* 8 (1973–74): 1–28.

Bruel, Alexandre. "Notes de Vyon d'Herouval sur les baptisés et les convers au temps de saint Louis." *BEC* 28 (1867): 609–21.

Brundage, James. *Medieval Canon Law and the Crusader.* Madison, 1969.

Brussel, Nicolas. *Nouvel examen de l'usage des fiefs in France.* 2 vols. Paris, 1750.

Caro, Georg. *Sozial- und Wirtschaftsgeschichte der Juden im Mittelalter und der Neuzeit.* 2 vols. Frankfort, 1908–20.

Cartellieri, Alexander. *Philipp II August, König von Frankreich.* 4 vols. in 5. Leipzig, 1899–1922.

Catane, Mosche. *Des Croisades à nos jours.* Paris, 1956.

Chantereau-Lefebvre, Louis. *Traité des fiefs et de leur origine.* 2 vols. Paris, 1662.

Chapin, Elizabeth. *Les villes des foires de Champagne.* Paris, 1937.

Chazan, Robert. "The Blois Incident of 1171: A Study in Jewish Intercommunal Organization." *PAAJR* 36 (1968): 13–31.

——. "The Bray Incident of 1192: *Realpolitik* and Folk Slander." *PAAJR* 37 (1969): 1–18.

——. "Jewish Settlement in Northern France, 1096–1306." *REJ* 128 (1969): 41–65.

——. "1007–1012: Initial Crisis for Northern-European Jewry." *PAAJR* 38–39 (1970–71): 101–18.

——. "The Persecution of 992." *REJ* 129 (1970): 217–21.

——. "A Twelfth-Century Communal History of Spires Jewry." *REJ* 128 (1969): 253–57.

Cochard, Théophile. *La juiverie d'Orléans.* Orléans, 1895.

Cohen, Gerson. "Esau as Symbol in Early Medieval Thought." *Jewish Medieval and Renaissance Studies.* Edited by A. Altmann. Cambridge, Mass., 1967.

——. "Messianic Postures of Ashkenazim and Sephardim." *Studies of the Leo Baeck Institute.* Edited by Max Kreutzberger. New York, 1967.

Cohn, Norman, *The Pursuit of the Millenium.* Rev. ed. New York, 1970.

Dan, Joseph. *Torat ha-Sod shel Ḥasidut Ashkenaz.* Jerusalem, 1968.

d'Arbois de Jubainville, Henri. *Histoire des ducs et des comtes de Champagne.* 7 vols. in 8. Paris, 1859–69.

Darmesteter, Arsène. "L'Autodafé de Troyes (24 avril 1288)." *REJ* 2 (1881): 199–247.

Delaborde, H.-François. "Le texte primitif des enseignements de Saint Louis à son fils." *BEC* 73 (1912): 73–100, 237–62.

de l'Epinas, E. *Histoire de la ville et des sires de Coucy.* Paris, 1848.

de Lespinasse, René. *Le Nivernais et les comtes de Nevers.* 3 vols. Paris, 1909–14.

Delisle, Léopold. "Des revenus de la Normandie au XIIe siècle." *BEC* 10 (1848–49): 173–210, 257–89; 11 (1850): 400–51; 13 (1852): 105–35.

de Roover, Raymond. *Money, Banking and Credit in Mediaeval Bruges.* Cambridge, Mass., 1966.

de Sainte Marthe, Denis et al., eds. *Gallia Christiana in provincias ecclesiasticas distributa.* 13 vols. Paris, 1715–1876.

BIBLIOGRAPHY

de Vic, Claude, and Vaissète, Joseph. *Histoire générale de Languedoc.* 15 vols. Toulouse, 1872-92.

Douglas, David. *The Norman Achievement: 1050-1100.* Berkeley, 1969.

——. "The Rise of Normandy." *Proceedings of the British Academy* 33 (1947): 101-30.

Du Plessis, Toussaint. *Histoire de l'église de Meaux.* 2 vols. Paris, 1731.

Eidelberg, Shlomo. "The Community of Troyes before the Time of Rashi" (Hebrew). *Sura* 1 (1953-54): 48-57.

Emery, Richard. *The Jews of Perpignan in the Thirteenth Century.* New York, 1959.

Fawtier, Robert. *The Capetian Kings of France.* Translated by Lionel Butler and R. J. Adams. London, 1960.

Finkelstein, Louis. *Jewish Self-Government in the Middle Ages.* New York, 1924.

Fishman, Judah, ed. *Sefer Rashi.* Jerusalem, 1956.

Fliche, Augustin. *Le règne de Philippe Ier, roi de France (1060-1108).* Paris, 1912.

——, and Martin, Victor, eds. *Histoire de l'Église depuis les origines jusqu'à nos jours.* 24 vols. Paris, 1924-present.

Funkenstein, Amos. "Changes in the Patterns of Christian Anti-Jewish Polemics in the 12th Century" (Hebrew). *Zion* 33 (1968): 125-44.

Gauthier, Léon. "Les Juifs dans les deux Bourgognes." *REJ* 48 (1904): 208-99; 49 (1904): 1-17, 244-61.

Géraud, Hercule. *Paris sous Philippe-le-Bel.* Paris, 1837.

Golb, Norman. "New Light on the Persecution of French Jews at the Time of the First Crusade." *PAAJR* 34 (1966): 1-64.

Grabois, Aryeh. "L'Abbaye de Saint-Denis et les Juifs sous l'abbatiat de Suger." *Annales* 24 (1969): 1187-95.

——. "Du credit juif à Paris au temps de saint Louis." *REJ* 129 (1970): 5-22.

Grayzel, Solomon. *The Church and the Jews in the XIIIth Century.* Philadelphia, 1933.

——. "The Papal Bull Sicut Judeis." *Studies and Essays in Honor of Abraham A. Neuman.* Edited by Meir Ben-Horin et al. Leiden, 1962.

Gross, Henri. *Gallia Judaica.* Paris, 1897.

Güdemann, Moritz. *Geschichte des Erziehungswesens und der Cultur der abendländishen Juden während des Mittlelalters und der neueren Zeit.* 3 vols. Vienna, 1880-88.

Gutsch, Milton. "A Twelfth Century Preacher—Fulk of Neuilly." *The Crusades and Other Historical Essays Presented to Dana C. Munro.* Edited by L. J. Paetow. New York, 1928.

Hacker, Joseph. "About the Persecutions during the First Crusade" (Hebrew). *Zion* 31 (1966): 225-31.

Hailperin, Herman. *Rashi and the Christian Scholars.* Pittsburgh, 1963.

Halphen, Louis. *Le comté d'Anjou au XIe siècle.* Paris, 1906.

——. *À travers l'histoire du moyen âge.* Paris, 1950.

Haskins, Charles. *Norman Institutions.* Cambridge, Mass., 1918.

——. *The Renaissance of the Twelfth Century.* Cambridge, Mass., 1927.

Hefele, Karl. *Histoire des Conciles.* Translated and augmented by Henri Leclercq et al. 11 vols. in 22. Paris, 1907-49.

Holmes, Urban Tigner. *Daily Living in the Twelfth Century.* Madison, 1952.

Kahn, Zadoc. "Étude sur le livre de Joseph le Zélateur." *REJ* 1 (1880): 222–46; 3 (1881): 1–38.

Katz, Jacob. *Exclusiveness and Tolerance: Studies in Jewish-Gentile Relations in Medieval and Modern Times.* London, 1961.

——. "Martyrdom in the Middle Ages and in 1648–49" (Hebrew). *Sefer Yovel le-Yitzhak Baer.* Jerusalem, 1960.

Katz, Solomon. *The Jews in the Visigothic and Frankish Kingdoms of Spain and Gaul.* Cambridge, Mass., 1937.

Kisch, Guido. *The Jews in Medieval Germany.* Chicago, 1949.

Krauss, Samuel. "L'émigration de 300 rabbins en Palestine en l'an 1211." *REJ* 82 (1926): 333–43.

Kuk, S. H. "The Date of the Burning of the Talmud in France" (Hebrew). *Kiryat Sefer* 29 (1953–54): 281.

——. "R Yehiel of Paris and Erez Yisrael" (Hebrew). *Zion-Measef* 5 (1933): 97–107.

Labarge, Margaret. *Saint Louis.* Boston, 1968.

Langlois, Charles-Victor. "Doléances recueillies par les Enquêteurs de Saint Louis." *Revue historique* 92 (1906): 1–41.

——. *Le règne de Philippe III le Hardi.* Paris, 1887.

Langmuir, Gavin. "Community and Legal Change in Capetian France." *French Historical Studies* 6 (1969–70): 275–86.

——. "The Jews and the Archives of Angevin England: Reflections on Medieval Anti-Semitism." *Traditio* 19 (1963): 183–244.

——. " 'Judei Nostri' and the Beginning of Capetian Legislation." *Traditio* 16 (1960): 203–69.

Latouche, Robert. *Histoire du comté du Maine pendant le Xe et le XIe siècle.* Paris, 1910

Lavisse, Ernest, ed. *Histoire de France.* 9 vols. in 18. Paris, 1900–11.

Lazard, Lucien. "Les Juifs de Touraine." *REJ* 17 (1888): 210–34.

——. "Les revenus tirés des Juifs de France dans le domaine royal." *REJ* 15 (1887): 233–61.

Lebeuf, Jean. *Mémoires concernant l'histoire civile et ecclésiastique du diocèse d'Auxerre.* 2nd ed. 4 vols. Auxerre, 1848–55.

Le Nain de Tillemont, Louis. *Vie de Saint Louis, roi de France.* Edited by J. de Gaulle. 6 vols. Paris, 1847–51.

Leroy, Gabriel. *Histoire de Melun depuis les temps les plus reculés jusqu'à nos jours.* Melun, 1887.

Liber, Maurice. *Rashi.* Translated by A. Szold. Philadelphia, 1906.

Lifschitz-Golden, Manya. *Les Juifs dans la littérature française du moyen âge.* New York, 1935.

Little, Lester. "Saint Louis' Involvement with the Friars." *Church History* 33 (1964): 125–48.

Loeb, Isidore. "La controverse de 1240 sur le Talmud." *REJ* 1 (1880): 247–61; 2 (1881): 248–70; 3 (1881): 39–57.

——. "Deux livres de commerce du commencement du XIVe siècle." *REJ* 8 (1884): 161–96; 9 (1884): 21–50, 187–213.

——. "Les expulsions des Juifs de France au XIVE siècle." *Jubelschrift zum seibzigsten Geburtstage des Prof. Dr. H. Graetz.* Breslau, 1887.

Longnon, Auguste. *Atlas historique de la France.* Paris, 1888.

——, and Delaborde, H.-François. *La formation de l'unité française.* Paris, 1922.

Lot, Ferdinand. *Études sur le règne de Hugues Capet et la fin du Xe siècle.* Paris, 1903.

———, and Fawtier, Robert, eds. *Histoire des institutions françaises aux moyen âge.* 3 vols. Paris, 1957–62.

———. *Le premier budget de la monarchie française.* Paris, 1932.

Luchaire, Achille. *Louis VI le Gros.* Paris, 1890.

———. *Social France at the Time of Philip Augustus.* Translated by E. B. Krehbiel. New York, 1912.

Merchavia, Ch. *Ha-Talmud be-Rei ha-Nazrut.* Jerusalem, 1970.

The Metropolitan Museum of Art. *The Year 1200.* 2 vols. New York, 1970.

Molinier, Auguste. *Les sources de l'histoire de France des origines aux guerres d'Italie.* 6 vols. Paris, 1901–6.

Musset, Lucien. "Morel de Falaise." *Bulletin de la Société des Antiquaires de Normandie* 57 (1963–64): 559–61.

———. "Morel de Falaise, brasseur d'affaires du XIIIe siècle." *Bulletin de la Société des Antiquaires de Normandie* 50 (1946–48): 305–9.

Nahon, Gérard. "Contribution à l'histoire des Juifs en France sous Philippe le Bel." *REJ* 121 (1962): 59–80.

———. "Le credit et les Juifs dans la France du XIIIe siècle." *Annales* 24 (1969): 1121–48.

———. "Les Juifs dans les domaines d'Alphonse de Poitiers, 1241–1271." *REJ* 125 (1966): 167–211.

———. "Les ordonnances de Saint Louis sur les Juifs." *Les nouveaux cahiers* 6 (1970): 18–35.

Nelson, Benjamin. *The Idea of Usury.* Princeton, 1949.

Nicaise, Auguste. *Épernay et l'abbaye St.-Martin de cette ville.* 2 vols. Châlons-sur-Marne, 1869.

Noonan, John. *The Scholastic Analysis of Usury.* Cambridge, Mass., 1957.

Pacaut, Marcel. *Louis VII et son royaume.* Paris, 1964.

Paquet, A. E. *Histoire de Château-Thierry.* Château-Thierry, 1839.

Pegues, Franklin. *The Lawyers of the Last Capetians.* Princeton, 1962.

Petit-Dutaillis, Charles. *Étude sur la vie et le règne de Louis VIII (1187–1226).* Paris, 1894.

———. *The Feudal Monarchy in France and England.* Translated by E. D. Hunt. London, 1936.

Pfister, Charles. *Études sur le règne de Robert le Pieux.* Paris, 1885.

Pierquin de Gembloux, Claude. *Notices historiques, archéologiques et philologiques sur Bourges et la département du Cher.* Bourges, 1840.

Powicke, Frederick. *The Loss of Normandy,* 2nd. ed. New York, 1961.

Prawer, Joshua. *Toldot Mamlekhet ha-Zalbanim be-Erez Yisrael.* Rev. ed. 2 vols. Jerusalem, 1971.

Prévost, A. *La diocèse de Troyes, histoire et documents.* 3 vols. Domois par Orges, 1926.

Quantin, Maximilien. *Histoire anecdotique des rues d'Auxerre.* Auxerre, 1870.

Rabinowitz, Louis. *The Herem Hayyishub.* London, 1945.

———. *The Social Life of the Jews of Northern France in the XII-XIV Centuries.* London, 1938.

Rangeard, Pierre. *Histoire de l'université d'Angers.* 2 vols. Angers, 1877.

Regnault, Melchior. *Abrégé de l'histoire de l'ancienne ville de Soissons.* Paris, 1638.

Renan, Ernest. *Les écrivains juifs français du XIVe siècle.* Paris, 1893.

——. *Les rabbins français du commencement du quatorzième siècle.* Paris, 1877.

Richardson, H. G. *The English Jewry under Angevin Kings.* London, 1960.

Robert, Ulysses. "Étude historique et archéologique sur la roue des Juifs depuis le XIIIe siècle." *REJ* 7 (1883): 81–95; 8 (1884): 94–102.

——. "Les signes d'infamie au moyen âge." *Mémoires de la Société des Antiquaires de France* 49 (1888): 60–125.

Roblin, Michel. "Les cimetières juifs de Paris au moyen âge." *Mémoires de la fédération des sociétés historiques de Paris et de l'Île de France* 4 (1952): 7–19.

——. *Les Juifs de Paris.* Paris, 1952.

Rosenthal, Judah. "The Law of Usury Relating to non-Jews" (Hebrew). *Talpioth* 5 (1953–54): 139–52.

——. *Meḥkarim.* 2 vols. Jerusalem, 1966.

——. "The Talmud on Trial." *JQR* 47 (1956–57): 58–76, 145–69.

Roth, Cecil, ed. *The Dark Ages: Jews in Christian Europe 711–1096.* Tel Aviv, 1966.

——. *A History of the Jews in England.* 3rd ed. Oxford, 1964.

Runciman, Steven. *A History of the Crusades.* 3 vols. Cambridge, 1951–54.

Saige, Gustave. *Les Juifs du Languedoc antérieurement au XIVe siècle.* Paris, 1881.

Sars, Maxime, and Broche, Lucien. *Histoire de Braine.* La Charité-sur-Loire, 1933.

Schwarzfuchs, Simon. *Brève histoire des Juifs de France.* Paris, 1956.

——. "De la condition des Juifs de France aux XIIe et XIIIe siècles." *REJ* 125 (1966): 226–29.

——. *Études sur l'origine et le developpement du rabbinat au moyen âge.* Paris, 1957.

Setton, Kenneth, ed. *A History of the Crusades.* 2 vols. Philadelphia, 1955–62.

Shatzmiller, Joseph. "Towards a Picture of the First Maimonidean Controversy" (Hebrew). *Zion* 34 (1969): 126–44.

Smalley, Beryl. *The Study of the Bible in the Middle Ages.* 2nd ed. Oxford, 1952.

Soloveitchik, Haym. "Pawnbroking: A Study in *Ribbit* and of the Halakah in Exile." *PAAJR* 38–39 (1970–71): 203–68.

Southern, R. W. *The Making of the Middle Ages.* London, 1953.

Spiegel Shalom. "In Monte Dominus Videbitur: The Martyrs of Blois and the Early Accusations of Ritual Murder" (Hebrew). *The Mordecai M. Kaplan Jubilee Volume.* 2 vols. New York, 1953.

——. *The Last Trial.* Translated by Judah Goldin. Philadelphia, 1966.

Stein, Henri. "Les Juifs de Montereau au Moyen Age." *Annales de la Société historique et archéologique du Gâtinais* 17 (1899): 54–61.

Stein, Siegfrid. "The Development of the Jewish Law on Interest from the Biblical Period to the Expulsion of the Jews from England." *Historia Judaica* 17 (1955): 3–40.

——. "A Disputation on Moneylending between Jews and Gentiles in Me'ir b. Simeon's *Milḥemeth Miṣwah.*" *Journal of Jewish Studies* 10 (1959): 45–61.

——. *Jewish-Christian Disputations in Thirteenth Century Narbonne.* London, 1969.

Stengers, Jean. *Les Juifs dans les Pays-Bas au Moyen Age.* Brussels, 1950.

Strayer, Joseph. *The Administration of Normandy under Saint Louis.* Cambridge, Mass., 1932.

———. "Consent to Taxation under Philip the Fair." *Studies in Early French Taxation.* Edited by Joseph R. Strayer and Charles H. Taylor. Cambridge, Mass., 1939.

———. "Italian Bankers and Philip the Fair." *Explorations in Economic History* 7 (1969): 113-21.

———. *Medieval Statecraft and the Perspectives of History.* Princeton, 1971.

Synan, Edward. *The Popes and the Jews in the Middle Ages.* New York, 1965.

Tamar, David. "More on the Date of the Burning of the Talmud in France" (Hebrew). *Kiryat Sefer* 29 (1953-54): 430-31.

Twersky, Isidore. "Aspects of the Social and Cultural History of Provençal Jewry." *Cahiers d'histoire mondiale* 11 (1968): 185-207.

Urbach, Ephraim. *Ba'aley ha-Tosafot.* Jerusalem, 1955.

———. "Études sur la littérature polémique au moyen-âge." *REJ* 100 (1935): 56-72.

Veissière, Michel. *Une Communauté canoniale au Moyen Age, Saint-Quiriac-de-Provins.* Provins, 1961.

Vuitry, Adolphe. *Études sur le régime financier da la France.* Paris, 1878.

———. *Études sur le régime financier de la France. Nouvelle série.* 2 vols. Paris, 1883.

Wood, Charles. "Regnum Francie: A Problem in Capetian Administrative Usage." *Traditio* 23 (1967): 117-47.

Zeitlin, Solomon. "Rashi and the Rabbinate." *JQR* 31 (1940-41): 1-58.

INDEX

THE JOHNS HOPKINS UNIVERSITY PRESS

This book was composed in Baskerville text and display type
by Jones Composition Company, Inc. It was printed on Warren's
60-lb. Sebago and bound in Columbia Bayside Chambray by
Universal Lithographers, Inc.

Library of Congress Cataloging in Publication Data

Chazan, Robert.
Medieval Jewry in Northern France.

(The Johns Hopkins University Studies in Historical and Political Science,
91st ser., 2)
Bibliography: p.
1. Jews in France—History. I. Title. II. Series: Johns Hopkins University.
Studies in Historical and Political Science, ser. 91, no. 2.
DS135.F81C48   914.4'06'924   73-8129
ISBN 0-8018-1503-7